History on British television

D1614488

MANCHESTER
1824

Manchester University Press

STUDIES IN POPULAR CULTURE

General editor: Professor Jeffrey Richards

History on British television
Constructing nation, nationality and collective memory

ROBERT DILLON

Manchester University Press

Published by Manchester University Press
Altrincham Street, Manchester M1 7JA, UK
www.manchesteruniversitypress.co.uk

British Library Cataloguing-in-Publication Data is available

Library of Congress Cataloging-in-Publication Data is available

ISBN 978 0 7190 9985 4 *paperback*

First published by Manchester University Press in hardback 2010

This paperback edition first published 2015

Printed by Lightning Source

STUDIES IN POPULAR CULTURE

There has in recent years been an explosion of interest in culture and cultural studies. The impetus has come from two directions and out of two different traditions. On the one hand, cultural history has grown out of social history to become a distinct and identifiable school of historical investigation. On the other hand, cultural studies has grown out of English literature and has concerned itself to a large extent with contemporary issues. Nevertheless, there is a shared project, its aim, to elucidate the meanings and values implicit and explicit in the art, literature, learning, institutions and everyday behaviour within a given society. Both the cultural historian and the cultural studies scholar seek to explore the ways in which a culture is imagined, represented and received, how it interacts with social processes, how it contributes to individual and collective identities and world views, to stability and change, to social, political and economic activities and programmes. This series aims to provide an arena for the cross-fertilisation of the discipline, so that the work of the cultural historian can take advantage of the most useful and illuminating of the theoretical developments and the cultural studies scholars can extend the purely historical underpinnings of their investigations. The ultimate objective of the series is to provide a range of books which will explain in a readable and accessible way where we are now socially and culturally and how we got to where we are. This should enable people to be better informed, promote an interdisciplinary approach to cultural issues and encourage deeper thought about the issues, attitudes and institutions of popular culture.

Jeffrey Richards

For Halina, Charlotte, Oliver

Contents

List of illustrations

General editor's foreword

Around the middle of the nineteenth century, a fundamental split began to develop between academic history and popular history. Influenced by intellectual developments in Germany, a class of professional historians emerged in Britain. Their methods were critical, scientific and analytical, their approach professedly objective. They were committed to archival research and became increasingly specialised in their subjects of study. History in the academy, embodied in scholarly monographs, annual conferences and learned journals, became the province of the few, the initiates, the insiders. Popular history – history for the many – took a different route. Vivid, visual, immediate and often simplified, its vehicles became in succession painted artwork, the stage, the cinema and latterly television. It is from the last of these sources that most people now learn whatever history they know. History has been and remains a staple of television programming. Its popularity has led the public to turn a succession of programme presenters into stars, from Sir Mortimer Wheeler, Sir Brian Horrocks and Sir John Betjeman in the early days of the BBC, to Michael Wood, David Starkey and Simon Schama more recently.

The phenomenon of history on television is the subject of Robert Dillon's welcome new book. Drawing on a wide range of programme examples from a span of more than sixty years, he charts the evolution of history on television since 1946. Every change is carefully contextualised and analysed with reference to social, cultural, economic and technological developments in the country. He discusses the various forms and styles of television history programme, the approach to such topics as biography and war, the role and significance of presenters', audience and critics' reactions. No area of this subject escapes him and the book abounds in pertinent, nuanced and often revealing insights. Erudite, stimulating and admirably wide-ranging, this book constitutes a major contribution to an understanding of the role of television in the construction and transmission of history and the creation of national identity and collective memory.

Jeffrey Richards

Preface

History is not what we make of it, but what it makes of us. How we make sense of the world around us, the framework of the society we live in, the culture that we shape and form provides us with the basis for history, our history and the history of 'Others'. Engaging or interacting with the past can take many forms. Through education, by visiting museums, stately homes, and scenes of battle, all manner of opportunities allow individuals to connect with the past.

One of the most obvious connections, one almost taken for granted, under-estimated and undervalued as a teacher of history, is television. Factual history programming, in one form or another, has been on our television screens from 1946 until the present day. As one-off documentaries, award-winning series, quizzes or panel games, television history has developed alongside the television industry. This book is intended to chart how factual television has become such a consistent and long-lasting commodity on British television. More impor-tantly, the book attempts to explain and analyse how television history is a history of Britain as a nation-state. In its role of presenting the past, television is a collective storehouse of various underlying truths, misconceptions and false-hoods that have, over time, constructed our notion of nationality. These trans-mitted and inherited values contain and conceal myths and beliefs that support the concept of nation and nationality, essentially what it means to be British.

Motivated and derived from over ten years of teaching television and film studies – particularly documentary – the book is also heavily influenced by my Ph.D. thesis on collective memory and factual history on British television. One of the aims of my thesis was to try to explain, analyse and assess how and why the past and history as a subject has become not only a television commodity but also a form of popular culture that is consumed nationally by diverse audi-ence groups. To that end, a small-scale user survey was carried out targeted at three groups, from selected regional areas within the United Kingdom.

The first group, composed of students and staff at secondary, tertiary and higher levels of education, covered the Scottish Highlands, Northern Ireland and northwest England to South Wales. The second consisted of members from veterans' groups, local history/archaeological and family history societies from northeast Scotland, northern England and southern England. The third group featured a mixed spread across the United Kingdom, covering a range of professions and age groups including the over-sixties. Where reference is made to the findings from the groups, this will be in the form 'TV-user survey, All Groups'. Over five hundred questionnaires were distributed, with a return rate of 60 per cent.

The book also contains primary programme data from my thesis. A chronological survey of factual history programming on British television was undertaken in order to establish an overview of content, style and modes of presentation required to determine the definitive genre classification and genealogical development of factual history production.

Carrying out this survey was essential to pinpoint similarity and difference in the programme themes that have been produced from 1946 to 1986, the cut-off date for data collection. In some chapters in the book, I have included series or one-off programmes up to 2009, in order to spotlight how certain thematic values have continued to develop. By constructing this fundamental chronological survey, it has been possible to gain an insight into the contextual issues that influenced and shaped programmes at the time of their production, the nuts and bolts of nationality as it were. Finally, some references in the book refer to the British Broadcasting Corporation's (BBC), online Programme Catalogue. Unfortunately this excellent research resource is no longer available and the details are, according to the BBC, being incorporated into their general Archive/Programme website. The Archive site does feature some rare programmes in its themed collections that can be viewed online, including some of the programmes discussed in the book, such as *Bird's-Eye View* (BBC2, 1969–70) and *Morning in the Streets* (BBC, 1959). Several other series discussed and analysed in the book are available on commercial digital versatile discs (DVD).

Acknowledgements

There are many people who have provided enormous help and encouragement in ensuring that this book found its way to print. I would especially like to thank Jeffrey Richards for his time in ensuring my ambitious project reached fruition.

In taking the time and making the effort to provide written replies, talk over the telephone or agree to interviews, I am indebted to Laurence Rees, Creative Director of History for television at the BBC, David Starkey, Michael Wood, Bettany Hughes, Bamber Gascoigne and Adam Hart-Davis.

The staff at the BBC's Written Archive Centre, Caversham, also provided a valuable contribution in tracing scripts and programme files and in finding responses to sundry questions regarding the BBC's factual output. I am deeply indebted to James Feltham, picture archives manager, and Dave Woodward, picture archivist at Independent Television (ITV), for their help and assistance in locating images for use in the book. A special thank you is required for my family, who deserve recognition for their tremendous support, motivation at times of doubt, assistance with data recording and the battle to manage over forty years of factual programming that have made this book possible.

I would also like to thank the Manchester University Press team for the patience, encouragement and advice in turning my thesis into a real book. Lastly, I am extremely fortunate to have benefited from the original funding for my Ph.D. research project and I would like to thank the Arts and Humanities Research Council for recognising the importance of television as a producer and recorder of history. I sincerely hope that future research in this area continues to be encouraged.

Robert Dillon

List of abbreviations

ATV	Associated Television Ltd
BAFPU	British Army Film and Photographic Unit
BAFTA	British Academy of Film and Television Arts
BBC	British Broadcasting Corporation
BFI	British Film Institute
BSB	British Satellite Broadcasting
CBS	Columbia Broadcasting System
CFU	Crown Film Unit
CGI	computer-generated images
DVD	digital versatile disc
GCSE	General Certificate of Secondary Education
HTV	Harlech Television
ITN	Independent Television News
ITV	Independent Television
MoD	Ministry of Defence
NBC	National Broadcasting Corporation
Ofcom	Office of Communications
PSB	Public Service Broadcasting
RFPU	RAF Film Production Unit
SAS	Special Air Service
SNP	Scottish National Party
VCR	videocassette recorder
WS	wide shot

Introduction

Switching on the past

History has played a significant role in shaping the television landscape of Britain. Whether it has been screened as costume dramas, literary adaptations, period films, documentaries or in one of its other variant formats, including panel games, television history has proved a popular genre on British television since 1946.

If other popular programme genres have encountered hostility concerning their format and presenters, facing charges of poor taste and telephone vote rigging scandals, television history has encountered different criticism. By attempting to appeal to the lowest common denominator in order to recruit a large enough audience-share to justify production costs, some formats inevitably attract stinging rebukes. The issues raised tend to always orbit not very far from the contention that television cannot be trusted not to place entertainment above education when producing history programmes.

On one level the book attempts to understand how something that we take at face value, television, can be capable of teaching history and teaching it in a certain way. At the same time, the book will explore and address some of the criticisms levelled at television history.

The implications of television serving as a significant custodian of our history are extremely important. As individuals, as groups, as a nation, we need to connect more with the past or society faces the prospect of stagnating and fracturing, of losing not only its national identity but also its core values of citizenship. Perhaps that point has been reached; perhaps not even television has the magnetism to appeal to certain audience groups any more.

Surveys carried out in 2004 suggested that certain groups found the past something they increasingly preferred to turn off, rather than turning on, as they 'confused myth with history or treated what they saw in Hollywood films as historical fact'.[1] History, for all the importance it serves as connecting past and present together, remains a mystery to some people. When a young visitor was informed by an English Heritage guide that Queen Victoria had nine children, the visitor wondered: 'Did they all have the same dad?' And another visitor was mystified why so many ruined castles had been built.[2]

If certain groups are being bypassed by history at school and bypassing history on television, we really are in danger of losing touch with the past. History on television is vital then, not only as a means of visualising how society has evolved but in reaching individuals who shun history in other formats. This is no easy feat, and not always successful, but television transforms dates, events, people and places into entertaining one-off documentaries and riveting series.

The problem with television in the early twenty-first century as it copes with the digital changeover, a shrinking of advertising revenue and calls for the public service broadcasting (PSB) licence fee to be shared, is that it has lost sight of what audiences want, which, unsurprisingly, is to be entertained and informed. In his 2008 MacTaggart Lecture at the Edinburgh International Television Festival, Peter Fincham, Director of Television for ITV, accused Channel 4 and the industry's independent regulator, the Office of Communications (Ofcom) of attempting to use PSB as 'social engineering'.[3] Conversely, the BBC has also come in for criticism for not doing enough to 'tackle the big broken society issues'.[4] The suspicion of 'social engineering' and a failure to provide visual role models suggests that television is, after all, a powerful conduit for propaganda.

History has always been propaganda in one form or another, and when it is combined with television it is manifestly capable of entertaining and informing as social and cultural propaganda. Television history provides a highly motivated form of propaganda capable of justifying and explaining how social and cultural codes have become modified or rejected as motivational goals of citizenship. In fact, citizenship is a prime requirement of the BBC, written into its Royal Charter in the section detailing 'Incorporation and Purposes' with one of the BBC's 'Public Purposes' defined as 'sustaining citizenship and civil society'.[5]

What has become apparent from writing this book is that television has become a historian in its own right by using history as a commodity. With its prime convention of entertaining paramount, television has become a free agent in how it manages the past, how it retold the story of England, then Britain, as an island. In short, television functions as a visual barometer of what it meant to be English or British, what national characteristics counted, how a national outlook formed. Television organises and motivates how national character has been valued, presented as fact, reality, reconstruction and myth.

Two central concepts of national character that have been present since British television resumed transmission after the Second World War are heritage and tradition. Treated as not very useful, or very valuable by-products of history by some historians, television, even in its early high-cultural and didactic BBC days, did not turn its nose up at heritage and tradition. These are the twin pillars of what is accepted as the foundations of mainstream, popular history. This is what Winston Churchill referred to as 'Long History' and what Humphrey Jennings attempted to capture as aspects of 'Deep England' in *Listen to Britain* (Crown Film Unit, 1942), with his eloquent articulation of regionality forming a cohesive picture of Britain. A very inclusive and restrictive picture it may have been, but one that had what television cannot function without, and that is popular appeal.

When popular appeal is added to heritage, to tradition, to television images and sound, its combination produces a powerful visual stimulus: the sort of stimulus recognised and utilised highly effectively by Dr Joseph Goebbels in Nazi cinematic propaganda campaigns. Television is not an adjunct to culture and society, but a fundamental core of national values. It not only reports, presents, re-presents – in the case of the past – it also promotes a dynamic visual insight into Britain that history books cannot match.

Attempting to define what it means to be English or British has long been a theme of history before television. Not only does the message need to strike a popular chord, to tap into the social and cultural values of the time, it has to utilise a form of communication, a medium, a genre, an organisational structure that enhances and amplifies shared concerns, values and beliefs. Jeffrey Richards has written how Victorian history paintings presented a very singular view of the past representing national ideals. Likewise, Henry Newbolt (1862–1938), committed his vision of what it meant to be English in his own vibrant, stylised, but often ridiculed poem *Vitaï Lampada*. Capturing the cultural nuance of the day in popular styles takes many forms, but it has become second nature to television.

Clearly, popular history has many guises, many formats. Some, such as the ITV drama *Lost in Austen* (ITV1, 2008) employs a plot that actually fuses past and present together through time travel, or, as in the adaptation of Dickens' *Little Dorrit* (BBC1, 2008), the conventions of thirty-minute soap opera episodes are borrowed for its fourteen-part run.[6] At first glance, they may not appear to be history, but that is one of the advantages of television, it can disguise the past as sheer entertainment, as fiction posing as fact. Television achieves this through spectacle, characterisation and narrative in the same way that Victorian history paintings attempted to define a national outlook by celebrating the nation's achievements.

Both history paintings and romanticised notions of duty are products of their time, controlled, shaped and transmitted by the medium available to their creative producers. It is this defining of a particular moment, of harnessing dominant technological codes and conventions, where television excels as a teacher of history. Television has displaced cinema as an electronic canvas that teaches individuals about their past, their culture and society. Much in the same way that television eroded cinema's position as a favoured point of exchanging leisure time for entertainment, the computer is threatening to supersede television as a personal space where information can be controlled and produced to suit our own needs. History is becoming personalised depending on individual tastes, individual values and how people choose to assemble it.

When individual, collective or popular memory, popular culture, television and history are combined they become a potent mixture. Their interaction and influence on British history programming should neither be taken lightly nor ignored. By critically examining the concept of collective memory and the production of history programming, the book aims to reveal how the past has become an important popular cultural commodity, shaped to satisfy the demands of a competitive, volatile and rapidly changing marketplace.

For some individuals, television represents their only contact with history in formats that they understand and enjoy. Creating formats that make history popular and educational as well as entertaining is certainly not new. Increasingly, the struggle in the twenty-first century is to find new audience groups willing to interact with history in any form whatsoever.

In many ways, television serves the same function as Victorian paintings in their depiction of events for a largely non-academic audience in the way of affordable prints and textbook illustrations.[7] Two artworks by Daniel Maclise (1806–70), *The Death of Nelson* and *The Meeting of Wellington and Blücher at Waterloo* commissioned for the Palace of Westminster, demonstrate this appropriation of the past as a commodity. As manufactured views of history, texts are wholly determined by the social cultural context formed around the chosen medium, genre and anticipated audience.

Television, from its post-war resumption in 1946, has gradually monopolised the visual articulation of the past as it has displaced painting and

photography as popular formats. As cinema outdid the theatre for visual spectacle, so too has television developed new uses for the past, including drama,
advertising and comedy.

It is this increasing generation of meaning about the past through history
programmes on British television that many academic historians regard as the
onslaught of popular history, which by its very definition, is out of their remit
and control.[8] Exactly who controls the past is an essential factor in determining how much or little of it is made into 'public history', how much of it has
relevance for the present.

Producing and managing the past

As with any contentious dispute, there is inevitably a trigger, a catalyst to be
identified as a motivating force behind the event. Published by Macmillan in
1961 and Penguin in 1964, Edward Hallett Carr's *What Is History?* proved to
be an agent of change in its own time. Almost half a century later, it is still
capable of producing numerous claims, counter-claims and ongoing polemical
debates that seek to resolve how the past should be produced and managed.

Carr's cardinal sin was to propose that professional history might not be best
served by a purely empirical 'commonsense view'.[9] Instead, it should embrace
an open approach to the past, encompassing more of a science-orientated methodology.[10] This proved a provocative slight to historians trained in the Rankean
techniques of 'rigid objectivity' and the primacy of documentary evidence as a
means of closely re-producing the past.[11] If this radical thrust against academic
historians was not bad enough, Carr compounded his assault by proposing
that social science could and should make a valuable contribution to history;[12]
initiating a controversy that has not significantly diminished.

What Carr did not touch on directly, however, was the role that television
history programmes have to play in manufacturing the past. In many ways,
television is a central mediator in what Carr claimed to be an ongoing dialogue
between the past and the present.[13] Any attempt at opening up avenues of communication requires what Martin Baker describes as a dialogical contract.[14] For
this contract to be effective, there needs to be a common understanding of, and
trust in, cultural and social values through which meaning is produced.

Although documents and records provide a valuable bridge from the present
to the past for historians, television as historical text and textual producer of
history is viewed as a suspicious or dubious record. Its failure in this sense
comes from what historian Arthur Marwick, a founding member of the Open

University, regarded as the frippery of 'general service television' and its fetish for visual incident, often leaving history programming marginalised.[15]

Much criticism of television history is aimed at its technical conventions, the very framework it has to use to produce television programmes. The disappointment of Felipe Fernández-Armesto, that production 'logistics' are more important than content,[16] can only serve to enforce professional animosity towards history programming. Bracketed off from 'good' academic history, television history has been shunted into a popular history siding, along with heritage, family history, collective memory and oral history. Keeping popular history quite separate from the mainline of academic history can only intensify the debate on what constitutes history and who should be entitled to manage the past.

From the number of history-based textbooks in circulation, numerous historians have devoted endless pages to deciphering this knotty puzzle on how a dialogue expected to span different generations can be set up and effectively operated. With so much disagreement about exactly how any act of communication between past and present takes place likely to rumble on in academia, history programme-makers can continue to create access to the past through informative and entertaining popular formats.

Never absolutely defined, nor fast and fixed in its interpretation, the past is a continuing site of a power struggle for control. The main protagonists are professional historians who vie to impose authority and decree who has the necessary qualifications to acquire the rights and mantle as gatekeepers to the past.

The popularity of history programming on British television is not surprising given its transition from a single terrestrial black-and-white broadcast system following the Second World War. With the introduction of colour transmissions bringing the past vividly to life and the proliferation of cable, satellite and digital channels, the amount of history available – original and repeat – has increased substantially.

Equally, throughout its evolution into a professional area of study, history has gone through distinct phases where the fundamental issues of historical facts and their interpretation have undergone a process of revision and development. As with television, these phases, reflecting economic, political and intellectual trends, beliefs and values of society, have by turn influenced cultural meaning.

The professional study of history as part of the Western tradition has also progressed, transforming how we utilise our past. More importantly, the way in which vital events have been visually told has developed from primitive iconic recordings, celebrating and commemorating events, such as the ritual depiction of animals recorded on the cave walls at Lascaux, in southwest France, to the computer-generated recreation of a different age in the docudrama *Egypt* (BBC1, 2005).

Images alone can never explain fully how events have unfolded; they always require anchoring through captions, scripts or speech. The oral tradition for instance, may have its roots in the work of Herodotus and Thucydides, yet oral history primed, fed, and sustained by memory is a lynchpin in many history programmes. This is evident not merely in series such as *Time to Remember* (ITV, 1968–72), *Flashback* (C4, 1983) and *People's Century* (BBC, 1995), where individual memory operates as a bridge to the past, but also as a presentational storytelling device that can be traced back to Sir Mortimer Wheeler's authoritative style in *The Grandeur That Was Rome* (BBC, 1960).

Making television history for people like us

It is easy to divide off audiences from the producers and practitioners of television history, creating a model of binary opposed interests, overlooking the fact that producers and practitioners are also members of audience groups. Disagreement on audience interaction with television texts, the various modes of reception and interpretation have vexed researchers on how accurate 'audience' is as a lexicon for analysing television viewing activity.[17]

Attempting to find an adequate, alternative definition for viewer/audience, what I propose to employ in place of viewer/audience throughout the book is TV-user and TV-users. This is neither original nor meant to be theoretically cutting edge, but is a term, I believe, that denotes levels of autonomy, choice and, crucially, television's technological development and output. The very act of transmitting is an agent of production and reception that alters the nature of its contract with its users, a flexible interface that is capable of modifying levels of satisfaction or need such as companionship or as an information point for commercial television's Teletext and the BBC's Ceefax.

Television history in Britain must have achieved some levels of success with its TV-users or it would not have survived against other forms of popular television programming for as long as it has done. It has achieved this by offering a compelling invitation for TV-users to virtually step into the past through reconstruction and dramatisation or as a fellow traveller accompanying the presenter. Historical facts, in as far as television reworks history, are believed by some historians to be largely taken at face value,[18] unquestioned and presented as starkly and as simply as possible.

This of course is the dilemma of history programming, caught between the pressure from professional historians for in-depth analysis and programme-makers working within television's codes and conventions of providing cost effective television that appeals, entertains, informs and educates. For historians, the fundamental concern has never shifted far from the issue of historical facts and their interpretation. Programme-makers on the other hand have largely concentrated on creating programming formats, TV-user appeal, channel share and ratings.

How far television history programming has travelled from a mass-TV-user broadcast system to a narrowcast, niche market system incorporating specialist history channels is of critical importance. Increased diversity does not necessarily equate with an increase of quality programming unless there is a strong belief and commitment in the future of history programming. More channels simply brings more repeats, not original programming, and destroys the creative possibilities of television. This is a failure Peter Fincham alluded to in his MacTaggart lecture, when he observed:

> I don't suppose Lord Reith would have been familiar with the phrase 'less is more', but he might nevertheless have raised one of his menacing eyebrows if he'd heard what his simple prescription had grown into.[19]

Any advantage to be gained by television history through the opening up of the marketplace should not be squandered on endless repeats recycled on specialist digital channels. With increased scheduling opportunities, commissioning editors and programme-makers need to revisit parts of the past that are capable of attracting TV-users who would not normally engage with history. One area that opens up distant events in a dynamic, accessible platform is in the direct experiences and shared narratives based on collective and personal forms of memory.

Television, history and memory

Memory as a means of accessing the past causes many historians problems in terms of its reliability and accuracy. There are considerable arguments that suggest collective memory is an active element in constructing cultural values and an understanding not only of the present but also of the past.[20] Memory has become a staple convention in many history programmes, as eyewitness testimony, and as oral history, becoming a contributing factor in the production of the past for successive history series and one-off programmes.

Collective memory, popular memory and social memory often refer to how group narratives bound by mediated, second-hand memories form a distinct impression of the past. Collective memory, for instance, is never formed from isolated individual viewpoints but is generated from what Maurice Halbwachs describes as 'frameworks' that organise how various groups remember events collectively as a means of maintaining their own group identity.[21]

One of the central concerns with collective memory, and perhaps a valid reason why many historians reserve judgement on its value, is that it can become a seductive term that supposes and suggests that memory is governable and a shareable commodity within a community that enjoys uniform, popular values. Memory, in fact, is constantly in revision and modification. Individual memory often works alongside collective memory, particularly during the production of narratives that make sense of remembered events by filling gaps, providing a coherent structure that renders each memory capable of 'reinterpretation',[22] for different purposes.

For us to make sense of not only the world around us but also the past, individual and collective memory operate with the approval of each other. They are both open to modification, review and transformation, depending on the demands of society, particularly the revising of personal memories when these are shared publicly.[23] What does appear to condition memory duration, the process of remembering and forgetting, is the power of emotional resonances produced at the time of memory formation. This creates, in certain circumstances, an intense attachment to an experienced or witnessed event,[24] a binding resonance.

Another aspect of collective memory – collective institutional memory – is often overlooked. It does not only involve re-circulating stories and experiences, or the handing down of myths from one generation to another that become locked into the past;[25] it also influences the content, type of shots and editing of film and television.[26] Memory, either individual or collective, relies for its structure, in the same way that television does, on the bonding of images, words and sounds around a narrative structure. Giambattista Vico, for instance, places image formation within the realm of memory.[27] For Leon Battista Alberti, the concept that memory and image are related and interdependent can also be found in the visual aesthetics of the early Renaissance. Alberti's treatise on perspective records that the *istoria*, the emotive content of a painting, is derived from an artist's inspiration, imagination and memory.[28]

To some extent, an institutional collective memory operates within history programming. This consists of creative production values that include a typology of narratives, stock shots, cutaways, framing, camera work and editing based on what Vico regards as the perpetual reinvention of history as a facet of memory as imagination.[29] In this cycle of reinvention, each generation of history programme-makers may create their own variations on how events from the past should be told and look, but those selections have their traces, their creative roots, in the given 'look' of previous British and Hollywood films and television programmes.

By not deviating from an accepted production formula where time constraints, budgets, logistics and TV-user expectations are paramount, this institutionalised, hereditary visual memory can unconsciously or consciously determine the look of a programme. This inherited look draws on dramatic cinematic conventions, early archive material and newsreel footage, particularly where the Second World War features as a theme, just as the codes and conventions of historians lead to a prescriptive range of styles.[30]

Television is the perfect conduit for collective memory within history programming. In many ways television history formats are ideal channels for collective memory with characters, presenters and archive footage functioning as a cultural 'bard'.[31] As a bardic form, television production mediates, controls and creates meaning through images and language grounded in the oral tradition. This tradition is a predominant feature of documentary, and given the already ambitious scope of the book, it will be only possible to largely concentrate on factual television history.

Where possible, examples of one-off dramas, series or films will be included where appropriate as comparisons to factual history programming. This is particularly important when fictional productions are based on historical accounts, such as letters and diaries. What I do hope the book ultimately succeeds in doing, however, is to trace and reveal how history on television produces and teaches a stylised representation of nation, nationality and citizenship.

Notes

1 'Hitler a Real Person? Who Do You Think You're Kidding?' *Daily Mail* (5 April 2004), p. 31. The results of a survey commissioned by Blenheim Palace highlighting a worrying lack of basic historical insight. This is echoed by the findings of a BBC poll revealing confusion and gaps in knowledge of British history. '1066 and All What?', *Daily Mail* (5 August 2004), p. 37.

2 Andy Bloxham, 'Do the English Build Castle Ruins?', *Daily Telegraph* (11 August 2008), p. 9.

3 Peter Fincham, '2008 MacTaggart Lecture at the Edinburgh International Television Festival', p. 6. http://image.guardian.co.uk/sys-files/Media/documents/2008/08/22/MacTaggartLecture2008.pdf.

4 Andrew Porter, 'BBC Must Help to Heal the Broken Society, Says Tories', *Daily Telegraph* (29 September 2008), p. 6.

5 Department for Culture, Media and Sport: Royal Charter for the continuance of the British Broadcasting Corporation, p. 2. www.bbc.co.uk/bbctrust/framework/charter.html.

6 Cole Moreton, 'What the Dickens?', *Independent* (26 October 2008), p. 28.

7 Jeffrey Richards, 'Popular memory and the construction of English history', *The Ninth Annual Bindoff Lecture, Queen Mary and Westfield College, University of London* (London: University of London, 1998), p. 7.

8 Ludmilla Jordanova, *History in Practice* (London: Arnold, 2000), p. 141.

9 Edward Hallett Carr, *What Is History?* (Harmondsworth: Penguin, 1964), p. 9.

10 Carr, *What Is History?*, p. 85.

11 John Warren, *The Past and Its Presenters* (London: Hodder and Stoughton, 1998), p. 104.

12 Carr, *What Is History?*, p. 66.

13 Carr, *What Is History?*, p. 30.

14 Martin Baker cited in Dominic Strinati, *Popular Culture* (London: Routledge, 1995), p. 253. Although Barker employed the concept of a dialogical contract on the study of comics as popular culture artefacts, it has equal validity when applied to factual history programmes.

15 Arthur Marwick, *The New Nature of History* (Basingstoke: Palgrave, 2001), pp. 232–3.

16 Felipe Fernández-Armesto, 'Epilogue: What is history now?', in David Cannadine (ed.), *What Is History Now?* (Basingstoke: Palgrave Macmillan, 2002), p. 159.

17 Muriel Cantor, 'Audience control', in Horace Newcomb (ed.), *Television, The Critical View* (New York: Oxford University Press, 3rd edn, 1982), p. 311. See also Tamar Liebes, 'Viewing and reviewing the audience: Fashions in communication research', in James Curran and Michael Gurevitch (eds), *Mass Media and Society* (London: Hodder Arnold, 4th edn, 2005), pp. 358–9.

18 Marwick, *New Nature of History*, p. 234.

19 Fincham, 2008 MacTaggart Lecture, p. 7.

20 Maurice Halbwachs, *On Collective Memory*, ed. and trans. Lewis A. Coser (Chicago: The University of Chicago Press, 1992), p. 59.

21 Halbwachs, *On Collective Memory*, p. 53.

22 Elizabeth Jelin, and Susana G. Kaufman, 'Layers of memory. Twenty years after in Argentina', in David E. Lorey and William H. Beezley (eds), *Genocide, Collective Violence, and Popular Memory* (Wilmington: Scholarly Resources, 2002), p. 48.

23 Bernice Archer, '"A low-key affair": Memories of civilian internment in the Far East, 1942–1945', in Martin Evans and Ken Lunn (eds), *War and Memory in the Twentieth Century* (Oxford: Berg, 1997), p. 46.

24 Lucien Febvre, *A New Kind of History*, ed. Peter Burke (London: Routledge and Kegan Paul, 1973), p. 14.

25 Halbwachs, *On Collective Memory*, p. 137.

26 Halbwachs, *On Collective Memory,* p. 139.

27 Giambattista Vico, *On the Most Ancient Wisdom of the Italians*, trans. L. M. Palmer (Ithaca: Cornell University Press, 1988), pp. 95–6.

28 Leon Battista Alberti, *On Painting*, trans. John R. Spencer (New Haven: Yale University Press, rev. edn, 1966), pp. 70–85.

29 Giambattista Vico, *The New Science of Giambattista Vico*, trans. Thomas Goddard Bergin and Max Harold Fisch (Ithaca: Cornell University Press, 1984), p. 264, para. 699.

30 Stephen Davies, *Empiricism and History* (Basingstoke: Palgrave Macmillan, 2003), p. 127.

31 John Fiske and John Hartley, *Reading Television* (London: Routledge, 1989), pp. 85–8.

1

Whose past is it anyway?

The first obstacle that historians and producers of television history have to deal with when working with the past is defining what can be classed as history. What is a valid subject for study, for a one-off programme, a series? What is the distance between then and now for an event to be deemed worthy of being regarded as history?

There is of course an eclectic range of areas that make up historical study. These include, in no order of prestige or preference: political, religious, economic, military, feminist, social, oral, cultural, intellectual, philosophical, industrial and popular history, to name but a few of the major and sub-brands of research and study. Given the range of areas included under the mantle of history, perhaps in the future the question posed should be, 'What isn't history?' The distinguished historian A. J. P. Taylor sums up this dilemma with his view on what European history entails: 'European history is whatever the historian wants it to be.'[1]

Recreating the past is always going to be problematic. History as a concept, as a way of connecting the present with the past is based on national events and personal events. These are histories of two very different kinds, the former usually coming as indirect mediated experiences, the latter direct and first-hand. It is in this overlap between direct experience and recreated experience where issues of representation, truth, memory and accuracy contained within British television history programming become sharply defined.

To begin with, however, it will be valuable to assess the various stages of historiography in order to lay down a base from which it will be possible to evaluate and analyse points of divergence and similarity between academic history and popular history. At the core of popular history sits the production and consumption of television history as a major form in the popular recreation of the past.

Tracing the evolution of the modern European idea of history, R. G. Colling-wood, in *The Idea of History*, refers to early attempts at historical writing as recording the actions of individuals under the influence of divine power and its agency. This he believed to be a ceremonial control of society through myth, a period of pre-scientific history, what he termed 'theocratic history and myth' which predominated until the Greco-Roman period.[2]

This phase of iconic recording, commemoration and celebration has reso-nances in history programming by the fact that television as a medium repre-sents totemic values and rituals in the home. The type of television set owned acts as a status symbol, the programmes watched as a cultural index and the programmes themselves offer the potential to leave the safety of the home to indirectly experience travel, danger, excitement and reward.[3]

Tracing where, in Western historiography the first influences on factual history programming on British television came from, a distinct line exists between the Greek historians Herodotus and Thucydides and the eyewitness accounts that form the platform for so much television history. This 'oral' tra-dition, whereby great events were recorded as a future legacy, as a commemo-ration of what had taken place,[4] became the cornerstone for a twenty-six part series regarded by many as marking the beginning of a television history genre that presented war and conflict in a totally different form.

The Great War (BBC2, 1964) is credited as setting the 'look' for television history.[5] Its narrative mechanism of oral testimony interwoven with actuality footage capped by authorial and regal narration generated a definitive pro-gramme style, setting the norm for many factual history genres. One of the series' unquestionable strengths is in its development of the history and mode of telling practised by Herodotus and Thucydides. This entails having a clear chronological structure of beginning, middle and end to record the actions of individuals, unlike theocratic history's reliance on myths and their dateless events.[6]

History programming may have its base in oral testimony, yet many pro-grammes have also woven the didactic, reinterpretation practices of Bede into their narrative structures. Bede's revisionist policy in the middle ages is quite evident in his *The Ecclesiastical History of the English People*. Here, the past is not only revised but reworked to form history as Christian dogma.[7] Under Christian influence, historiography moved from the particular to the universal, with providence and the life of Christ as essential organising features of events. This chronological recording of events through a tightly controlled trajectory of causality–resolution–causality and systematic closure has become a central device of television history scripted and screened as stability/unrest/conflict/disaster and resolution.

Following the medieval eclectic approach to the past, a radical shift towards modern history took place in the Renaissance with humanism.[8] For Niccolò Machiavelli, history could no longer be accounted for through Divine agency with events determined by fate, the supernatural or the imagination. 'So leaving aside imaginary things about a prince, and referring only to those which truly exist',[9] Machiavelli drew on antiquity and classic scholars to illuminate his writings. History, in other words, was entirely earthbound, the direct result of individual action.

Recognising how influential individuals are in forming the past, Vico's concept of contextual history emphasised that individuals do not work or live in isolation, so therefore their story, their history, must take into account the world in which they lived.[10] This is an inclusive concept, one that is clearly at work in *Times Remembered* (BBC2, 1970–73), a *Man Alive* production billed as:

> Treasured memories of other times – firm views about present times. In the race for today few of us spare enough time to listen – even to learn from people who also know about yesterday, as they talk to the *Man Alive* reporters.[11]

Scheduled to run for ten minutes on Wednesday evenings, *Times Remembered* introduced some of the BBC's major presenters and journalists – Gillian Strickland, James Astor, Harold Williamson, John Pitman, Denis Tuohy, Jonathan Dimbleby and Esther Rantzen – as they interviewed a variety of individuals from different backgrounds as a means of exploring the individual composition of the nation.

In a similar vein, *Yesterday's Witness* (BBC2, 1969–80) was 'a series which explores living memory'.[12] The series evolved from a chance meeting in a South Wales public house between the series' producer Stephen Peet and an elderly miner. The miner, 'gripping his pint with some determination, said "I am going to tell you a story"'.[13] Recognising that this represented a 'direct link with the past',[14] Peet put together the series where individual programmes and small-part specials allowed eyewitness accounts to become the frame for 'Stories from the past, unexpectedly worth hearing'.[15] Expanding the concept of the past being witnessed from the present as in *The Great War*, this personal connection with the past was a significant breakthrough that would prove to be an extremely popular strand of television history.

In historiography, it was the Enlightenment that distinguished its approach from the Renaissance's humanist ethos of the spirit and soul by reason galvanised

1   A. J. P. Taylor, the first telly-don

by logic, embraced by Pierre Bayle, Voltaire, Montesquieu, Hume, Gibbon and Kant. History had a new motivation, a different perception of individual inspiration, action and reaction that enabled 'history of a new kind' to be written, based on the relationship between individuals and their landscape.[16]

Television history has also enjoyed its own Enlightenment, commencing in the 1950s when A. J. P. Taylor demonstrated his mastery of television as a medium for history and his subject in *Challenge* (ITV, 1957), covering the Russian Revolution.

Throughout his television career, Taylor, hailed as the first 'telly-don',[17] delivered lectures for both the BBC and ITV, completing his career with a lecture series for Channel 4 in 1985 before his death in 1990. Taylor's style fused reason, with Gibbon's style of effortlessly linking past and present, encouraging a dominant position of privilege alongside the historian as they ventured into history together.

As a 'typical Enlightenment historian' whose version of history was motivated by 'human irrationality',[18] Gibbon illuminates this causality through strong narrative structure. In his *Decline and Fall of the Roman Empire,* this structure is judiciously punctuated by stereotypical two-dimensional morality-engaged characters, measured by their 'virtues' 'faults' or 'failings',[19] rather than as true individuals. A similar range of character types are employed within programmes, such as *Great Britons* (BBC1, 1978), *Late Great Britons* (BBC1, 1988) or *Great Britons* (BBC2, 2002), where individuality is consumed by stereotypical national values. Learning from the past rather than the present formed an important and influential bridge between the rationality of the Enlightenment and the emotive nature of Romanticism.

Increasing turmoil in Europe, with wars and revolution accompanied by Britain's position as an industrial nation, made the rapid progress of the present an opportune moment for the cultivation of Romanticism as a philosophy and an ideal in 'cultural practices'.[20] After the French Revolution in 1789, understanding the past without nostalgia and fabrication was central to the movement away from Romanticism to realistic history. In an approach developed by the work of Barthold Georg Niebuhr and Leopold von Ranke, the authenticity of facts was the motivating principle. Held in high esteem as being 'the founding father of empirical historiography',[21] Ranke determined to move from the fictional, Romantic, concept to concentrate only on verifiable documents and evidence.

Television history production seems to have adopted Ranke's famous assertion that historians should 'simply show how it really was (*wie es eigentlich gewesen*)',[22] in its extensive use of eyewitnesses and the later developments of highly dramatised reconstructions and computer-generated images (CGI). Whilst Ranke may have initiated the launch of contextual, realistic history, Hegel added impetus through his concept of 'historicity'.[23] Based on necessary progressive movements from one age to another, this launched historiography well on its way towards Marxism and its current modern orbit.

History for Marx and Engels involved the interaction of economic, political, social and cultural strands of the past as a single history,[24] which is constantly restructuring itself through different phases of development.[25] At the beginning of their critique of Feuerbach in *The German Ideology*, Marx and Engels define history as a derivative from and dependent on production,[26] creating a history between individuals linked through modes of production.[27] In effect, individuals produce history and they consume it,[28] quite separately from institutional forms of history formed up and above their daily lives.

This Marxist materialistic approach has its roots in a culture and society gripped by attempts to unravel problems and issues through scientific study and observation. What came to be classed as Positivism had Auguste Comte as one of its central advocates, proposing that there were laws defining the causes of historical development.[29] If Positivism and Materialism are the genesis of scientific methodology,[30] then Thomas Babington Macaulay preferred to practise the principles of what would become the ethos of PSB delivered by the BBC. Macaulay wrote history in order to educate and entertain through the promotion of Englishness as a measure of freedom attained through democracy. In his introduction, to volume 1 of *History of England* (1848–55), Macaulay states his intention with an assured hand, confident that he is embarking on a historical journey that is designed to illuminate the present as much as the past.

> For the history of our country during the last hundred and sixty years is eminently the history of physical, of moral, and of intellectual improvement.[31]

Writing for a wide audience as Macaulay did is not reserved for professional historians, as the BBC journalist Andrew Marr's book, *A History of Modern Britain* (Macmillan, 2007) accompanying his BBC2 series, testifies. Influences from American 'New History', coupled with disenchantment with grandiose national histories after the First World War, saw history broaden out and adopt a more flexible stance. Central to this expansion was the *Annales* School formed by Marc Bloch and Lucien Febvre, who urged for a wider study of the past, incorporating social sciences.

Heralding a move away from the dynastic to the ordinary, the focus was on the thoughts, beliefs and values held by individuals. In this sense, history for Febvre 'extends beyond the "local" and the "national" context and reaches out to that which is truly human'.[32] Development of focused history following the *Annales* School's championing of a truly interdisciplinary approach increased the proliferation of sub-history subjects. These concentrated on ever decreasing and more specific topics centred in cultural, social and other aspects of history such as intellectual, economic, political, feminist, cultural, social and colonial themes for example.

It also introduced new methodologies centred on prosopography and quantitative and econometric analysis.[33] In many ways, it is Lewis Namier who is regarded as the classic practitioner of professional academic history through setting the precedent for painstaking archival work. Namier instigated a move away from studying the great and the good as being responsible for parliamentary power,[34] opting instead for a type of forensic history. Concentrating on multiple biographies of members of parliament, Namier was able to reveal the mechanisms of self-serving party politics.

In contrast to archive work, philosophical history practised by Benedetto Croce and R. G. Collingwood evaluated how the past was activated in the mind of the historian, the very method by which the historian engages with the past. Collingwood sets out his concept of philosophy by suggesting that it involves not merely thinking about something but the thinking of why the original thinking is taking place, what might be deemed reflective philosophy.[35]

The historian, insisted Collingwood, can successfully re-enter the past only through re-enacting it in their own mind, of trying to contextualise, as much as possible, the source material they have to work with.[36] Television history programmes are in one sense this imagination and thought process externalised and brought onto the screen. They represent Collingwood's fundamental proposition that 'all history is the history of thought',[37] hence justifying different interpretations and modes of presentation. The prospect of the past and history being classed as a science rankled in certain circles, with Edward Hallett Carr entering the debate with his usual gusto,[38] though by the 1970s a science of a kind had gradually made an appearance in historiography, if not a favourable impression.

Expanding into previously uncharted territory during the 1960s, by the 1980s, history was reduced to statistical charts based on economic theory. Cliometricians prefer to deal with statistical data rather than with problematic eyewitness, biographies, diaries, letters and other standard historical documents. Their 'econometric' techniques perhaps come closest to history's search for a truly scientific, objective model, leading to another cliometric phase of study termed 'Cliodynamics',[39] drawing on biology and physics.

History also began to emerge from the margins during this period. Feminist history, or women's history, grew from the 1960s and 1970s women's liberation movements, proving influential in questioning aspects of labour history that developed into issues concerning the role of women in industry and the home as equal contributors to social history. The essential concept is not merely concerned with discovering facts that promote the role women played as history makers but also questions how and why those facts have been ignored or suppressed.[40]

An important feature of feminist analysis can be found in the application of Ferdinand de Saussure and Roland Barthes' work on linguistics and structuralism. Language, for Saussure and Barthes, is an arbitrary system that shields its own ideological composition and values,[41] with its social value recognised by Febvre: 'Languages are in fact the most powerful of all means by which groups can act upon the individual.'[42] In *Elements of Semiology* Barthes describes language as an 'unclassifiable reality'[43] where, therefore, meaning can never be stable and is available for appropriation each time a text is written, each time an image is produced,[44] essentially securing a means of controlling the past as well as the present.

Texts spanning diverse spectrums of knowledge and appeal offer broad or multiple levels of preferred readings because each and every word has its own history. Semantemes produced in the past are carried into the present as units in myth systems, their value already prescribed. Myth is created as a second-order semiological system,[45] so that language or images are reused, redefined. In the case of the programme ident that leads *Falklands: When Britain Went to War* (C4, 2002) in and out of commercial breaks, the images already constitute signs in their own right. Symbolic icons of Britain's national character – a Union Jack and a clasp of Second World War medals taken from the programme's opening sequence – become reissued as contemporary signifiers, illustrating a strand of ideological anti-war sentiment.

In this visual act of appropriation, a veteran, resplendent in regimental beret, tie and blazer displaying his clasp of medals, a souvenir Union Jack in hand, is positioned between two 'characters' representing the programme-maker's concept of the 'then' generation at the time of production. The characters – one female, one male – are dressed in street-style fashion: the male in a black T-shirt, leather jacket, studded belt, short hair, with a choker around his neck, and the female in a dark top worn off one shoulder, a scarf around her neck, her hair cut in an 'edgy' style.

There is something faintly retro-punk about the pair: the way they have been posed slightly to the side of the veteran, the female twisted towards the camera, the male behind the veteran, one hand proprietarily on the veteran's shoulder. Both characters are also waving souvenir Union Jacks, and the female has something close to a smile to compare to the warm smile of the veteran.

However, it is the contemptuous sneer on the face of the male that emphasises the deep structural meaning of the programme-makers. At a surface level, there is a visual bridge between different generations, but the values of one generation have become usurped, appropriated and modified to represent the values of an artificially represented generation that stands for the ideological position of the programme-makers.

Each time language, either as written texts or as images, are appropriated, they are framed by different textual anchors. Whether in a magazine, article, book or television programme, it is this contextual framing that produces myth systems that gather additional meaning and mythical units as it progresses. The more language and images are reproduced, the more their original traces are written over, what Barthes deems to represent myth as being 'speech *stolen* and *restored*'.[46] In this instance the Union Jack, a potent symbol of British military success in the Second World War, connects different meanings of Britain's military roles together.

This appropriation and control of the past through discourse production sits centrally in the Postmodernism debate, with Michel Foucault, amongst others, questioning the power-knowledge relationship between language and objects. This can apply to factual history programme equally well. When a character or event appears on television, it carries the suggestion of validation, of being privileged above other characters or events. These hierarchical inclusions imply that selections have authority, that they are somehow invested with absolute, unquestionable power that blocks or refutes challenges on authenticity.

Foucault's assertion is that by concentrating on those individuals wielding power, historians overlook the mechanisms that generate it,[47] failing to confront who has the right to control the past and how history is presented and told. Ignorance of these mechanisms of power sits at the centre of what Collingwood asserts is the 'common-sense' concept of history.

This concept presupposes that any source has to be taken as fact. If the historian deviates from using these facts absolutely unaltered from when they were discovered, the historian provides a misleading insight into the past through his or her interpretation. Common-sense history places the historian in an impossible position, operating as nothing more than a chronicler, a scribe faithfully recording someone else's history without question.[48] Postmodernism is the natural antithesis to the common-sense approach to history, widening the historical landscape and horizon by including the marginal groups, the previously ignored individuals isolated beyond the standard searchlight beam of historical enquiry.

By extending the illuminating arc of historiography, 'Microhistory' developed from the work of postmodernist, Jean-François Lyotard. Historical events, according to Lyotard, adopting a Kantian perspective,[49] become reductive, mystified when categorised by language. The whole concept of being able to produce a reliable, all encompassing 'grand narrative' favoured by Marxists was rejected by Lyotard, who argued that the very nature of modernity meant that these 'grand narratives', the act of 'narrative legitimisation',[50] could not accurately include every event and every action.

Historiography saw a shift of emphasis towards personal histories examining the minutiae of an individual's life to construct a wider view of the period. Microhistory and factual television do share a similarity in their retelling of the personal story, the individual profile with its popular roots in cinema's biographical picture (biopic). The immediacy and intimacy of television heightens these personal accounts.

These can range from a woman accused of murdering her lover in *The Trial of Madeleine Smith* (BBC, 1949) to memories of tragedy, disaster and achievement in the BBC's nine-part series *First Hand* (BBC, 1956–57). Personal bravery on the battlefield in *Victoria Cross Centenary Review* (ITV, 1956) and the six-part series *For Valour* (BBC2, 1979) also provide tight biographical packages – as do political and social development in *As I Remember* (BBC2, 1987) featuring Lady Asquith. Allowing TV-users to connect at such an intimate level is the very reason that television history excels with the personal biography.

One series that does come close to microhistory by positioning the personal narrative in contrast to a perceived public linear history is *Who Do You Think You Are?* (BBC1, 2004–). In the series, the family history of celebrities is neatly investigated as they attempt to discover their cultural and national roots by tracing their family tree.

This format is not without its drawbacks as it compresses the painstaking archival genealogical search for ancestry into sixty minutes, much in the same way as a television 'make-over' show defies the usual time span of building and decorating projects to achieve a transformed room, home or garden. The 'reveal' in *Who Do You Think You Are?*, is often a shock or surprise. The television chef Ainsley Harriott found out in the 2008 series that not only were his ancestors slaves, one was actually a slave owner.

In the same series, the foppish interior designer, Laurence Llewelyn-Bowen discovered that his great-great-grandfather had lied in order to obtain his master's ticket enabling him to captain merchant ships. Whether the production team are lucky in finding unusually suitable celebrities with interesting family histories or preliminary archival work weeds out the less interesting possibilities is hard to tell.

It would be naïve, if not entirely foolish, to claim that factual television history programming completely mirrors and represents the various phases of history. One important difference is that historiography has been in production far longer than television history programmes; secondly, television is *a priori*, a visual medium attracting large groups of heterogeneous TV-users and, in consequence, is deemed a popular cultural form.

One form of popular history where texts come in a variety of formats or as objects to be viewed is that practised by museums. Museums represent another popular form of 'public' history, delivering selected aspects of the past 'framed' for viewing, complete with audio or written narratives. Museums and television share a common strand and similar parallels in their production of the past that Lucy Noakes alludes to in her analysis of the Blitz in two of London's museums. The factors Noakes highlights as intrinsic to these displays of the past, being 'powerful sites of cultural transmission and public education', forming an 'embodiment of knowledge and power' as an 'exhibition of national beliefs' making national characteristics visible,[51] are shared by television.

The role of popular history and academic history has, it would seem, the same overarching concept and shared goal of making the past visible. How they achieve that visibility differs quite considerably. For museums, local history groups, family historians, restoration enthusiasts, re-enactment groups and producers of factual history programming, the aim of popular history is to offer wide and open access to anyone who has an interest in the past; whereas, on the other hand, academic history is concerned primarily with research, teaching and publication for a limited market that may or may not lead to its practitioner's work being made available to a wider audience.

A people's past?

In this ongoing schism between popular history and academic history there is common ground in the need to 'tell', narrate and re-present the past in the kind of recognisable format expected by respective targeted users of specific texts. Through 'telling' the past, history as a subject and television as a visual medium share a close affinity. Each in its own way deals with the recording of events deemed to be noteworthy and significant.

Both rely on discourse frameworks such as narrative structure, modes of narration and linear time management in order to present their 'stories'. Because popular history challenges academic history by opening up the past to groups previously suppressed by 'elitist, over-professionalised history', popular history is regarded as radical.[52] It is also dismissed as a commercial venture that colonises and sanitises history by placing a value on the past as a commodity.

Television, following on from cinema, cannot stand accused of suddenly transforming history into a popular commodity. A subject so rich in characters involved in the unfolding of dramatic events has always had its roots in popular narratives created to attract a mass-market such as the almanacs, flyers and chapbooks of the eighteenth century and the Victorian penny novel, or penny dreadful.[53]

Popular culture is not a recent mass media invention. Every period has a popular tradition, from the oral ballads of the Anglo-Saxons, such as *Beowulf* in the eighth century,[54] to the epic poems, chivalrous tales and romances that the troubadours of the medieval period recited.[55] In many respects, television has borrowed and adapted some of these early conventions, redefining and reworking them as a means of layering moral lessons and knowledge within an entertaining format.

Entertainment is one of television's most attractive components, working on a number of different platforms from light entertainment and comedy to factual programming that gratifies through insight, as a presentation of knowledge not intended to overwhelm. Seen as a factor in low cultural production, entertainment has a populist ring that does not sit comfortably with a serious academic study of history.

Historians who shun factual history programming as damaging or irrelevant, might wish to consider that television history is created for TV-users who have an extended choice of what to view,[56] whereas their work does not face such a blunt selection process at its point of delivery at lectures, conferences or through publication. The whole debate on masses and mass communication seems to have a natural outlet in popular culture, with Raymond Williams suggesting there is some truth in the association of mass as a concept for audiences and consumers with the poor-taste consumerism they display. 'After the Education Act of 1870, a new mass-public came into being, literate but untrained in reading, low in taste and habit. The mass-culture followed as a matter of course.'[57]

Here the crucial point is that television history, heritage and other forms of popular history are core ingredients of mass-culture, and therefore must be of low taste. At the core of this professional, academic versus popular debate sits the issue of training, empiricism and the use of facts.

Empiricism, facts and gatekeeping

According to R. G. Collingwood, the past is accessed through four fundamental, pertinent methods that combine experience, training and thought not just of history and its events but also of why those events matter. In short, what is the point of history?[58] In other words, a return to the question posed at the beginning of this chapter – what is history?

My own loose interpretation, offered with no claims to validity, consists of defining history, in its rawest form, as anything that occurred in the preceding second as belonging to the past. News journalism is made entirely of instant history, and as Hew Strachan notes, 'Today's media are fond of describing the most trivial events as historic'.[59] Deciding who or what makes any event noteworthy or memorable as history, who has the right to select facts and turn them into history, is a different matter and another conundrum tackled by Carr.[60] The art of admitting the past into the present through gatekeeping applies to historians and the makers of television history equally well.

Whether facts sit unselected in the margins or positively vibrate with importance from repeated selections, historians always approach facts with their own ideological preconceptions. By steering a sharp plough across the hallowed ground of facts, some historians refusing to forgive him for such desecration,[61] Carr devoted a considerable number of pages in *What Is History?* to facts and their selection and usage by historians. The past is, for Carr, never absolute but unordered, consisting of a lottery of facts collected at random for different reasons across various periods.

Taken together, they do not provide a whole, despite 'vanished generations of historians' having ordered the past in a systematic way,[62] their selections scrutinised, revised or abandoned by successive gatekeepers. This, for academic history, attests to a validating process of ongoing scrutiny, a constant asserting of professional standards, whereas television's ultimate gatekeepers, the commissioning executives, work to very different criteria.

With so much of Britain's past unseen and unknown by TV-users, there does seem to be an extremely narrow repertoire of history assumed to provide good television. The shadowing of formative or successful series by competing broadcasters has consistently occurred in television history. Following neatly in the footsteps of the BBC, Channel 4 screened two series exploring the formation of Wales and Scotland with *The Dragon Has Two Tongues* (C4, 1985) following the thematic lead set by the BBC's *Wales! Wales!* (BBC2, 1984). Running fourteen years after *Who Are the Scots?* (BBC1, 1971), Channel 4 turned its attention to national identity with its *Scotland's Story* (C4, 1984), and this shadowing of themes in major series does tend to suggest a very narrow commissioning perspective.

As much as television producers prefer to suggest that programmes and series are only commissioned and aired to meet the demands of TV-users, driven by quasi-scientific, though ultimately misleading and misrepresentative, rating figures, the real power rests with commissioning executives. Controlling which aspect of the past becomes available and viable as television history belongs in the higher executive ranks of commissioning editors who practise gatekeeping at its most influential and primary level.

Turning the story of national development into factual television history during the 1970s and 1980s reflects how commissioning executives reacted to an identity crisis that permeated the very roots of British politics. Nothing short of a constitutional crisis was aptly revealed by the Scottish National Party (SNP), claiming eleven seats at Westminster with 30 per cent of the Scottish vote in the 1974 General Election.[63] With Scotland finally having its own parliament in 1999 and a seemingly unstoppable resurgent SNP in power with forty-seven seats following the 2007 Scottish election, the question of Scottish independence was once again being raised.

With Scotland's separatism back on the political agenda, BBC Scotland did not squander the opportunity to re-evaluate national identity in its ten-part series, *History of Scotland* (BBC, 2008). Hailed as a 'landmark' series, and 'one of the most ambitious historical series ever created',[64] its production was not without complaints of bias towards English sensibilities in Scottish history. Resignations from the series' advisory board over the content being too Anglo-centric, and a further academic's refusal to join the board because Neil Oliver, a Scot and seasoned presenter from *Two Men in a Trench* (BBC2, 2002) and *Coast* (BBC2, 2005), was an archaeologist rather than historian,[65] demonstrate the fracture lines between creating popular television history and academic history.

The important issue in what Carr proposes as the crux of his argument is the validity and significance given to some events over others. Essentially, who is to be a gatekeeper of historical facts, determining which facts are worthier than other facts? Acting as a gatekeeper is never a simple process of selection but involves elements of career pressure, social pressure, personal and group perception that has to vie with impartiality.

Controlling which aspect of the past reaches TV-users is no common-sense straightforward choice between factual accuracy and discrepancy. As the Creative Director of BBC History Laurence Rees is acutely aware, facts are not objective and programme-makers have to be even more guarded when dealing with a good deal of their source material, which happens to be, in many instances, living witnesses.[66] At the commissioning level, decisions must also take into account a channel's brand identity for factual history, its reputation for innovative and successful formats and, strategically, whether this selection from the past will have enough appeal for its TV-users.

Memory and oral history

Standing as a central convention of *The Great War*, and what marked Herodotus' contribution to historiography, was his intention to produce historical inquiry 'so that human achievements may not become forgotten in time',[67] derived as it was, from oral sources. Television history and academic history have had an uneasy, tempestuous relationship when it comes to oral eyewitness-based narratives. The question of oral testimony's reliability as a primary source is often given for this divergence between academia and popular history, including television formats, with one of the fundamental reasons concerning the validity of eyewitness testimony and accounts based on individual and collective memory.

Memory as a concept is problematic. Its formation and function as a long-term cognitive system are in continuous revision through ongoing studies concerning its structure and means of assessment. A consistent factor with individual memory formation is that memory is never constant. Memory is forever shifting, changing its boundaries, modifying its narrative depending on the circumstances surrounding its formation, the influences on it and its accuracy when recalled or modified for specific purposes.[68]

In the same way that the past is not exclusively private, it is always framed by associated events as causal correlatives; intense personal memories are also extremely vulnerable to seepage or elaboration from external sources such as cinema and television. This in itself is not reason or motivation enough to dismiss memory as having no part to play in history. In its collective or popular form, it becomes an adhesive that bonds the filaments of nation and nationality tightly together.

When memory has strong contextual anchors and can be cross-referenced, its value should, Trevor Lummis argues, be accepted as 'good historical evidence', creating a personal view of the past to be interwoven with other sources.[69] Memory, in its first instance, as a deposited trace, is derived through sensory contact, filtered through perception, judgmental configurations and the imagination. For my purposes, I intend to concentrate on collective memory, attempting to define how television functions as a modifier of collective memory, based on the 'hyper-integrative model' which proposes that 'television is seen as a major instrument in the shaping of collective memory, especially national, and sometimes global'.[70]

If individual, personal memory is directly experienced, the result of participatory experience of an event, collective memory can be classed as memories removed from direct experience, constituting secondary spectatorship of some kind. Individual memory is endemic, collective memory pandemic; that is to say, one is entirely located with personal contact and experience, whereas the other is located in the wider public sphere largely dominated by professional mediated discourses, of which television is a substantial provider.

Compiling individual memories comes through perception of external visual signs matched against an internalised, highly personal series of references compiled as we develop as individuals. At key moments, triggered by stimuli, logical and emotive experiences are stored as raw memory. When TV-users interact with television, a judgemental interface, consisting of similarity and difference, based on past sensory experiences comes into play.[71] The present, if this proposition is extended, is always negotiated and formed from previous experiences,[72] from personal memory dependent on the strength of each trace.

Television provides both logical and emotive stimuli that can attach themselves to personal memory, enlarging or redefining individual memory into group or collective memories, where personal and public slide into each other,[73] forming a conglomerate memory. When television meshes with an individual TV-user's life story at a particular point, interconnecting with other memory frameworks, other 'vehicles of memory' allows the past to be shared as a collective concept.[74] For television this meshing and fusing of memory acts as a 'reconstructive' agent,[75] and factual history programming is no exception.

If conglomerate memory is a *bricolage* of individual and collective memories, historians play an active part, as Raphael Samuel recognises, as 'memory-keepers',[76] though some historians distrust collective memory, regarding it as liable to produce 'dubious' history.[77] This stance also, to some extent, rejects a natural product of memory, that of its transference into oral history. Perhaps it is distrusted because it stands uncomfortably with, and challenges , officially sanctioned memories, as it 'allows the voice of ordinary people to be heard alongside the careful marshalling of social facts in the written record'.[78]

Yet, memory and the past are never free. They always function as commodities, appropriated, modified or transformed in a specific way to attain a specific goal,[79] which marks off memory as being regarded more a popular history covenant than an academic history form. More than books, radio and other mass forms of communication, television, is, for Robert Hanke, a major outlet for popular memory.[80]

When television history deals with a specific past reality, the truth of that reality is lost in its translation, it becomes modified by memory and can never be a perfect mimetic version of its original. What television history produces, is a socially constructed reality understood by both programme-makers and TV-users. Television has the ability to make objects, actions, sound, dialogue, movement, colour and characters appear natural and acceptable because television and its technology are 'where mass media, history and memory do not exist within neatly defined boundaries. The boundaries are blurring and each of these domains is overlapping and influencing the others'.[81]

As John Fiske explains, television 'presents itself as an unmediated picture of external reality ... television is seen either as a transparent window on the world or as a mirror reflecting our own reality back to us'.[82] Pre-war British television, however, offered neither a mirror nor a window, but a small keyhole through which a modest number of TV-users could watch a public service broadcaster set about reinforcing a collective vision of national identity.

Notes

1 A. J. P. Taylor, 'What is European history…?', in Juliet Gardiner (ed.), *What Is History Today?* (London: Palgrave Macmillan, 1988), p. 143.

2 R. G. Collingwood, *The Idea of History* (Oxford: Oxford University Press, 1961), p. 16.

3 David Morley, 'Television: Not so much a visual medium, more a visible object', in Chris Jenks (ed.), *Visual Culture* (London: Routledge, 1995), p. 181.

4 Vico, *New Science*, p. 53, para. 101.

5 Taylor Downing, 'Bringing the past to the small screen', in David Cannadine (ed.), *History and the Media* (Basingstoke: Palgrave Macmillan, 2004), p. 9.

6 Collingwood, *Idea of History*, p. 18.

7 Bede, *The Ecclesiastical History of the English People*, ed. Judith McClure and Roger Collins (Oxford: Oxford University Press, 1998).

8 An in depth study of the Renaissance can be found in Jacob Burckhardt, *The Civilisation of the Renaissance in Italy*, trans. S. G. C. Middlemore (London: Penguin Books, 2004).

9 Niccolò Machiavelli, *The Prince,* trans. George Bull (London: Penguin Books, 2003), p. 50.

10 Vico, *Ancient Wisdom of the Italians*, pp. 60–1.

11 *Man Alive, Radio Times* (hereafter, *RT*) (12–18 September 1970), p. 37.

12 *Yesterday's Witness, RT* (22–28 March 1969), p. 19.

13 *Yesterday's Witness, RT*, p. 30.

14 *Yesterday's Witness, RT*, p. 30.

15 *Yesterday's Witness, RT*, p. 30.

16 Norman Hampson, *The Enlightenment* (London: Penguin Books, 1990), pp. 107–8 and p. 239.

17 Geoffrey Wansell, 'A Profile of A. J. P. Taylor: "A Pyrotechnic Academic." How Vanity Led an Unquiet Don into New fields', *The Times* (30 August 1971), p. 6.

18 Collingwood, *Idea of History*, p. 79.

19 Edward Gibbon, *The Decline and Fall of the Roman Empire*, a one-volume abridgement by D. M. Low (London: Book Club Associates, 1979), pp. 393 and 748.

20 Stephen Bygrave, 'Introduction', in Stephen Bygrave (ed.), *Romantic Writings* (London: Routledge/Open University, 1996), p. vii.

21 Davies, *Empiricism and History*, p. 27.

22 Carr, *What Is History?*, p. 8.

23 Eric Hobsbawm, *The Age of Revolution: Europe 1789–1848* (London: Abacus, 1992), p. 302.

24 Karl Marx and Frederick Engels, *The German Ideology, Part One*, ed. C. J. Arthur (London: Lawrence and Wishart, 2nd edn, 1974), p. 59.

25 Marx and Engels, *German Ideology*, p. 57.

26 Marx and Engels, *German Ideology*, p. 48.

27 Marx and Engels, *German Ideology*, p. 50.

28 Marx and Engels, *German Ideology*, p. 131.

29 John Tosh, *The Pursuit of History* (London: Longman, revised 3rd edn, 2002), p. 166.

30 Arthur Marwick, *The Nature of History* (Basingstoke: Macmillan, 2nd edn, 1981), pp. 43–4.

31 Thomas Babington Macaulay, *History of England vol. 1* (London: Heron Books, 1967), p. 2.

32 Febvre, *A New Kind of History*, p. 3.

33 Marwick, *New Nature of History*, p. 97.

34 Peter Thomas, 'Reappraisals: The structure of politics at the accession of George III', Institute of Historical Research. www.history.ac.uk/reviews/reapp/lewis.html.

35 Collingwood, *Idea of History*, p. 1.

36 Collingwood, *Idea of History*, p. 282.

37 Collingwood, *Idea of History*, p. 115.

38 Carr, *What Is History?*, pp. 69 and 85.

39 'Ernest Labrousse and the rise of Cliometrics', Cambridge Forecast Group. http://cambridgeforecast.wordpress.com/2008/04/06/ernest-labrousse-and-the-rise-of-cliometrics.

40 Joan Wallach Scott (ed.), *Feminism and History* (Oxford: Oxford University Press, 1996), p. 3.

41 Roland Barthes, *Elements of Semiology*, trans. Annette Lavers and Colin Smith (New York: Hill and Wang, 1967), p. 31.

42 Febvre, *A New Kind of History*, p. 4.

43 Barthes, *Elements of Semiology*, p. 13.

44 Roland Barthes, *Mythologies*, trans. Annette Lavers (London: Vintage, 1993), p. 109.

45 Barthes, *Mythologies*, p. 109.

46 Barthes, *Mythologies*, p. 125.

47 Michel Foucault, *Power/Knowledge, Selected Interviews and Other Writings 1972– 1977*, trans. Colin Gordon, Leo Marshall, John Mepham, Kate Soper; ed. Colin Gordon (Harlow: Longman, 1980), p. 51.

48 Collingwood, *Idea of History*, pp. 234–5.

49 Jean-François Lyotard, 'The sign of history', in Derek Attridge, Geoff Bennington and Robert Young (eds), *Post-structuralism and the Question of History* (Cambridge: Cambridge University Press, 1987).

50 Jean-François Lyotard, *The Postmodern Condition: A Report on Knowledge*, trans. Geoff Bennington and Brian Massumi (Manchester: Manchester University Press, 1986), p. 36. Lyotard covers the concept of language, its use, modification and suppression in chapters 8–10, pp. 27–41.

51 Lucy Noakes, 'Making histories: Experiencing the blitz in London's museums in the 1990s', in Evans and Lunn (eds), *War and Memory*, pp. 90–1.

52 Jordanova, *History in Practice*, p. 141.

53 R. K. Webb, 'The Victorian reading public', in Boris Ford (ed.), *The New Pelican Guide to English Literature, vol. 6, From Dickens to Hardy* (Harmondsworth: Penguin, 1982), p. 203.

54 *Beowulf*, trans. Michael Alexander (Harmondsworth: Penguin, 1973), p. 11.

55 Ingeborg Glier, 'Troubadours and Minnesang', in Boris Ford (ed.), *The New Pelican Guide to English Literature, vol. 1, Medieval Literature, Part Two: The European Inheritance* (Harmondsworth: Penguin, rev. edn, 1982), pp. 171–8.

56 Laurence Rees, Creative Director BBC History, interview with the author (26 October 2005), BBC Television, White City, London.

57 Raymond Williams, *Culture and Society 1780–1950* (Harmondsworth: Penguin, reprinted with a postscript, 1963), p. 295.

58 Collingwood, *Idea of History*, pp. 9–10.

59 Hew Strachan, 'Forward', in Svetlana Palmer and Sarah Wallis, *A War in Words* (London: Simon & Schuster, 2003), p. x.

60 Carr, *What Is History?*, p. 11.

61 Marwick, *New Nature of History*, p. 155.

62 Carr, *What Is History?*, p. 14.

63 Allan Massie, 'The Final Highland Fling?', *Daily Telegraph* (14 April 2007), p. 20.

64 Paul Bignell, 'BBC Hit by Row Over "History of Scotland"', *Independent on Sunday* (9 November 2008), p. 9.

65 Bignell, 'BBC Hit by Row', p. 9.

66 Rees, interview with the author.

67 Herodotus, *The Histories*, trans. Aubrey De Sélincourt (London: Penguin Books, rev. edn, 2003), p. 3.

68 Pierre Sorlin, 'Children as war victims in postwar European cinema', in Jay Winter and Emmanuel Sivan (eds), *War and Remembrance in the Twentieth Century* (Cambridge: Cambridge University Press, 1999), p. 105.

69 Trevor Lummis, *Listening to History: The Authenticity of Oral Evidence* (London: Hutchinson, 1987), p. 130.

70 Jérôme Bourdon, 'Some sense of time', *History and Memory*, 15:2 (2003), 6.

71 M. L. J. Abercrombie, *The Anatomy of Judgment* (London: Free Association Books, 1989), p. 27.

72 Abercrombie, *Anatomy of Judgment*, pp. 34–5.

73 Abercrombie, *Anatomy of Judgment*, p. 34.

74 Alon Confino, 'Collective memory and cultural history: Problems of method', *The American Historical Review*, 102:5 (1997), 1386.

75 Bourdon, 'Some sense of time', *History and Memory*, 7.

76 Raphael Samuel, *Island Stories, Unravelling Britain, Theatres of Memory, Volume II*, ed. Alison Light (London: Verso, 1998), p. 37.

77 Marwick, *New Nature of History*, pp. 31–2.

78 Tosh, *Pursuit of History*, p. 299.

79 Carr, *What Is History?*, p. 12.

80 Robert Hanke, 'Quantum leap, the postmodern challenge of television as history in television's historical fictions', in Gary R. Edgerton and Peter C. Rollins (eds), *Television Histories, Shaping Collective Memory in the Media Age* (Lexington: The University Press of Kentucky, 2001) pp. 61–2.

81 Alejandro Baer, 'Consuming history and memory through mass media products', *European Journal of Cultural Studies*, 4:4 (2001), 499. http://ecs.sagepub.com/cgi/content/abstract/4/4/491.

82 John Fiske, *Television Culture* (London: Routledge, 1987), p. 21.

2

Post-war television and history: from sound to vision

Converting Britain from sound to vision before the outbreak of the Second World War was slow, to say the least. Muddle, fudge, corporate and government power play bedevilled the dash to become the first provider of a television service to Britain. Transmitting its first officially branded programmes from 22 August 1932,[1] the BBC had chosen John Logie Baird's pioneering system, though it was far from convinced of the picture quality.

Television was viewed by an estimated 10,000 enthusiasts,[2] whose initial interaction with the medium was through a nine by four inch screen that produced dim, flickering and crude pictures.[3] Regardless of a new high-definition system being introduced, the move from radio to television measured by set ownership was exceedingly sluggish. Only around 20,000 television sets were owned by 1939.[4] This can be attributed in some way to how mass media entertainment in pre-war Britain offered a straightforward choice between radio and the cinema.

When the BBC resumed its transmissions in 1946 those diligent pre-war enthusiasts were treated to multiple runs of *Television is Here Again*, a 'pot-pourri of TV production, past, present, and future for use as a test film by engineers installing new television receivers'.[5] If TV-users in pre-war Britain had experienced the world through a small flickering keyhole, their post-war television was about to resemble a mirror on their world, rather than a window on the world outside London.

The post-war London-based TV-users of 1947, estimated at 15,000 to 25,000 sets located within 'roughly forty miles of Alexandra Palace, though there are many reports of good reception at much greater distances',[6] represented the first form of class bias associated with the BBC. As 1947 drew to a close, almost half of all television sets were owned by the 'top twelve percent of the income distribution'.[7] A rapid increase of television ownership, measured by the number of licences issued, rose from 240,000 in December 1949, to 1,900,000 at the end of 1952 as new regional BBC transmitters came on line.[8]

With the 1943 Hankey Committee rubber stamping the Selsdon Committee's 1934 findings that the BBC be the sole provider of television and radio after the war, the BBC's domination of the airwaves were guaranteed for the immediate future.[9] Controlling both radio and television, the BBC may have regarded itself as an influential institution, though outside its growing empire, it was viewed by the *New Statesman* as early as 1934 as having an unfair monopoly on radio and television programming as it went about 'civilizing the population'.[10]

As far as its television service was concerned, it had become an institution misunderstood and feared by 'theatre managements, sports promoters, and the film industry, which leads them to deny the BBC facilities'.[11] Secure in its belief of building *the* framework for a national television service, the BBC, in its progression through the 1950s, suggested a resolute indifference to a society in flux: 'Despite difficulties not of its own making, the BBC television service is still pre-eminent in the range and quality of its programmes'.[12]

Programmes ranging from demonstration films, ballet and drama[13] to 'expository programmes as "News Map" and "Foreign Correspondent"'[14] and popular entertainment in the form of *The Grove Family* (BBC, 1954), the United Kingdom's first soap opera, albeit with an aspirational middle-class family, became the basic orthodox formula for PSB. With the first 'provincial relay station at Sutton Coldfield' operating by the end of 1949,[15] a steady commissioning of transmitters throughout the 1950s finally brought most regions, including Northern Ireland within receiving distance of BBC Television.[16] Ironically, this availability of BBC transmissions to nearly all parts of the country would prove to be the high-water mark of its television service monopoly. Unease at the BBC's stranglehold on sound and vision broadcasting, its corporate size, its dominance by management biased towards radio, were all factors presented to the Beveridge Committee on Broadcasting in 1949 and 1950.[17]

One challenge to the BBC's continuation as *the* single broadcaster came from the Liberal and Fabian Research Groups, with the Liberals noting how the BBC represented 'the biggest single bureaucracy in the world concerned with the propagation of ideas'.[18] A majority report by the Beveridge Committee did indeed note that an unchecked BBC would assume a 'Divine Right', that it posed 'dangers of Londonization' and staff 'favouritism and injustice' were likely to be more of an 'evil in a monopoly' than if competition existed.[19]

Unwilling to recommend a break-up of the BBC or introduce competition, the Beveridge Report called for the appointment of a 'Director of Public Representation' to oversee the corporation,[20] though this was never implemented.

A much more damaging minority report by Selwyn Lloyd did little to diminish the debate, and a 1952 White Paper on Broadcasting set out to introduce competition,[21] though rather paradoxically recommended continuing the 'ban on commercial broadcasting', yet allowing for an 'element of competition in television'.[22]

A rival broadcaster finally arrived in September 1955, following the Television Act of 1954, ending the BBC's monopoly with the introduction of ITV, Britain's first commercially funded broadcaster. Launched with a remit from the outset to provide elements of public service broadcasting, ITV came under the commercial channels' regulatory body, the Independent Television Authority (ITA), and was to be funded entirely by advertising.

It was hardly a shock to find ITV's output as different from the BBC's high cultural orbit as possible. By concentrating on programmes that would not simply inform and educate, ITV created the added advantage of being shamelessly entertaining through popular appeal. Not only did the emergence of ITV threaten to take TV-users from the BBC, it also led to BBC staff being offered high incentives and inducements to move across to the commercial sector.[23] This tangible threat from ITV was taken seriously within the BBC because of ITV's determination to differentiate itself on the screen, making a concerted effort to lure more TV-users over from the BBC. What TV-users received on the opening night of ITV transmissions was a preview of good and not so good television interspersed with commercial breaks. The first advertisement to run on British television was for Gibbs S. R. toothpaste.[24]

Offering something new was a strategy that also bore fruit in an increase of TV-users overall, the average number of daytime TV-users rising from 1.6 per cent in 1952, to 3.0 per cent in 1955, and evening TV-users increasing from 5.8 per cent in 1952, to 13.7 per cent by 1955.[25] That ITV had struck a popular chord with its appeal to certain TV-users can be measured in the rate of television set purchases. At the end of 1954, upper middle-class TV-users accounted for 40 per cent of the television public, but only represented 12 per cent of the population, the lower middle classes registered 38 per cent of TV-users, accounting for 20 per cent of the population, whilst the working class made up 68 per cent of the population, yet only recorded 22 per cent of TV-users. Television, before the launch of ITV, was nothing close to being a cross-section of British adults.[26] What posed a greater threat to BBC programme output – based, as it was, on quality – was that although the proportion of working-class TV-users had risen on a par with middle-class purchases, from 1955, middle-class television set acquisition began to decline as working-class purchases increased.[27]

The BBC may have been technologically forward looking, but institutionally, it was antediluvian, a monolith, unprepared for the success of ITV and finding it difficult to change direction, revealing the BBC to be stuck firm and fast in a different era. Whilst the BBC may have lost its way when faced by the populist challenge of ITV, that challenge did force the corporation to assess its position with regard to what TV-users preferred. As its position as sole provider of television was challenged, the BBC was to become bedevilled by ITV competition from 1955 onwards. The BBC now found itself in the same position as British cinema had, when faced with severe competition from Hollywood during and after the war. Figures for 1957 revealed that where TV-users had a choice between BBC and ITV programming, 72 per cent preferred the commercial output.[28]

As a direct descendant of BBC radio and the ethos of its first Director General, Sir John Reith, BBC television adopted his vision as a means of offering a dignified air of public broadcasting based on providing education, information and a moral lead. This was intended to underpin and weld the country together as a whole, unified by a sense of national spirit.

Safeguarding and maintaining any standards meant the BBC adopted a role as the arbiter not only of taste and quality but also of national identity, inheriting the Reithian ethos that it should serve as a beacon of enrichment for all its viewers and listeners by maintaining, promoting and presenting a discernible national identity at home and overseas. This was a mandate that its factual history programming between 1946 and 1949 be scrupulously upheld, producing programmes based around the central themes behind the concept of a nation-state (see table opposite).

It can be no coincidence that the BBC's first two factual history programmes, *Germany Under Control* and *The Heart of an Empire* offer reassurance that a bitter enemy has been tamed and that London is still functioning as *the* capital city of the world. *The Heart of an Empire*, originally released in 1935, consisted of a static rooftop camera survey of the historic architecture of central London targeted at 'younger viewers'.[29] Though how many of them would be aware of the Empire's impending fragmentation is hard to say.

This stirring over of the coals of past glory a year later in *Song of Ceylon*, Basil Wright's 1934 documentary for the Empire Tea Marketing Board, is com-

BBC factual programming 1946–49
One-off programmes and series based on the past

1946

Sunday 1 September	*Germany Under Control* (BBC, 1946)
Saturday 16 November	*The Heart of an Empire* (BBC, 1946)
Tuesday 19 November	*The War Underwater* (BBC, 1946)
Tuesday 10 December	*Early History of the Film* (BBC, 1946)

1947

Friday 10 January	*Early History of the Film* (BBC, 1947)
Monday 17 March	*Early History of the Film* (BBC, 1947)
Monday 16 June	*Early History of the Film* (BBC, 1947)
Wednesday 10 September	*Britain Can Make It* (BBC, 1947)
Monday 13 October	*Digging up the Past* (BBC, 1947)
Tuesday 11 November	*The Palace of Westminster* (BBC, 1947)
Friday 12 December	*Berlin* (BBC, 1947)
Sunday 14 December	*Song of Ceylon* (BBC, 1947)

1948

Sunday 4 January	*Death at Newtownstewart* (BBC, 1948)
Tuesday 27 January	*Music Through the Centuries* (BBC, 1948)
Thursday 25 March	*Coastal Command* (BBC, 1948)
Tuesday 20 April	*Close Quarters* (BBC, 1948)
Monday 11 October	*Secret Mission* (BBC, 1948)

1949

Sunday 9 January	*The Trial of Madeleine Smith* (BBC, 1949)
Friday 5 August	*London Town* (BBC, 1949)
Monday 28 November	*London Town* (BBC, 1949)
Friday 30 December	*London Town* (BBC, 1949)

Source: Radio Times.

plemented by other themes of nationality and civilisation running in diverse series. These include a series on the history of film, a pilot for a series on music and the first television brush with archaeology in *Digging up the Past*. As dominant features of the 1946–49 scheduling these formative programmes and series would establish some of the most popular history formats on television. What they also clearly delineated was where Britain stood in the post-war world and where it had come from.

Exactly where Britain was going with a promise of coming prosperity was not left to chance either in *Britain Can Make It*. The dark side of society, brutal murder and love affairs leading to murder, providing the theme of justice so much needed for national values, also made their first television debut, though it would be far from their last.

The Trial of Madeleine Smith, based on court transcripts, represents the formation of the reconstruction framework at the centre of docudramas. The first of two live transmissions on Sunday 9 January from 8.30 to 10.10 p.m., the second on the following Thursday, reconstructed Smith's trial as she stood accused of murdering Pierre Émile L'Angelier, her illicit, and socially inferior, lover. As the BBC announcer makes clear, the programme was breaking new ground:

> ANNOUNCER: This is the B.B.C. Television Station at Alexandra Palace. Good evening, everyone. Our programme this evening consists of something which we ask you to consider as a kind of experiment. We have selected a well-known murder trial and we have tried to present it to you in such a way that you may be able to assess the weight of the evidence exactly as the jury had to do. The actual trial we are dealing with lasted for nine days, and of course we have had to do a very great deal of compression. But we believe that all the important facts will be put before you. We hope that you will find it possible (without too great an effort of concentration), to follow the various points as counsel make them.[30]

Having been given the privileged role of participants as individual jury members, TV-users were also drawn into a collective re-examining of the past in the early schedules. This role of revisiting the past reiterated a sense of national values and national esteem in reissuing and emphasising victory contained in Second World War documentary films.

Originally produced by the British Army Film and Photographic Unit (BAFPU), the Crown Film Unit (CFU) and the RAF Film Production Unit (RFPU), the films cemented the post-war television experience with the wartime cinematic experience of Britishness the films had depicted for many TV-users. *Desert Victory* (BAFPU and RFPU, 1943/BBC, 1947), *Coastal Command* (CFU, 1942/BBC, 1948), *Close Quarters* (CFU, 1943/BBC, 1948) and *Target for Tonight* (CFU, 1941/BBC, 1950) re-celebrated victory by capitalising on 'the tradition of painstaking, didactic British documentary realism which had been planted and watered between the wars by John Grierson and others'.[31]

Adamant that ITV competition would not interfere with its 'aims and obligations',[32] the BBC asserted that programme competition 'must be met when it comes'.[33] A hiatus in the BBC's factual history output appears to reflect how the BBC was re-thinking its strategy on how best to deal with ITV by monitoring what its commercial rival actually delivered.

What ITV and its programme-producing franchise companies actually delivered was a string of factual history programmes that maximised their entry into a new marketplace, the hallowed BBC territory of factual programming where the BBC had stoically ensured that 'every aspect of national and international life seems to be touched upon one way or another'.[34] Aspects of anthropology, religion, heritage, antiques and collective memory – *Kaye Webb's Scrap Book* (1955) – defined ITV's challenge and set the pattern for its factual history production that mirrored much of the BBC's programming built around the concept of the nation-state.

ITV also included wartime documentaries in its schedules – *The True Glory* (BAFPU, 1945/ITV, 1957), *Fires Were Started* (CFU, 1943/ITV, 1960) and *Desert Victory* (ITV, 1959) divided into two parts to accommodate a commercial break. During its early output, ITV did in fact show a marked attempt to build a distinctive identity after producing a range of programmes similar to those broadcast by the BBC.

Speaking for the nation?

The escalating spiral of competition between the BBC and ITV led to an intransigent belief in PSB on the one hand versus an overwhelming populist approach on the other. For the BBC, this saw it adopt a significant role in attempting to structure the cultural complexion of the country as the 'voice of Britain' or the 'voice of the nation'. An institutional perception inherited from BBC radio and Reith's idealism of patriotic duty. For BBC television, this idealism is enshrined in its sombre coverage of events and anniversaries of national importance that celebrate and commemorate pageantry, heritage and tradition. This is evident in its coverage of royal weddings, state funerals, Trooping the Colour, the Lord Mayor's Show and the wreath-laying ceremony at the Cenotaph in Whitehall.

One common theme that unites television and academic history in a consensus revolves around the intricate, perennial question of nationality. This has been particularly relevant to what it means to be British, a theme serving as a dominant presence in television schedules since the 1950s for all broadcasters.

The physical manifestations of national characteristics in the landscape and the people function as a conduit, which circulates, forms and re-establishes inherited collective memories within concepts of tradition and heritage. Factual television history in this way provides a subtle but continuous form of citizenship. As a result, television as an institution is in effect a cultural dynamo, powered by institutional and individual forces that produce ideological values.

If television in general is part of the 'political geography' mapping a national collective identity, then factual history programming helps to 'determine the very nature of national allegiances, attitudes towards place, family, government and state'.[35] An interesting theme to emerge during 1955 was the personal narrative format that gave precedent to individual testimony, the eyewitness account. One of the early oral history formats, *Looking Back* (BBC, 1955), dealt with 'Nationalism' from the individual viewpoint of Patrick O'Donovan in part two of the series, with other personal memories being brought to the surface that spanned motor rallying with Sheila Van Damm and transport with Paul Jennings. The series returned briefly in the 1960s, covering more weighty issues such as the two-part recollections of Leonard Woolf – 'An Unredeemed Intellectual' and 'Remembering Virginia' (BBC1, 1967) – and 'Palme Dutte: Professional Revolutionary' (BBC1, 1967).

The success of this first person-orientated programming, is its ability to get below the institutional level of ideology to form an intimate, binding relationship with groups and individuals where collective memory is at its most powerful. At this level, the views and values expressed differentiate individual and group memories, forming positive or negative relationships.

Some of the one-off programme themes in this format that deal with measuring the present against the past represent 'looking back', 'being there', 'remembering' or 'growing up'. This theme is redolent of the twelve-part series *The Curious Character of Britain* (BBC1, 1970). Directed by Philip Trevelyan and Trevor Vibert, and narrated by Derek Jones, the aim of the series, repeated as the *Sights and Sounds of Britain* (BBC1, 1971/1972), was to travel 'somewhere different each week in search of the British – and [to get] involved with their feelings about the place they call home – somewhere on our island'.[36]

The problem of series designed to explore concepts of nationality or regionality, is that national identity can be regarded as an irksome myth. It cannot account, it is argued, for the fault lines of individuality based on gender, religion, class or politics.[37] In his attempt to define how a national identity is constructed, David Miller proposes that national identity is organised around shared beliefs and a sense of commonality that 'embodies historical continuity. Nations stretch backwards into the past, and indeed in most cases their origins are conveniently lost in the mists of time'.[38] Issues of nationality are complex, made up of institutional and individual values that mean: 'To be British is to be a mass of contradictions and competing loyalties.'[39] Of course, national identity is formed from core values that can be appropriated and institutionally organised to promote a cohesive, collective mentality when national interest demands it.

Usually these are in times of war, national emergency, economic crises or terrorist attacks. The officially issued 'patriotic poems and prose pieces' to boost troops' morale during the First World War,[40] attempted to define the need to fight and provide reasons for self-sacrifice. Re-invoking and calling on the same concept of a shared purpose redolent in so many British propaganda films from the Second World War, validating the Falklands War in 1982, and the first invasion of Iraq in 1991, represent an institutional appropriation and commodification of the past.

This is entirely different from group or personal concepts of Britishness, though these resonating traces of victory can be part of a collision of values at work in multilayered narratives within collective memories. This multilayering of different voices, of different values in collective memory, collides personal memory with public or group memory.

In television history, this collision is brought about by the visual power of a particular image privileging the presenter's view, or that of an eyewitness, narrator or specialist account or testimony as being commonly shared and therefore a valid position to hold. This position of shared, accepted national values, represent an assumed position of truth that has the collective power to modify personal memories when they collide with a common perception or myth of what has taken place.

In this way collective memory is never original, it is a second-hand compass shifting position between the unknown points on a map of the past, and the known territory of personal memory. Consequently, collective memory is only activated by the present concerns of society, the modern topography of thought and reason, forming sites of personal and public remembrance. Memories as a means of charting the past are always incomplete; some features are more pronounced, more visible and memorable than other features.

Where collective memory interacts with individual memory, it is always as a modifying agent sanctioned by group pressures and group ideals. Individuals react to group values and ideology as groups offer structured systems of acceptance where memories have strategic value and can be shared within an agreed consensus of what is and is not acceptable. One of the most cohesive elements of collective memory as national identity is gained from buildings, the landscape, heritage and tradition. The landscape, an established powerful motivator for artists and poets attempting to externalise their own feelings of place and time, became particularly loaded with exaggerated personal significance during the Romantic period.[41] This quasi-taming of the landscape to demonstrate cultural, educational, in some cases political, empowerment and control,[42] defines England/Britain as an insular island race that has mastered its island environment to produce order and stability.[43] Once again, BBC programmes and series mapped out the theme for others to follow.

The initial concept behind *Historic Houses of England* (BBC, 1950–53) was not without its problems, encountering one of the determining factors in the production of factual history, the availability of actuality footage. Resolving this dilemma required a letter from producer John Read to confirm what library film of 'famous houses' was available.[44] In setting a historical criterion for the series, Read sums up the definition of a 'historic house' thus: 'The term, "Historic House" should include the best of the any period, short of the immediate present.'[45]

This was a pioneering encounter with the landscape as nationality, and there were technical limitations for location work that dictated the format. On the proposed inclusion of Wightwick Manor, Read notes that the programme would have to consist of photographs with voice-over commentary, accounting for 75 per cent of the content, and interviews with the owners would make up the remainder.[46] In some cases – Luton Hoo in part five, for example – exhibits from the house were boxed up and transported to the Alexandra Palace studio.[47] Houses themselves, however great or historical, are not enough to form a lasting impression of national identity.

The concept of ownership within the confines of the physical landscape drew together natural features alongside sites of spatial growth. Houses, villages and cities become apposite records of cultural periods as tokens of nation and nationality denoting achievement. This celebration of the present through the past provides the format for *At Home* (BBC, 1955), where famous figures such as Field-Marshal Montgomery of Alamein and other celebrities of the day, including the journalist and radio and television presenter Gilbert Harding, discussed their homes. Equally, in a symbolic paradigm, the home becomes a figurative motif for national character in *The Englishman's Home* (BBC, 1957) and *The Englishman's Country Home* (BBC, 1957), where England and Englishness stand out as defining criteria of nation and nationality in the 1950s.

How far bricks, stone and mortar represented nation and nationality, and how far society had moved on from the 1950s was identified by Channel 4's *Caves, Castles and Council Houses* (C4, 1993) tracing the evolution of British housing and its social effect. At the opposite spectrum, Lady Victoria Leatham used *Heirs and Graces* (BBC2, 1988) in a mid-afternoon slot to explore nine stately homes. This personal link to property was reinvigorated with *House Detectives* (BBC2, 1997–2002), Channel 4's *No 57: The History of a House* (C4, 2003) and is still a feature of factual history with *Hidden House History* (History Channel, 2006–), presented by Nick Barratt and Jonathan Foyle. The series' objectives of making the past personal, based on a genealogical approach, is gained thus:

> Combining the social and personal history of a house with its architectural back-ground Jonathan and Nick will chart the story of the nation and the day-to-day lives of our ancestors through its houses.[48]

As much as it may have held itself to be the 'voice of the nation', the BBC did not have exclusive rights to programmes exploring national identity. ITV gave the idiosyncratic Daniel Farson free rein to roam through the bastions of traditional English values in his series *Keeping in Step* (ITV, 1958), which assesses the institutional class system and hierarchies in its variant forms, including 'The Women's Institute', 'The Stock Exchange' and 'The Brigade of Guards'. In 1959, Farson went beyond the institutions with *Farson's Guide to the British* (ITV, 1959), a twelve-part foray into the peculiar characteristics of the British, including the British as cat lovers, a visit to the working-class holiday resort of Blackpool and the 'Jews of Commercial Road'.

Both ITV's and the BBC's probing of nationality through institutions and the physical landscape reinforced a sense of what it meant to be English in their different ways. It is these educational and entertaining visual themed classes in national citizenship, that are redolent of what Wordsworth described as 'spots of time' in Book XII of the *Prelude*.[49] These topographical junctions of past and present are where the landscape is fused with associative values and meanings affixed to a period in British history as times remembered. They function as a moral and aesthetic guide to the formative development of Britain, a logical and emotive means of creating powerful receptors in an inherited collective memory.

Disparate landscape elements, a natural feature such as a river, great houses, churches, cathedrals, homes and public buildings act as tangible 'spots of time' in the formation of a nation-state and also as symbolic sights that fuse together the collective memory framework required to 'imagine' the concept of Britain as a nation.[50] Heritage, with its sights of remembrance in the national psyche, is the most popular form of factual television history, constituting what can be thought of as a journey into history typology.

Where geographical features, houses or buildings do appear as avatars in television history programming, their representational paradigm constructs a literal picture of nation and national heritage. Utilising the same visual and physical manifestation of the distant and not so distant past as employed by the tourism and heritage industries, popular forms of television history have capitalised on the landscape as a means of branding and selling the past.

Creating these nostalgic journeys into the past, *Outlook: Time and Place* (BBC2, 1967) employed these metonymic tropes to integrate heritage into a visual assemblage of 'Deep England' and its 'Long History' as in part eight, 'Constable Country' and part eleven, 'Shakespeare's England'. Anglia Television's contribution to the popular *About Britain* series, with its *In Constable's Country* (ITV, 1975), clearly indicates that commercial television was equally adept at utilising heritage and tradition as a means of being seen as a broadcaster that understood the importance of a reassuring 'Golden Age'. In fact, what the BBC's and ITV's most popular factual history formats share is a metonymical and synecdochical rhetoric that circulates a mythical national identity.

There can be little doubt how the coastline, landscape and buildings of Britain provide visually stunning opportunities to make good television history. There also seems no shortage of presenters willing to explore and explain once more how we built Britain. Fred Dibnah's *Building of Britain* (BBC2, 2002), Simon Thurley's *Building Britain* (C4, 2005), *Coast* (BBC2, 2005) and David Dimbleby's *How We Built Britain* (BBC1, 2007) all re-cover traditions, heritage and genius that celebrate the unique features of how Britain has developed as a nation-state.

The pictorial overview of building Britain, however, began with what was an innovative series for its time, *Bird's-Eye View* (BBC2, 1969–71). Filmed from a helicopter, it attempted to reintroduce the landscape and its history to a population who, it believed, were unaware of what heritage was actually around them. The *Radio Times'* feature for the new series offered a forthright statement on what these aerial tours were designed to achieve:

> What can they know of England who only England know? Or for that matter, only Scotland, Ireland or Wales? The trouble is, people who live in a country tend all too often not to take much notice of it. So now a new series of fifty-minute documentaries – to be screened not at regular intervals but on high days and holidays – is being mounted with the aim of directing the eyes of the inhabitants of these places back to their native soil. [51]

With some parts written by John Betjeman, others by Correlli Barnett and John Terraine, the series covered iconic aspects of 'Deep England', from the coast to industrial heartlands. The first part, written and narrated by John

Betjeman, ran on 5 April 1969 and was, unsurprisingly, titled *The Englishman's Home*.

Once again, aerial history is a concept the BBC has returned to with Andrew Marr's *Britain from Above* (BBC1, 2008) in a series where Marr explores the changing face of Britain. To spice up the three-part series that delved sporadically into the past, Marr skydives and takes to a microlight as part of this aerial survey, though his efforts to give the multiplatform project any real meaning is not wholly successful, as Alison Graham, the television editor of the *Radio Times*, points out:

> Very nice, but there's not a great deal else to *Britain from Above*, apart from these admittedly impressive gimmicks … but this is another 'Oooh, isn't Britain marvellous and fascinating?' sort of documentary that doesn't demand his incisive mind … What's next, I wonder – Britain from the Drains?[52]

What Marr's series does in fact do, is to seamlessly fit into the tourism and heritage industries' strategy that commodifies the past as a marketing device that carries an inherent value of what it means to be British. Turning Britain into a commodity is a factor Catherine Palmer succinctly highlights as a central concept for constructing national paradigms; 'the tourism industry relies upon a form of nationalistic rhetoric as a way of conveying images and meanings about what it considers to be the nation's communal heritage'.[53]

Rhetoric as a representative index of nation-state values is not a convention developed by television. History has always been doctrinaire in one form or another as it re-presented the past. Television's direct predecessors in presenting visual narratives meant to represent a national history are the Victorian history paintings that 'provided a permanent visual memory of a highly selective and romanticized past'.[54] With visual representation always a product of technological and cultural change, television has become the electronic canvas through which the past is now framed.

Because television quickly colonises other social practices such as the theatre, doing as cinema did in providing more spectacle than in earlier modes of visual representation,[55] it transforms existing narrative forms into distinct elliptical paradigmatic metonymical and synecdochical codes – nothing less than television shorthand for what it means to be British. Evidence of this is paramount in the way the format of landscape heritage history on television developed in the 1970s and 1980s in the series *Day Out* (BBC1, 1977–88).

A regional BBC production, a good deal of it from BBC West in Bristol, *Day Out* used heritage as a platform to explore well-established portals of collective memory as regional contributions that constructed a sense of national identity. The series' format consisted of a portmanteau approach to regional links with the past. Each episode embarked on a quest, with river journeys, tours of the countryside, or investigating ancient customs, myths and museums. An updated version of this format can be found in *Castle in the Country* (BBC2, 2005–), with John Craven and Gloria Hungerford presenting its fourth series. The pair, usually 'explore', 'discover', 'learn about', 'find a tale', sometimes 'tragic', concerning regional history,[56] with its anodyne format not intended to needlessly ask very much involvement from its TV-users.

During these heritage quests, the narrative and images visibly connected present and past in the same way that 'tourism's use of the natural landscape is another means by which identity can be constructed within the imagination'.[57] Regional identity is important in forming a framework to feed into a collective memory of why Britain has developed and unified in spite of, or through difference and diversity. A series in the 1990s had a title that left little to the imagination with an impassioned plea: *Think of England* (BBC2, 1991), unpicking elements of race and language as defining nationality, whilst Channel 4 ran a British Transport film, *The Coast of Clyde* (C4, 1991), that nostalgically connected regionality with English and Scottish perspectives of nationality. The importance of the landscape as a core block of nationality also featured in *Landscape and Memory* (BBC2, 1995), examining how geographical features and culture have influenced each other.

In *Day Out* and the other one-off programmes and series dealing with the physical landscape, its geographical features and its buildings, this core of paradigmatic nationality evolved from the Second World War when it was essential to reinforce and reiterate a sense of national identity and ongoing achievement. In many ways, the range of locations in the programmes pick up where Humphrey Jennings left off in *Listen to Britain*, in capturing and evoking the essence of Britain through symbolic connections constructed through the landscape.

Regional history inevitably feeds into the regeneration of national identity as the *Radio Times* and *TV Times* reveal dedicated slots for regional programming. Designed initially for local TV-users, ITV had *About Britain*, with *Network*, *Homeground*, and the *Northern Documentary* produced by regional BBC centres. *The Noble Game* (BBC, 1962), dealt with cricket memorabilia, listed in the *Radio Times* as 'an edited version of a programme seen last spring by viewers in the south'.[58] In a similar vein, Denis Mitchell's *Night in the City* (BBC, 1962), a 'Northern Regional Film Unit production',[59] and *Spitfire!* (BBC2, 1978), first shown in the south, demonstrate not only the BBC's

production of regionally centred history but also the crossover of these programmes into the national schedule.

ITV's chief contributions to regional diversity, was its popular and populist *About Britain* (ITV, 1970–88). The series cannot claim to be entirely new
or innovative, as the BBC had experimented with the format in 1952 with
Richard Dimbleby in *About Britain* (BBC, 1952–53). ITV's version was a
thirty-minute travelogue/history/human interest format produced by regional
television companies for the lunchtime, early afternoon network slot. In its
own unique way, the series was a distinct forerunner of Richard Holmes' and
Simon Schama's style of using the landscape to bring the past vividly into the
living room.

Using history as a core theme, the series offered a diverse insight and range of
presenters covering subjects that included Scottish Television's 'Burns Country'
(ITV, 1973) and Southern Television's 'Such a House is Goodwood', presented
by Max Robertson (ITV, 1974). Anglia Television offered 'Royal Sandringham'
(ITV, 1977), and Harlech Television (HTV), the history of Welsh iron-making
in 'Men of Iron' (ITV, 1980) with Wynford Vaughan-Thomas. Scottish Television's 'Weir's Way … The Seven Men' (ITV, 1981) had Tom Weir attempting
to walk in the footsteps of Bonnie Prince Charlie. To sustain an eighteen-
year run on a commercial network, *About Britain's* success does indicate that
daytime TV-users preferred their regional history to be heritage-based and not
duly demanding.

Factual history production by the Northern Ireland Film Unit provided
'A Study of Principal Ernest Davey 1890–1960' for *View Point: The Rounded
Mind* (BBC1, 1964). Ulster Television's eleven-part series *Ulster Landscapes* (C4, 1983) and its six-part series *A Heritage From Stone* (ITV, 1986),
examining Ulster's architectural legacy, written and presented by Brian Boyd,
equally demonstrates regional history for local and national TV-users. Border
Television's history quiz series *That's History* (ITV1, 1991), hosted by Andy
Craig, had different stately homes in the north of England and Scotland as a
weekly backdrop for its contestants to join battle over the past during its Friday
afternoon run. Granada Television's *Lost Treasures* (ITV1, 2008), broadcast
during the early evening network split on Sundays, investigated and explored
regional history, archaeology and mysteries in the northwest. The series was
fronted by Mark Olly, a man of myriad talents as 'a musician, artist, photo-
grapher, writer, and archaeologist, [who] holds a Certificate of Ministry and
a Diploma of Biblical Studies. He trained in field archaeology with Liverpool
University in the 1970s and 1980s'.[60]

Promoted as an 'exciting six-part "adventure archaeology" series … presented by charismatic antiquarian Mark Olly',[61] it contains countless re-enactments and a style of presentation that has Olly dressed in a flowing black highwayman's coat, black fedora and elaborate boots as he over-dramatises his discoveries. Nevertheless, behind the on-screen distractions of Olly, there is regional history in the series that reconnects the story of northwest England into the larger panorama of British development.

Nationalism is not by any means a modern phenomenon. Its roots can be traced back to Herodotus and 'the oldest written histories',[62] and it can be found in the dominant paradigms of representation motivating the work of humanist French photographers following the Second World War. Working within the parameters of a collective memory of what France should constitute, the photographers attempted to re-represent the concept of France. This drew together the myths of Frenchness in order to reaffirm the social fabric of France as a newly emerging nation-state.[63]

As a visual articulation of collective identity, this called up previous myths of Frenchness to be overwritten with new social and cultural imperatives as the country attempted to heal its crisis in identity and national pride. Myths are not pure fabrication or without foundation; they are rooted in the structure of culture and society, an expression of collective memory and values that are expressed as facts.[64] History, including factual television history, plays an important part in creating and sustaining myths. In the case of television, myths are the product of the society that has invested them with privilege, status and a means of circulation.[65]

Myth, its formation, its conditions for usage and its longevity all depend on the culture and society where it finds its sources and forms. Like strands of collective memory, less popular myths become forgotten, abandoned as no longer relevant,[66] though they always leave behind traces around which new myths are constructed. As Roland Barthes recognised, images are an ideal vehicle for the generation and circulation of myths because of their immediacy and impact.[67]

Factual history production as it moved through periods of social and cultural change from the 1950s to the present day is both a destroyer and circulator of myths. Television production has always been as much a social construct as a technical one, responding to the ideological beliefs of those working within the industry. Therefore, the construction of national identity is as much a personal statement as it is an institutional statement, and neither can ever be divorced from the circulating myths of Britishness.

By building 'inclusive representational' categories of what the country and the world can perceive as a nationality,[68] factual history television creates a definitive world view for consumption at home and, in the case of co-productions and exports, overseas. Representations of nationality, even when revisionist, produce classifications of 'Other' because understanding is established by difference. This is particularly apposite when 'identity is linked to spectatorship',[69] the very mechanism that engages TV-users with the past.

If national identity is constructed and brought about by difference, then it is always a difference marking then and now, here and then. Measured as time past and as a different landscape, the past becomes a truly 'Other' collective, inherited world. Moving between cultural and social landmarks of difference is entirely feasible and possible with television because of its immediacy.

Television is more than an apparatus that reflects a world beyond the home back to its users; it is more sophisticated, and it has an altogether higher level of complexity in its intimacy with TV-users. As a virtual time machine, it is capable of transporting viewers globally into any aspect of the past, present and future.

This implied authority to move through time is founded on trust, TV-user experience and levels of personal gratification that factual history programmes can create. It enhances any view of the past as being both accurate and reliable, or for some TV-users, it delivers a direct contradiction to their own 'first-hand' experiences.

When manufacturing nationhood through television, a struggle between dominant and contradictory discourse voices takes place on the screen. The screen becomes a contested space where claims that one form of heritage as a rightful representation of the past, contest others, inevitably producing counter discourses revealing myth structures. By making claims on heritage, to effectively declare ownership on certain aspects of history creates a vacuum. In the end, programme-makers often have nothing more substantial to work with than the layers of myth that amplify a public perception of a nation-state.

Recreating history with the intention of providing fresh evidence, knowledge and insight is a practice television history programme-makers have to balance with the ability to make the past an interesting experience for TV-users.

As early as 1948 BBC television was well aware of its need to produce programmes that would generate viable TV-user numbers as well as ensuring loyalty. In a memo from Cecil McGivern, Head of Television Programmes, to James Hartley, producer of *Music Through the Centuries*, McGivern lambasts the second programme as being too 'arty-crafty' and warns that the series will not run again if drastic revisions are not made. 'I feel sure we had very few viewers left by 9.45 p.m. on Sunday. And I should have hated to hear some of their language.'[70]

As soon as TV-user research began to play an integral role in shaping BBC programming strategy spurred on by competition with ITV, this intensified scheduling policy. Offering a balanced evening's viewing with a range of programmes was now all-important.

This mind frame exists in the Viewer Research Report on the second programme of the *Historic Houses of England* series, featuring West Wycombe. The report notes that the disappointing feedback seems to arise from its being scheduled to follow immediately on from another documentary, *Gateway to Europe* (BBC, 1950), unlike part one of the series *Luton Hoo* – which followed the 'variety show' *Kaleidoscope* (BBC, 1950).[71]

To ensure that it could get the balance right between popular less demanding programmes and the 'highbrow' programming would put tremendous strain on the BBC. Following the austerity of the Second World War and the limbo of the early to mid-1950s, Britain was desperate to progress but not sure how to do so, which mirrored the BBC's position. The end of the decade through to the liberal movement of the 1960s created a cultural hiatus from where the past was no longer taken as a model to be adapted and developed. A progressive push was underway for cultural and social systems to be abandoned and opposed in every conceivable way possible with the BBC caught in this cultural riptide.

Television from 1955 onwards concerned direct competition between the BBC and ITV franchise companies spread across regional lines throughout the United Kingdom. However, it was only after these original companies and new companies had bid for the second franchises that their financial security and profit were established,[72] and by the 1960s, the BBC was forced to accept that viewers preferred more choice. With changes at the BBC including the appointment of Sir Hugh Greene as Director General and the start-up of BBC television's second terrestrial channel, BBC2, in April 1964, television history programming had its own channel from where its ascendancy as a popular form of history and commodity would be spearheaded.

From 1955 until the launch of BBC2 and Channel 4 in 1982, the two terrestrial giants of British broadcasting would be locked into a ferocious battle for ratings. With advertisers' demands for larger numbers of TV-users, ITV franchise companies were propelled on a popular but downward spiral as they appealed to the lowest common denominator. For some critics of commercial television, a base level had already been reached in 1955, summed up as 'the taste-less, the time-wasting and the trivial'.[73] Caught in this competitive system, factual history in the 1960s would enter one of its most formative and enduring phases, a period when many formats were created that have provided genealogical roots still evident in 2009 programming.

Notes

1 Ronald H. Coase, 'The development of the British television service', *Land Economics*, 30 (1954), 209.

2 Coase, 'British television service', 209.

3 Coase, 'British television service', 209.

4 Coase, 'British television service', 211.

5 *Television Is Here Again*, BBC Programme Catalogue.

6 *BBC Yearbook 1947* (London: The British Broadcasting Corporation, 1947), p. 80.

7 A. D. Bain, 'The growth of television ownership in the United Kingdom', *International Economic Review*, 3:2 (1962), 146.

8 Coase, 'British television service', 211.

9 Coase, 'British television service', 212. See also the *BBC Year Book 1950* (London: British Broadcasting Corporation, 1950), p. 151.

10 Coase, 'British television service', 211.

11 *BBC Year Book 1950*, p. 152.

12 *BBC Year Book 1950*, p. 152.

13 *BBC Year Book 1950*, p. 152.

14 *BBC Year Book 1950*, p. 153.

15 *BBC Year Book 1950*, pp. 151–2.

16 B. P. Emmett, 'The television audience in the United Kingdom', *Royal Statistical Society Journal*, 119:3 (1956), 284–5.

17 Coase, 'British television service', 212.

18 Norman Collins, 'The nature of "competitive" television', *Political Quarterly* (1953), 371.

19 Collins, 'Nature of "competitive" television', 371.

20 Collins, 'Nature of "competitive" television', 372.

21 Collins, 'Nature of "competitive" Television', 372–3.

22 Coase, 'British television service', 218.

23 'BBC's "Critical Phase" After Lavish Rivals Offers to Staff', *The Times* (29 July 1955), p. 3.

24 'First Night of the I. T. A. Emphasis on the "Stars"', *The Times* (23 September 1955), p. 5.

25 Emmett, 'Television audience', 299.

26 Emmett, 'Television audience', 295.

27 Emmett, 'Television audience', 296.

28 Asa Briggs, *The History of Broadcasting in the United Kingdom, Volume V. Competition*

(Oxford: Oxford University Press, 1995), p. 20.

29 *The Heart of an Empire, RT* (10–16 November 1946), p. 35.

30 BBC Written Archives, Caversham (hereafter, WAC), Microfilm copy of the script – *The Trial of Madeleine Smith*, written by John Gough, produced by Royston Morley (transmitted BBC Television, 9 January 1949).

31 Angus Calder, *The People's War 1939–1945* (London: Pimlico, 1992), p. 368.

32 *BBC Handbook 1956* (London: British Broadcasting Corporation, 1956), p. 115.

33 *BBC Handbook 1956*, p. 116.

34 *BBC Handbook 1956*, p. 116.

35 Monroe E. Price, *Television: The Public Sphere and National Identity* (Oxford: Oxford University Press, 1995), p. 3.

36 *Sights and Sounds of Britain, RT* (10–16 January 1970), p. 42.

37 Bernard Porter, 'My country. Right or wrong?', *History Today*, 56:7 (2006), 32–3.

38 David Miller, *On Nationality* (Oxford: Clarendon Press, 1997), p. 23.

39 Alan Cochrane, 'A Britishness Day Is Not the British Way', *Daily Telegraph* (4 June 2008), p. 22.

40 A. P. Foulkes, *Literature and Propaganda* (London: Methuen, 1983), p. 9.

41 Noël Carroll, *Philosophy of Art* (London: Routledge, 1999), p. 59.

42 John Barrell, 'The public prospect and the private view: the politics of taste in eighteenth-century Britain', in Salim Kemal and Ivan Gaskell (eds), *Landscape, Natural Beauty and the Arts* (Cambridge: Cambridge University Press, 1993), p. 81.

43 David Lowenthal, 'European and English landscapes as national symbols', in David Hooson (ed.), *Geography and National Identity* (Oxford: Blackwell Publishers, 1994), p. 21.

44 WAC T32/189, letter from John Read, 29 January 1952.

45 WAC T32/189, report from John Read, undated.

46 WAC T32/189, memo from John Read, undated.

47 WAC T32/189, undated.

48 *Hidden House History* www.hiddenhousehistory.co.uk/press/view.php?Id=88.

49 William Wordsworth, *Selected Poems,* ed. Walford Davies (London: Dent, 1975), p. 148.

50 Benedict Anderson, *Imagined Communities* (London: Verso, rev. edn, 1991), p. 6.

51 *Bird's-Eye View, RT* (5–11 April 1969), p. 32.

52 Alison Graham, 'Britain from Above', *RT* (9–15 August 2008) p. 66.

53 Catherine Palmer 'Tourism and symbols of the identity', *Tourism Management*, 20 (1999), 316.

54 Richards, 'Popular memory and the construction of English History', p. 7.

55 Williams, *Culture and Society: 1780–1950*, pp. 290–1.

56 *Castle in the Country* www.bbc.co.uk/programmes/b006mk00.

57 Palmer 'Tourism and symbols of identity', 317.

58 *The Noble Game, RT* (18–24 August 1962), p. 23.

59 *Night in the City, RT* (21–27 July 1962), p. 45.

60 Mark Olly biography www.media53.co.uk/clizone/treasures/series1/mo.html.

61 *Lost Treasures* www.media53.co.uk/clizone/treasures/series1/index.html.

62 Samuel, *Island Stories*, p. 5.
63 Peter Hamilton, 'Representing the social: France and Frenchness in post-war humanist photography', in Stuart Hall (ed.), *Representation, Cultural Representations and Signifying Practices* (London: Sage/The Open University, 1997), pp. 76–7.
64 Barthes, *Mythologies*, p. 143.
65 Barthes, *Mythologies*, p. 110.
66 Barthes, *Mythologies*, p. 110.
67 Barthes, *Mythologies*, p. 110.
68 Hamilton, 'Representing the social', pp. 76–7.
69 Rey Chow, 'Film and cultural identity', in John Hill and Pamela Church Gibson (eds), *The Oxford Guide to Film Studies* (Oxford: Oxford University Press, 1998), p. 171.
70 WAC T13/78), memo from Cecil McGivern, Head of Television Programmes, to James Hartley, producer of *Music Through the Centuries*, undated.
71 WAC T32/189, viewer research report on programme 2, West Wycombe (week 31) VR/50/315, undated.
72 Arthur Marwick, *Culture in Britain Since 1945* (Oxford: Blackwell, 1991), p. 86.
73 'The End of the Monopoly', *The Times Radio and Television Supplement* (19 August 1955), p. xi.

3

The making of a popular commodity

Television history has not suddenly emerged from the late night shadows of scheduling or as daytime 'fillers' to reach its position of an exceedingly successful popular television commodity. Within the industry, its appeal and success has always been evident since 1946. Year on year, the figures for new series and one-off programmes demonstrate a rise in commissioning and output – including repeats – that emphasise consistent TV-user commitment and loyalty to the genre.

The transmission of *Germany Under Control* in 1946, credited as being the first factual history programme that 'inaugurated television documentaries',[1] was one of only seven factual history programmes broadcast that year. Since then, professional history and television history on British television have undergone significant changes in their treatment and re-presentation of the past.

Programming produced by BBC television since 1946 was, by the 1960s, still extolling the virtues, morals and standards that marched to a different tune. This was in stark comparison to the modern beat of the 1960s, regardless of a cultural climate that, for some, was seen as an opportunity for rebellion. Teddy boys, hippies, mods and rockers, Hells Angels, skinheads and punks generate a distinguished line of anti-establishment 'youth culture', beginning in the 1950s, as a means of constructing a different physical, musical and culturally symbolic identity from the 'older generation'. Allying specific dress codes with particular pop music genres and bands – mods and *The Who*, punks and the *Damned* and the *Sex Pistols* for instance – provided a means by which each generation could stand apart from parents, or anyone old enough to be regarded as parents, through defined cultural tastes in music and fashion.

If these manifestations of rebellion marked out each youth culture as sections of society cast adrift, for many, their only roots lay primarily in a working-class culture. This was a culture that, from the 1950s onwards, witnessed its traditional manufacturing role and self-esteem shrinking, a factor television programming largely ignored. Television programmers contented themselves by presenting a world of parental values and authorised cultural views remote from the interests of each generation's youth culture, preferring to broadcast what was essentially adult-orientated scheduling.

ITV may have had to provide factual history programming from its launch to satisfy its regulatory obligations, though its appeal to TV-users was largely confined to its imported Hollywood films, which cost Associated Television Ltd (ATV) £89,300 in 1957.[2] Balanced by dramas and game shows branded around less formal, people-like-us hosts, they inevitably drew more TV-users across from the formal BBC.

As far as the commercial sector was concerned, history could be given a popular framework in compilation programmes and quizzes such as *Flashback*, which a year later returned to the schedules as *Answers Please!* (ITV, 1958) together with further nostalgia centred newsreel compilations *This Day* (ITV, 1956), and *This Was Today* (ITV, 1956).

This same strategy of combining popular, peripheral history and serious history continued throughout the 1960s for ITV. The channel presented diverse series ranging from *The Origins of Man* (ITV, 1962) to *Early Musical Instruments* (ITV, 1977), demonstrating that it could balance popular history formats with in-depth examination of the past. This was a shrewd tactical strategy, ensuring that the ITV network satisfied its statutory requirement to provide quality programming at a period when television provision was under intense public and government scrutiny once more.

The enquiry into television provision in this case came within the remit of the Pilkington Committee, under the chairmanship of Sir Harry Pilkington, which commenced work on 13 July 1960. Its task was to examine every aspect of the BBC except its external services. The BBC's Charter would expire on 30 June 1962, but Harold Macmillan, Conservative Prime Minister, and his Postmaster-General Reginald Bevins extended the Charter to 29 July 1964, to coincide with the ending of the ITA's original ten-year period of control over commercial television. Both the ITA and BBC were informed that they would continue to operate after 1964, but it would be the Pilkington Committee's task to assess how and in what form. The key question soon revolved on the possibility of a new third television network and how this might be controlled and managed. The BBC had high expectations of being given the new network.[3]

After all the evidence, the doubts and uncertainties, the recommendations of the Pilkington Committee called for a completely new structural relationship between the ITA and ITV companies and for the BBC to take responsibility for a new network.[4] Commissioning two White Papers on the future of broadcasting following the Pilkington Committee's findings, the Government rejected the recommendation of Pilkington for a revision and overhaul of the ITA structure, but did accept the White Papers' endorsement for the BBC to be given a second network and introduce colour television.[5]

Far from cutting the BBC free from its competition, the 1960s heralded a worrying time for the corporation, with Hugh Greene, the Director General, overseeing decisions that attempted to steer the broadcaster in a new direction, though this fresh strategy proved unpopular and 'alienated a substantial section of the listening and viewing public, particularly the latter'.[6] Despite this, during October to December 1962, the BBC's viewing figures exceeded those of ITV for the first time since the commercial channel's launch in 1955 in areas where TV-users had a choice between the two broadcasters. The BBC captured 52 per cent compared with ITV's 48 per cent.[7]

If ITV's scheduling strategy highlights an attempt to go head-to-head with the BBC in terms of factual history, then it never achieved its objective, and once BBC2 had joined the fray in 1964 and established itself as the BBC's iconic factual channel by 1969, ITV would never be able to compete. Faced by the combined forces of BBC1 and BBC2 from 1964, which accounted for 68 per cent of factual history scheduling compared with ITV's 32 per cent, inclusive of repeats, it gained only a meagre three per cent increase on the 29 per cent it had achieved in the 1950s. Between 1970 and 1979, ITV could only manage a paltry 29 per cent compared with BBC1 and BBC2's 71 per cent.[8]

By the 1960s the BBC, unfettered at least by commercial pressures, could afford to experiment. Commissioning series such as *Monitor* (BBC, 1958–65), the BBC covered the arts and culture with a remit that never expected a large TV-user share.[9] This flew directly in the face of ITV's ethos of attracting large numbers of TV-users through programmes that appealed to the widest tastes. Producing the award-winning *Elgar* (BBC, 1962) a film biography written and directed by Ken Russell, *Monitor* helped to establish the BBC's trend for producing history from as wide a base as possible.

> Made for *Monitor* in 1962, Elgar has proved the most popular of all Ken Russell's television films. Old newsreel film, photographs, and specially shot material are combined with Elgar's music to reconstruct the life of this great English composer. The film won Ken Russell his first Screenwriter's Guild Award for the best documentary film script of the year.[10]

It proved such a success that it was placed forty-eighth in the British Film Industry's 'Top 100' programmes and fourth in the British Film Industry's 'Top 100' Factual category.[11] Repeated in 1963, 1966 and 1968 as part of the *Omnibus* series, this demonstrates the diversity of production strands capable of delivering history-based programming for the BBC that has never been really matched by ITV.

Above all, the 1960s created a platform for a radical revision of what society consisted of and its future direction and role, with the BBC attempting to realign itself within the changing cultural and social upheaval. Rapid social and economic restructuring during the 1950s, initially impeded by the Korean War in 1950, was driven by Labour and Conservative governments with their own idealistic visions for forming a New Britain to rise from the ashes of Empire as a technological force to be reckoned with.

If the Second World War had already begun to establish a dominant collective voice in shared memories as a key tabular of nationality, real social cohesion founded on class came to be challenged during the 1950s and 1960s. This was perhaps nowhere more true than on television, with satirical programmes that questioned the inherited 'official, class-secure social system and its attendant inequalities'.[12] Satirical programmes such as *That Was The Week That Was*, 'TW3' (BBC, 1962–63), evoked and captured this sense of change more readily than most. Relishing its role in challenging the establishment, a similar stance was adopted by *The Frost Report* (BBC1, 1966–67) featuring the often-repeated class sketch performed by John Cleese, Ronnie Barker and Ronnie Corbett, questioning the entire concept of class as a ruling paradigm.

History programming too showed a marked move towards exploring social and cultural tensions at home and overseas that had begun to surface in the factual output of the 1950s. This increased dramatically through the 1960s and was to become a dominant fixture of the 1970s. One series that emerged from the 1960s that entertained and informed different groups of TV-users and forged an indelible genealogical footprint was the BBC's archaeology/history series *Chronicle* (BBC2, 1966–89). Archaeology, uncovering the past or fitting lost or fragmented pieces together has formed an important programme and series strand for factual television history since the late 1950s. In his paper for the Institute of Historical Research 'Television archaeology: Education or entertainment', Don Henson, an archaeologist, writes:

> I think it is noteworthy that the earliest archaeology on television had to fit into an entertainment format to be accepted. *Animal, Vegetable, Mineral*, which began in 1952, was a copy of an American TV show called *What in the World?*,

and featured Glynn [*sic*] Daniel, Sir Mortimer Wheeler and some of the other key archaeologists of the day.[13]

Animal, Vegetable, Mineral? (BBC, 1952–58) was indeed a panel game, but it was a good six years behind the first archaeological programme on British television. The BBC's 1947 transmission of *Digging up the Past* set in motion a television fascination for unearthing or discovering 'finds', 'clues' or 'treasure' in order to interpret how Britain developed as a nation. Other early one-off programmes derived from, or based on archaeology included *The Elgin Marbles* (BBC, 1950), *Roman City* – 'Colchester' (BBC, 1950), and *Bygones* – 'Medieval London' (BBC, 1951).

Television archaeology has never lost its appeal for TV-users or programme producers – the BBC's *Buried Treasure* ran from 1954 to 1958 – and has set a distinguished route through different decades, forming a demand demonstrated by the success of Channel 4's *Time Team* in 1994.

The popularity of television archaeology owes its success to *Chronicle*, a series very much a product of the 1960s. It is perhaps the vision and skill of the early production team – Paul Johnstone, producer; Julia Cave, director and on-screen presenters Glyn Daniel and Magnus Magnusson – that provided *Chronicle* with such a flexible format, ensuring that it remained a flagship series for over twenty years. One of *Chronicle's* enduring strengths came from Magnusson's magnetic on-screen persona, one that did not simply carry authority and weight in its delivery of facts and intricate details but fizzed with a passion for the past.

Stripping away myth makes for good television history, yet there is a dilemma here that an early episode of *Chronicle* had to confront and surmount. One of the problems of creating popular history without having all the pieces present is evident in Magnusson's opening delivery in a 1968 *Chronicle* episode, 'The Death of the High King'. Using the same dramatic sobriety that later underpinned the BBC's hugely successful twelve-part fictional series, *I Claudius* (BBC2, 1976), 'The Death of the High King' is a forty-five minute reconstruction based on acknowledged academic research. Viewed today, the programme's pace is ponderous, the acting formulistic, the transitions between studio sets and exterior actuality location, and atmospheric cutaways burden an already heavy narrative with a laborious style. This particular reconstruction embodies the very substance of contextualisation of then and now, of attempting to dispose of myth, which in turn inserts an artificial barrier of dramatisation.

Of course the programme should not be measured by today's highly complex and sophisticated production techniques and values, for 'The Death of the High King' is a piece of history itself in the way that it encapsulates its period, critical thinking and knowledge about the subject it is dealing with. Equally, Magnusson testifies to a major flaw in television history reconstructions by honestly and openly admitting that the programme can only deal with the unknown of the past through applying modern assumptions. What this means is that the past has to be forced through an archaeological sieve shaken by whatever television drama techniques are available at the time to separate fact from myth.

There are only a finite number of possibilities for television to present TV-users with artefacts being recovered from below ground in what is a tedious and painstaking process not suited to the rapid dynamics of television production. The producer of *Time Team* (C4, 1994–), Tim Taylor, has adapted a dramatic television format that uses the traditional archaeological quest for finds within a given time frame with a regular team of specialists that have become characters in their own right. In this attempt at introducing a modern take to archaeology, the prosaic ritual of a 'dig' has been given a dynamic edge by imposing a two or three-day limit on the excavation.

Heightening the sense of a 'challenge', the team tackle the past, not once, but twice for the cameras as they come to terms, dictated by television, of making sense of past events spread out along a diachronic axis. This visual search for discovery and explanation is then squeezed not only into a production-designated synchronic chronology but further compressed into edited screen time of fifty-minutes. Compression of this kind accentuates the sensation of a quest controlled by a game show convention of winning or losing. Attempting to further the tension and challenge of television archaeology, Channel 4 also aired *Extreme Archaeology* (C4, 2004), where digs were undertaken in precarious locations on cliffs, down copper mines and inside cave systems, as though a small-screen Indiana Jones dicing with danger would move archaeology up another gear.

> A new Channel 4 series takes archaeology to the edge as a team of experts tackles sites across the country that are beyond the reach of normal investigations … Using some of the most advanced scientific equipment available, and high-tech miniature cameras and communication systems to record the action, *Extreme Archaeology*'s experts are dropped into extreme and inaccessible environments under time and other pressures that test their personal and professional skills to the limit.[14]

Despite the series coming from Tim Taylor, with its promise of extreme endeavours designed to provide a 'further twist guaranteed to make a commissioning editor salivate',[15] neither the format nor the extreme team managed to make archaeology any more exciting. However precarious the site, however audacious and daring the team, each programme could not disguise the fact that the end result was still a 'find' of the sort destined to undercut the format's hyperbole. The experiment with sending archaeologists into environments where no one else dared to tread was wisely not recommissioned.

A nation in decline

Television is continuously redefining itself through its technological developments, programming themes, and its relationship with TV-users. This progression highlights how social and cultural conflicts are worked through in a cycle of reproduction,[16] ironing out tensions in order for society to move forward. Series and one-off programmes that provide this key point history in the shaping of Britain, and its relationship with other nations would have been forgotten if, first and foremost, they were not eminently worth watching and remembering.

TV-users as members of society act as a catalyst for cultural shifts and change, leading to new innovative, creative television formats that attempt to articulate or address society's regeneration. Factual history programming does have an intrinsic part to play here, as does academic history, in examining and emphasising sections of the past as significant waymarkers on the development and progress of Britain and Britishness which was becoming detached from its collective, institutional roots.

As demands for social progress increased, programmes in the 1960s began to examine how a distinct break with the past was being added to the weave of a society heady on the endless possibilities afforded by new technology. In *Intertel Presents* – 'Postscript to Empire: Britain in Transition' (ITV, 1962) and *Where Have all the Teddy Boys Gone?* (BBC2, 1969), this process of social transition sought to sever as many outdated links with the past as possible. But, by the 1970s, Britain's technological revolution had become mired in industrial unrest that had been slowly gestating since the Labour government of Clement Attlee came to power in July 1945.

Although Attlee's government oversaw the formation of hugely popular welfare reforms leading to the National Health Service and National Insurance, it had also set about a process of nationalisation that by the 1950s had claimed the Bank of England, coal mines, gas and electricity supply, steel production and public transport as government-controlled industries. However determined Attlee's government and the Labour Party may have been to redistribute economic prosperity in order to ensure growth and stability, their vision for continuing 'the peaceful revolution'[17] was not shared by an electorate whose confidence had been shaken not only by the Korean War but the Partition of India, its subsequent independence and the question of Palestine.

Not even a sustained turn in power by the Conservatives from 1951 to 1964 would prevent a fermenting of industrial ill will in nationalised industries that, by the General election of 1964 marking the end of thirteen years of Conservative rule, was already seeping into other industrial sectors. The growing industrial discontent of the 1970s, a decade dominated by strikes and power shortages, brought disruption to BBC transmissions over disagreement on working hours.[18] However, this was not the BBC's only encounter with a trade union: its first ever official strike with members of the Association of Broadcasting Staff Union had occurred nine years earlier in late 1969.[19] The seeds of unrest driven by international tensions that brought down the Labour government of James Callaghan in 1979, when the country 'was literally grinding to a halt',[20] also created a mood of introspection. This saw a much more cynical questioning of British society from Establishment policies to working practices, immigration, the role of women, the nature of the family and everyday life. Ultimately, the oil crisis of 1973 became a millstone for Labour politics and government through the mid- to late 1970s.

Deepening debt eroded confidence in a party that had pledged to reduce the gap between the rich and poor but could only manage to bring the country to short-time working – even television had a 10.30 p.m. shutdown – and union unrest led to a series of bitter strikes.[21] The miners carried out their first strike in 1972, followed by a second in 1974, coinciding with the oil crisis sparked by the Israeli–Egyptian War. For the most part, television attempted to produce a range of programmes that ignored the deep-rooted divisions in British society, as though distraction would make things better.

Disillusioned by a government unable to break the cycle of strikes, the electorate took the opportunity to change direction, leading to a Conservative victory in the 1979 election.

Following the appointment of Britain's first and, so far, only female Prime Minister Margaret Thatcher, little time was wasted in lopping back what had been seen as the protective boughs of state intervention in favour of an economy, welfare infrastructure, society and culture powered by market forces. A lack of social equilibrium in the 1970s brought about a sense of fragmentation between past and present. This led to a collapse in a belief in a shared collective identity instigating a marked increase in factual history programmes themed on collecting and museums. For these programmes, the past was no longer an embarrassment, a stigma of an elitist imperialist society but a reassuring bridge between objects symbolising development that represented national strength and stability. *Collector's World* (BBC2, 1973) and *Antiques Roadshow* (BBC1, 1979–) demonstrated in their own way that objects had become historical commodities directly linking individuals with the past.

Valuing the past in this way saw ITV swing between the highbrow *Treasures of the British Museum* (ITV, 1974) and the popular, optimistic quest-formatted *Trash or Treasure* (ITV, 1976). With the past always affixed to the present as a convenient sought-after commodity that can be utilised for a variety of reasons as an organisational resource,[22] it is hardly surprising that factual history programmes of the 1970s contain an ongoing search for reassurance regarding Britain's then shaky present and uncertain future. In series such as the oral history-based *Yesterday's Witness*, the eight-part *Man in his Place* (BBC2, 1972), exploring working-class culture, the eight-part *A Place in History* (ITV, 1974) examining British towns and institutions, *Six English Towns* (BBC2, 1978) and the three-part *Heritage in Danger* (ITV, 1979), the past became an anchor for the drifting present.

If there was any persuading, moralising and cajoling to be done in factual history programming in the 1970s, it was, by and large, left to the BBC. From the 1960s to the 1980s, British culture and society attempted to reinvent itself not only according to which political party held the reins of government but also as a deliberate means of ending a profound break with the past. Whilst the BBC may have perceived itself as part of the cultural foundations of the country, at the cusp of the 1950s, it was believed that ITV's increasing share of ratings was slowly but surely displacing the BBC as the 'national broadcaster'.[23] Asa Briggs regards the state of the nation as being inexorably linked with the output of British television,[24] particularly the BBC as the self-appointed guardian of culture.

A sense of continuity with the past in terms of preserving and displaying heritage rose sharply in programmes and series dealing with museums in the 1970s as more of Britain's heritage appeared in series and one-off programmes during this disruptive period. An increase of factual history programming themed around industrial relations and disputes also occurred during the 1970s, rising from five programmes in the years 1950–59, to thirty-two in 1960–69 and fifty-eight in 1970–79.[25]

Disillusionment, revolution and questions of equality in the home and workplace provided thematic indexes in factual history programming during the 1970s, for an introspective assessment of what Britain had become. *So You Think You Know Britain?* (BBC1, 1971), or what it actually means to be British, *Who Are the Scots?* This disenchantment with the present also opened up opportunities to confront accepted dogma, tradition and interpretations of the past within the confrontational framework of series and factual documentaries. Political reputations were evaluated, strategies raked over, allegations re-evaluated and allegiances scrutinised at home and overseas. These included *That Day in Dallas: LBJ Speaks* – 'Tragedy and Transition' (BBC1, 1970) and *On Trial: Roger Casement* – 'A Question of Allegiance' (BBC1, 1970), revisiting the case of the Irish patriot born in Dublin, who served as a British diplomat and stood accused of dealing with Germany prior to the Easter uprising in 1916.

As Britain's manufacturing industries went further into decline during the 1970s, a rather different industrial endeavour from the past underpinned BBC2's 1972 ten-part *Industrial Grand Tour*.

> The first of a series of ten looking at Britain's industrial heritage – the richest legacy in Europe of monuments of the Industrial Revolution. A Grand Tour of memorials not to statesmen and soldiers but to the skills and labours of ordinary men whose work gave Britain the title 'workshop of the world'.[26]

Touring symbolic points on the Industrial Revolution's compass, the series attempted to reconnect a lost sense of pride and achievement with a 1970s era that had 'forgotten' its collective roots of nation and nationality. Just how detached industrial glory had become from 1970s Britain formed its own strand of collective memories in *The Melter's Tale* (BBC1, 1970), piecing back together the working life of a redundant steel worker.

At the core of *This Week – 1844* (ITV, 1975) lay a direct parallel between the working landscape of the 1970s and the pay and conditions faced by the nineteenth-century Durham miners. In what was ostensibly claimed to be a documentary, though scripted dramatically by Richard Broad, a news crew reported the 1844 Durham strike in the way that the 1970s disputes were reported. The 'us and them' opposition so redolent of reporting industrial action in the 1970s had Freddie Jones as Lord Londonderry, symbolic of a class-bound system unmoved, uncaring and unconcerned about the plight of working men. For Derek Parker in his critical review for *The Times*, the Thames Television production was 'altogether a success – showing among other things how little life has changed'.[27] Making industrial and technological connections, James Burke's ten-part *Connections* (BBC1, 1978) sought to trace the inter-relationship and development of technology as the instigator of a series of related changes that may have taken place in the past but have the power to alter the present.

A loss of direction in a collective remembering of national identity and characteristics during the 1970s can also be a direct explanation for the diminishing number of factual history programming themed on religion during this period. From a modest total of six programmes, including series, produced in the years 1950–59, religious history reached its peak of 115 programmes, including repeats, in 1960–69, before slumping to seventy-five in 1970–79. There was to be little improvement in the 1980s, perhaps signifying that material considerations were outweighing divine ones, with a total of sixty-seven programmes, between 1980 and 1989, including Channel 4's repeat of Bamber Gascoigne's thirteen-part *The Christians* (ITV, 1977/C4, 1986).[28] How far faith is 'imagined' to be tied into the fabric of nationality can be gauged by the *Daily Telegraph's* 2008 front page headline, 'Decline of Christian values "is destroying Britishness"', that cited the Bishop of Rochester blaming the liberal attitude of the 1960s for creating a 'moral vacuum'.[29] Accusations that the BBC 'spent far less on religious and ethical programmes than on entertainment shows',[30] or that the journalist and BBC2 presenter Jeremy Vine claims 'it is becoming "socially unacceptable" to be a Christian in Britain',[31] highlights how Christianity has gathered an anachronistic stigma in terms of national values.

This is evident from the way that religion as factual programming was downsized during the 1990s. It featured sporadically if at all, as in the one-off *Secret History* repeat, *The Hidden Holocaust* (C4, 1995) revealing the 1915 slaughter of at least one million Armenian Christians, or Channel 4's 1993 further repeat of Bamber Gascoigne's *The Christians*. Questions of how far faith and religious values do reinforce or underpin notions of nationality have surfaced once more in Boris Johnson's *After Rome: Holy War and Conquest* (BBC2, 2008) and Channel 4's provocative series, *Christianity: A History* (C4, 2009). The series, based around 'eight public figures, eight different perspectives on Christianity,'[32] pitted the personal perspectives of believers, revisionists and sceptics together in an attempt to unravel the impact and influence of Christianity.

Cultural tensions concerning identity and immigration had also become a key feature of the 1970s.[33] *The Black Man in Britain 1550–1950* (BBC2, 1974) for instance, was one of a number of programmes re-evaluating questions of nationality, emigration and settlement that began in the 1960s. *The Colony* (BBC1, 1964) focused on West Indians living in Birmingham and was by no

Bamber Gascoigne, preparing for a piece to camera for his series *The Christians* in   **2**
St Peter's Basilica, Rome (ITV, 1977)

means the only programme or series to re-evaluate cultural divergence as a central unit of British nationality.

Even that doughty pillar of the BBC's light entertainment schedule, the *Black & White Minstrel Show* (BBC1, 1958–78), was not immune from charges of being degrading to black culture, as is made clear in a letter to a 1970s edition of the *Radio Times*.[34] The question of race and ethnicity had, by the 1980s, become an essential theme for programme-makers. Channel 4's *Passage to Britain* (C4, 1984) stoically examined the full cultural spectrum of immigration in its twelve-part series:

Part 1   *A Nation of Immigrants*
Part 2   *The Jews* – 'The Kosher British'
Part 3   *The Irish* – 'Using the Mickey'
Part 4   *World War Two* – 'Call to Arms'
Part 5   *Poles* – 'Betrayed!'
Part 6   *The West Indians* – 'Black Britons'
Part 7   *Hungarians* – 'How to Be the Alien'
Part 8   *Indian Origins*
Part 9   *The Sikhs* – 'Trimming the Turban'
Part 10   *The Bangladeshis* – 'Village Dreams'
Part 11   *The Chinese* – 'We Are Different'
Part 12   *The Legacy* – 'Rivers of Love'

Questions on the diverse nature of British society were still being asked in the 1990s with, for example, *Black Britain* (BBC2, 1991), and the gradual social changes that saw attitudes towards race change where examined in *When Black Became Beautiful* (BBC2, 2004).

But television as an industry in the 1970s was becoming quite adept at reacting to change, either as a result of industrial action – the early close-down during fuel crises – or brought about by government impositions. Up until 1972, broadcasting hours had been tightly regulated, but in response to pressure from the ITA, the Minister of Posts and Telecommunications, Christopher Chataway, agreed to end any broadcasting hours restrictions as a means of allowing for 'fuller use of ITV's programme making capacity'.[35] This in turn, 'would enable the authority to meet more adequately the needs of certain minorities, such as shift workers, and to provide greater opportunities for experimental programmes'.[36]

This move came only months before the Commons Select Committee on Nationalised Industries issued a report criticising the range of ITV programmes and the Independent Broadcasting Authority's (IBA) handling of the commercial network.[37] If ITV sensed another biased attack, as Sidney Bernstein, Chairman of Granada Television deemed had happened with the Pilkington findings,[38] this deregulation would also place pressure on the BBC to manage its resources more effectively whilst ensuring quality did not suffer.

This rise in the number of broadcast hours coincided with colour television becoming increasingly popular, so much so that government introduced separate colour licences in 1968 and by 1972 there was one and a half million colour sets operating, which by 1974 had risen to five and a half million and to eleven million by 1978. Working-class families outnumbered middle-class families in colour set ownership in 1972, standing at 52 per cent.[39] Colour television in itself did not guarantee a one-off programme or series' success. It may have provided initial novelty, adding impact to the screen spectacle, but for factual history programming, there has to be something more compelling to draw back TV-users on a regular basis. In Britain, since the first factual history programme was transmitted, this has been achieved through diversity in style and format.

Different tastes, different formats

To class all factual history programmes as documentary would be to do a disservice to both history and documentary. Most of the formative factual history programmes transmitted by the BBC came under the production banner of Television Talks. *Germany Under Control* may be regarded as the first BBC documentary, though as Jeff Walden, a member of the BBC research staff at Caversham points out:

> The programme has strong claims for being the first documentary, although there is always room for argument over points of interpretation (at which point does an illustrated talk become a documentary, etc?). This one was studio-bound, with live talking heads and film inserts from official sources (i.e. not specially shot by the BBC).[40]

Likewise, A. J. P. Taylor's three studio-based lectures *Challenge*, covering the Russian Revolution, or his five-part *Alan Taylor Lectures* (ITV, 1958) – 'When Europe Was the Centre of the World' – are both factual history programmes, but what they most certainly are not is documentary in the classic sense. Running during the 1960s in a five-minute slot on Sunday evenings between 6.45 and 6.50 p.m., the BBC's *Sunday Story* cast its net far and wide into past lives. Covering the stories of *Moses* in 1962, told by Kenneth Horne, *The*

Childhood of Helen Keller, told by Cyril Fletcher in 1963, *David Livingstone* in 1963, told by William Russell, *Edith Cavell* in 1964, told by Hattie Jacques, and *Abraham Lincoln* in 1965, told by Deryck Guyler, this is factual history programming well outside the conventions of documentary.

Popular history, an ambiguous and subjective classification in its own right, is not a spectre that has suddenly risen in the 1990s and 2000s but can claim a long heritage and tradition in making history an enjoyable television experience. Family history first appeared in 1979 as Gordon Honeycombe revealed the secrets of tracing and building family trees in *Family History* (BBC2, 1979), repeated on BBC1 in 1980, 1985 and 1986, reinforcing a natural development of programmes created around individual stories and oral history.

Any simplistic notion that all factual history programming comes under the generic banner of documentary or has to observe a classic documentary style epitomised in *The Great War* was undermined by David Attenborough's championing of a scholarly, yet informative, form of presentation when he was BBC2's Controller. The first example in Kenneth Clark's *Civilisation* (BBC2, 1969), the second in Jacob Bronowski's *The Ascent of Man* (BBC2, 1973), elevated history into an articulate, personal dimension with both series proving to be immensely popular.

Certainly voice-over documentary remains a central pillar of factual history programming, however there are many strands of factual history programming, including the five-minute oral history of *Times Remembered*, that push the genre as a whole, into new territory. A combination of drama and factual records is evident in *The Bristol Entertainment* (BBC2, 1971), offering a popular review of the city. The *Radio Times* listing makes no apologies for the programme pushing the past to the boundaries of fiction in presenting events derived from 'factual records, memoirs and newspapers of Bristol', with the rider, 'They may even be true'.[41]

Providing history with a quite different framework from documentary, musical evocations of the past contextualised major events by revealing how the Industrial Revolution or life in the trenches became a form of valid cultural and social expression through popular song, as *Songs for the Times* (BBC1, 1964) and *Something to Sing About* (ITV, 1972) clearly demonstrate. However unsatisfactory this creative interpretation of the past may be for some historians, it proves that the past is not, nor will be treated as, a sacrosanct commodity in television's constant desire for the new; leading to experimentation such as the past being afforded the Disney treatment in *Great – Isambard Kingdom Brunel* (C4, 1983), a cartoon set to music.

These forms of popular history are certainly outside the conventions of documentary, as is another diametrically opposed genealogy to 'proper history', containing the quiz, game show and chat show formats. These include the original *Animal, Vegetable, Mineral?*, with a reprised version running on BBC2 in 1971 for fourteen episodes. *The Balloon Game* (BBC1, 1976), *Domesday Detectives* (BBC1, 1986), *Looks Familiar* (ITV 1970–84/C4, 1984–86) and *Movie Memories* (ITV, 1981–84) all deal with the past but cannot be classed as serious history. What has to be considered is that TV-user tastes can and do vary enormously, and low-key, undemanding excursions into the past through factual history formats that entertain as much as they inform are still a valid means of engaging with history.

More freedom to access the past

Following the development and introduction of the video cassette recorder (VCR), the viewing regime around which TV-users patterned their social time was broken. The popularity of the VCR in the 1980s was to herald a transformation in viewing habits for households able to buy or rent VCRs. This enabled a change from regulated viewing through the schedules to viewing by convenience and choice, with 31 per cent of British homes equipped with VCRs in 1985, rising to 89 per cent in 2002,[42] creating the possibilities for 'time-shifting'.[43]

With more channels available and the use of VCRs freeing TV-users from the regime of seasonality and timing, many households effectively became their own schedulers, increasing the number of programmes they experienced through storing and free ranging between channels.

If new technology affects selection and preference for consumers, then marketplace differentiation at a supply level, that of channels, becomes more intense. An apparent proliferation of choices of programmes across terrestrial, satellite and cable channels is deceptive. More airtime usually results in less originality, as increased broadcasting capacity leads to the recycling of one-off programmes and series.

Although the ITA had lobbied for a second commercial channel to be made available as far back as 1972,[44] it was going to be 2 November 1982 when, much to the chagrin of ITV companies wanting an ITV2,[45] the independent Channel 4 began broadcasting amidst an industrial dispute concerning regional agreements over signal feeds for the new channel.[46] From its conception, Channel 4 intended to appeal to different demographic clusters of TV-users. As one documentary film producer saw it, their task was to 'serve the "ignored, the neglected and the overlooked"',[47] on the behalf of a commercial channel with a PSB remit that commissioned its entire output from external production companies.

If there is a decade when factual history programme production accelerated, it occurred in the 1980s, a period of transformation in how factual history programming became a powerful commodity for certain broadcasters as a means of ensuring their PSB remit.

The output of factual history programming from 1946 to 1949 amounted to 32 first transmissions and six repeats, totalling 38. In the period 1950–59, this had increased to a total of 765, with first transmissions rising to 745 and repeats to 20. The introduction of BBC2 in 1964 drove up the total between 1960 and 1969 to 2,772 with 2,369 first transmissions and 403 repeats. BBC2's scheduling accounting for 612 total broadcasts, 494 original and 118 repeats, giving it a 22 per cent share. During the 1970s, programming increased to a total of 4,064, with 2,917 first transmissions and 1,143 repeats. In the decade that Channel 4 entered the market, factual history programming rose during 1980–89 to 4,448, with 3,021 original transmissions and 1,427 repeats.[48]

Caught between its obligation to provide a percentage of factual programming and its commercially rewarding output, ITV's factual history series gradually diminished as Channel 4 strove to prove its PSB ethos with an increasing quota of factual history production that had become a burden to ITV.

There is nothing quite like the prospect of a major broadcasting overhaul by the government, however, to stimulate a burst of commissioning in a neglected area of production. This seems to be the case with ITV from 1986 to 1989, as British broadcasting prepared to enter its most radical phase of competition with the introduction of satellite transmissions. ITV started the decade with 87 first transmissions and 55 repeats, which had dipped to 28 original and six repeats by 1983, before rising dramatically to 180 original and 12 repeats in 1987. By 1989, the increase had peaked, with 105 original transmissions and five repeats.[49]

By the late 1980s, Channel 4 had made serious inroads into this competitive and high-risk marketplace of factual history production. Channel 4's output exceeded that of ITV's total of 1,116 including repeats, with 1,575 first transmissions and 832 repeats, totalling 2,407, representing a 31 per cent share of the market. Leading the factual output of the 1980s, BBC2 had 39 per cent of the share, with ITV and BBC1 having 15 per cent each.[50]

Channel 4's attempts to underscore its PSB remit relied heavily on a stable platform of factual history programming. To some extent Channel 4's attempts at creating a different, distinct view of the past meant initially imitating a concept already established by the BBC. Channel 4's *An Englishman's Home* (C4, 1986), bore an uncanny resemblance to *An Englishman's Home* (BBC2, 1986), a BBC format established in 1957. This reliance on the physical landscape of Britain has become a cyclic excursion back to its original thematic roots of nation and nationality.

As identifiable waymarkers of stability, history acts as a safety net capable of not only highlighting ordered development but also offering reassurance through difficult times of cultural change. For TV-users, this means a wholly manufactured nostalgic television timeline, punctuated by illusionary 'Golden Ages'.

That castles and examples of historic houses become expressions of England and Englishness with a limited syntax are evident in how frequently the same narrow selections of houses are held to be iconic examples of a national heritage by different presenters. *Arthur Negus Enjoys* (BBC2, 1981), *Personal Pleasures with Sir Hugh Casson* (BBC2, 1981), or Mark Curry with *Treasure Houses* (BBC2, 1984) re-crossed many of the thresholds of series from the 1950s and 1960s such as Blenheim Palace, Syon House and Saltram House.

An area where Channel 4 has created a strong presence in the formative years following its launch is with themes that fitted alongside its branded channel identity as an innovative broadcaster with series such as *The World: A Television History* (C4, 1983), or *Pillar of Fire: A Television History of Israel's Re-birth* (C4, 1986). The channel was also more than willing to take on and challenge the status quo with politically located series. These included *Claret and Chips* (C4, 1983), charting the formation of the Social Democratic Party, or *All the Prime Minister's Men* (C4, 1986), exploring how cabinet politics had become fractured and autocratic.

Now of course, the factual history most associated with its channel branding is that of *Time Team*, *Secret History* (C4 1991–2004), David Starkey's *Elizabeth* (C4, 2000) and *Monarchy* (C4, 2004–06). Picking up the mantle of factual history production from networked ITV companies, Channel 4's commissioning strategy combined the old with the new. New series included the six-part *The Spanish Civil War* (C4, 1983), produced by Granada, whilst one-off programmes such as the Canadian Broadcasting Corporation's (CBC) 1976 *Memories of Berlin* – 'The Twilight of Weimar Culture' (C4, 1983) joined successes from the ITV stable – *The World at War* (C4, 1983) and *The Christians* – as repeats.

In spite of Channel 4's controller Paul Bonner's belief that the new broadcaster would not be '*perceived* as a kind of BBC public service channel', the widespread view was that BBC2 was its 'direct rival'.[51] When it came to the production and screening of factual history programming, the rivalry and public service image of both broadcasters inevitably revealed that they did, in fact, share some of the same intellectual footprints when it came to reinterpreting the past.

Notes

1 *BBC Yearbook 1947*, p. 80.
2 'ATV To Pay £89,300 for U.S. Films', *The Times* (29 August 1957), p. 3.
3 Briggs, *History of Broadcasting*, p. 259.
4 Briggs, *History of Broadcasting*, pp. 294–5.
5 Briggs, *History of Broadcasting*, p. 305.
6 Briggs, *History of Broadcasting*, p. 308.
7 Briggs, *History of Broadcasting*, p. 313.
8 Figures derived from data collected from listed programmes in the *Radio Times*, *TV Times*, *The Times*, BFI Film and Television Database and the British Universities Film and Video Council TVTiP, online *TV Times* listings project from 1955 to 1985 (hereafter, Data from the *RT et al*).
9 Briggs, *History of Broadcasting*, p.167.
10 *Monitor: Elgar, RT* (13–19 July 1968), p. 21.
11 British Film Institute (hereafter, BFI) 'Top 100' www.bfi.org.uk/features/tv/100.
12 John Corner, 'General introduction: Television and British society in the 1950s', in John Corner (ed.), *Popular Television in Britain* (London: BFI Publishing, 1991), p. 2.
13 Don Henson, 'Television archaeology: Education or entertainment?' Institute for Historical Research. www.history.ac.uk/education/conference/henson.html.
14 *Extreme Archaeology* www.channel4.com/history/microsites/E/extremearchaeology/exa.html.
15 Peter Paterson, 'Angels Fail to Delight', *Daily Mail* (21 June 2004), p. 49.
16 Todd Gitlin, 'Prime time ideology: The hegemonic process in television entertainment', in Horace Newcomb (ed.), *Television, The Critical View* (New York: Oxford University Press, 3rd edn, 1982), p. 426.
17 Denis Richards and J. W. Hunt, *An Illustrated History of Modern Britain 1783–1964* (London: Longman, 2nd edn, 1965), p. 302.
18 'BBC Dispute Likely to Be Extended', *The Times* (13 January 1978), p. 4.
19 Briggs, *History of Broadcasting*, pp. 789–90.
20 Neil Tweedie, 'Taking On a Nation in Crisis', *Daily Telegraph* (10 January 2009), p. 21.
21 'TV Workers Protest at Early Close-Down', *The Times* (1 February 1974), p. 2.
22 Jordanova, *History in Practice*, p. 2.

23 Briggs, *History of Broadcasting*, p. 152.

24 Briggs, *History of Broadcasting*, p. 152.

25 Data from the *RT et al.*

26 *Industrial Grand Tour, RT* (22–28 July 1972), p. 39.

27 Derek Parker, 'This Week – 1844', *The Times* (22 January 1975), p. 11.

28 Data from the *RT et al.*

29 Martin Beckford, 'Decline of Christian Values "Is Destroying Britishness"', *Daily Telegraph* (29 May 2008), p. 1.

30 Martin Beckford, 'BBC Favours £18m Ross Over Songs of Praise, Say Bishops', *Daily Telegraph* (9 December 2008), p. 5.

31 Richard Eden and Jonathan Wynne-Jones, 'Why I Am Scared to Talk About My Christianity On Air, by Jeremy Vine', *Daily Telegraph* (18 January 2009), p. 7.

32 *Christianity: A History, RT* (10–16 January 2009), p. 38.

33 'Asians' Strike Threat Over Skinheads', *The Times* (27 May 1970), p. 3.

34 *Black & White Minstrel Show, RT* (11–17 April 1970), p. 58.

35 'Go-Ahead Given by Mr Chataway to 24-hour Radio and Television', *The Times* (20 January 1972), p. 7.

36 'Go-Ahead Given', p. 7.

37 Chris Dunkley, 'MPs Criticize Running of Commercial TV and Call for Inquiry into Broadcasting', *The Times* (28 September 1972), p. 4.

38 'Pilkington Report "Biased"', *The Times* (2 March 1964), p. 7.

39 Briggs, *History of Broadcasting*, p. 848.

40 Jeff Walden, BBC WAC, email reply to the author (13 January 2006).

41 *The Bristol Entertainment, RT* (27 November–3 December 1971), p. 67.

42 Office for National Statistics, Consumer durables – trends over time, table 4.19, consumer durables, central heating and cars: 1972 to 2002 www.statistics.gov.uk/lib2002/downloads/housing.pdf.

43 Office of Communications (hereafter, Ofcom), PSB Review Interactive Executive Summary: Glossary http://comment.ofcom.org.uk/summary/glossary.html.

44 'Go-Ahead Given', p. 7.

45 Peter Lennon, 'Lord Reith's Last Blast', *The Times* (1 November 1982), p. 8.

46 'Channel 4 Switch-On Despite Dispute', *The Times* (1 November 1982), p. 3.

47 Lennon, 'Lord Reith's Last Blast', p. 8.

48 Data from the *RT et al.*

49 Data from the *RT et al.*

50 Data from the *RT et al.*

51 Lennon, 'Lord Reith's Last Blast', p. 8.

4

Bringing the past alive

The Conservative Government of Margaret Thatcher determined that the 1980s would be remembered for their astute stewardship in steering Britain out of its industrial malaise. By drastically attempting to dismantle much of the Welfare State and privatising a whole raft of previously State-owned industries, Thatcher introduced a market-driven economy that became the central motivating force of Tory policy. The television industry would not be exempt or immune from the harsh realities of profit and loss. The industry, deemed too anti-government, too liberal and far too left wing, would benefit from a further bout of modernisation. As Douglas Hurd, Home Secretary at the time, put it:

> A little fresh air does no harm in broadcasting – indeed, I welcome the good,
> refreshing wind that has been blowing through broadcasting in recent years,
> through the restrictive practices and occasional complacencies in both the BBC
> and the independent sector.[1]

The 1980s may be recalled as an era of government financial experimentation, intended to curb inflation, though this merely fuelled the boom and bust cycle of an economy that was already overstretched, leading to the 1982 recession and the year-long miners' strike in 1984. Government intervention and deregulation had already brought the launch of Direct Broadcast Satellite (DBS) in 1986. British Satellite Broadcasting (BSB), backed by Granada, Virgin, Pearson and Amstrad, was awarded the franchise with Rupert Murdoch's Sky as its licensed competitor by 1989. Heavy losses for both companies ensured competition did not last for long, with Sky taking over BSB to become BSkyB in 1990 with what was, in effect, a government-approved monopoly.[2]

With the 1990 Broadcasting Act in place and franchises awarded to the highest bidder – not as previously done on terms of a company's existing provision or quality – by 2006, pay television cable and satellite penetration into the United Kingdom's households stood at 49 per cent.[3] With the industry already feeling the pinch from the arrival of niche providers such as Discovery in 1989, and the last terrestrial provider Channel 5 going on-air on 30 March 1997 – rebranded as Five in 2002 – terrestrial, cable and satellite channels were competing for an already saturated market share.

In such a voracious marketplace, it is not without good reason that the *Daily Mail* was reporting that in 2004, ITV1 had 'recorded its worst ratings figures since records began'.[4] It also revealed that viewing figures released for 1994–2004 showed an increase of 285.6 per cent for cable and satellite providers, with BBC1 unable to generate more than the 'symbolic benchmark of a 25 per cent share of audiences'.[5]

For the BBC, this diminishing of their guardianship of re-presenting history as a means of cementing the past and present together as national identity, reveals how far the television landscape has changed since the 1980s. Speaking for, and on behalf of, the nation is an integral part of establishing a channel's own perception of what and how nationality should be presented as a natural or alternative development of culture and society. For both the BBC and Channel 4, the 1980s had marked a challenge to re-present concepts of nation and nationality as a doctrine of their PSB policies.

The natural channel for history?

Any channel wishing to be taken seriously as a provider of quality factual history programming requires a significant bedrock of programming that underpins the occasional, authored series. The BBC's *Timewatch* (BBC2, 1982–) series set a formative magazine style for history and archaeology, creating opportunities for a number of professional historians to present self-contained pieces and to act as contributors and interviewees in each programme's three to four stories.

A similar format marked the arrival of *Today's History* (C4, 1982–84), commencing a battle between the BBC and Channel 4 during the 1980s to create and commission series that would confirm who held the right to lay claim to factual history programming as a central pinnacle of its PSB scheduling. As the BBC's flagship history magazine series created by Tim Gardam, *Timewatch* commenced its run on 29 September 1982 with John Tusa presenting three reports. The first was on the wartime role of the Duke and Duchess of Windsor, the second on Britain's first atomic test and the last on the history of Chatham Dockyard as its future lay in the balance. *Timewatch* quickly faced competition from *Today's History*, its first programme transmitted on 14 November 1982, focusing on an ambitious history of Poland presented by Neal Ascherson and Anne Fleming. Jointly produced by the *History Today* magazine and Visnews,[6] *Today's History* demonstrated a similar shared postmodern approach to *Timewatch*, in attempting to explode myths, dealing with the marginal aspects of the past previously overlooked.

For both series, this meant a concentration on the inclusion of the past that had been left dormant. They opened up investigations into minority groups or individuals who had remained without a voice, bereft of power to make their presence in the past recognised. *Timewatch* and *Today's History* invited new inter-referential assessments of meaning based on value structures and exposing spheres of power.

Quite unlike previous formats, their method of historical investigation bore resemblances to Michel Foucault's concept of genealogy:[7] a method that rediscovers the knowledge of struggles against systems of power rather than following a clearly defined linear pattern that ignores local struggles in favour of a unified, or dominant view of the past.[8] Although *Timewatch* may have inherited *Chronicle's* remit for outlining archaeological and historical investigation, even at times sharing the same presenter, David Drew, their boundaries were vastly different.

Timewatch, from its first series, concentrated more on history than archaeology, attracting a comparatively low number of TV-users to what Laurence Rees, its editor for ten years from 1992, describes as a format based very much on 'academic discussion'.[9] Whereas *Chronicle* devoted single episodes towards exploring history as a product of archaeology – 'The Vikings in North America' (BBC2, 1966), 'The Ashes of Atlantis' (BBC2, 1972), 'The Celts' (BBC2, 1975), and 'Life and Death in Ancient Egypt' (BBC2, 1983), *Timewatch* followed a different route into the past.

Taking a more specialised academic approach as its fixed point from which to investigate the past, *Timewatch's* magazine format had already begun to concentrate on one or two events, and when Laurence Rees took over as editor in 1992, the magazine format was dropped entirely.[10]

Defining different investigative criteria from the outset in its themes and presenters, *Today's History* demonstrated its credentials for social equality in its regular female presenters Anne Fleming and Juliet Gardiner, who were joined by specialist academic presenters and journalists who may or may not be professional historians. These included Stuart Hall, John Keegan, Rodney Mace and Clyde Jeavons.

Today's History's episodes too reiterated this search for difference, selecting a much more confrontational style in the themes chosen. Stuart Hall and Anne Fleming examined the question of truth and deception between real events and their portrayal in official film in 'Invisible History' (C4, 1982). John Keegan and Anne Fleming probed the reasons behind warfare in 'Why War?' (C4, 1982), and Juliet Gardiner and Rodney Mace questioned how history and historians have marginalised women in 'Women and Society' (C4, 1983).

Popular history also came in for scrutiny as Juliet Gardiner and Clyde Jeavons explored the creation of sporting legends in 'Love of the Game' (C4, 1983). *Timewatch* and *Today's History* may have delivered further diversification to the type of history broadcast, but the successful and popular framework of *Timewatch* proved to be a format that Channel 4 could not ignore. Channel 4's next attempt at creating a rival brand to *Timewatch* would see both broadcasters using the past as a central core of their factual programming into the 1990s and 2000s.

Channel 4's response to *Timewatch* was a new sixty-minute one-off documentary strand titled *Secret History* (C4, 1991–2004). Launched on Thursday 14 November 1991, *Secret History's* opening programme – 'The Hidden Hand' – was an investigation into political assassination in South Africa against anti-apartheid supporters and the clandestine operations waged in Mozambique.

By 1994, the two competing documentary strands were almost going head-to-head in the schedules. *Timewatch* running on Wednesday from 8 p.m. to 8.50 p.m., was followed on Thursday by *Secret History*. In its final 2004 series, *Secret History* still probed around the controversial aspects of the past. In *Britain's Boy Soldiers*, broadcast on 14 June 2004, the documentary examined the large proportion of underage British troops who fought and died during the First World War. The dark side to this documentary, gleaned from eyewitness testimony and fleshed out by reconstruction, had a profound effect in demystifying the institutional nation-state propaganda of troops betraying their comrades and country through cowardice. 'Shamefully, terrified boys who ran away from the horrors they witnessed were court-martialled and shot.'[11]

Times, television technology and the expectations of TV-users do change and formats reflect this. A recent *Timewatch* offering, 'Young Victoria' (BBC2, 2008), was noticeable not only for the insight into the intrigues of how Victoria became queen but also for its visual style.

Presented by broadcaster and historian Kate Williams, the documentary moved the art, craft and style of presenting into problematic territory. There were the usual inserts of period reconstructions to provide background interest and a visual dimension to the narrative of Victoria's troubled formative years, though the most powerful signifier within the frame was Williams herself. Highly photogenic and visually arresting, Williams became the dominant visual spectacle that motivated and powered the narrative forward.

Because television is a form of entertainment and education, forming a junction where past and present meet, the use of Williams as spectacle suggests that, where female presenters are concerned, society is still obsessed by and organised around appearance and age.[12] The way Williams was directed and shot actually expresses a visual rationale constructed in oil paintings, preserved and projected by film and television, that values appearance as much as, if not more than, knowledge.

> For what the spectacle expresses is the total practice of one particular economic and social formation; it is, so to speak, that formation's agenda. It is also the historical moment by which we happen to be governed.[13]

What is problematic here – and it does not bode well for the future style of female presentation of history formats – is that Williams, by adopting this screen persona, through her willingness to be framed in such a way, turns herself into an object. The camera clearly adores her, and the shots have a similarity to the historical depiction of women sexually objectified on canvas. Then as now, Williams becomes a gendered object, the female subject 'offering up her femininity as the surveyed',[14] producing nothing more than an edifice of image.

This structuring of the camera as symbolic of the male gaze is a convention of a world 'ordered by sexual imbalance'.[15] Accordingly, narrative space is divided between the active male and passive female that accentuates and heightens the pleasure of looking.[16] Williams may control the narrative as a storyteller, yet she remains in this sphere of regulated passivity as a sexualised object with a succession of shots and framing devices focused on her looks, as Williams the spectacle.

> In their traditional exhibitionist role women are simultaneously looked at and displayed, with their appearance coded for strong visual and erotic impact so that they can be said to connote to-be-looked-at-ness.[17]

Mid-shots and close-ups of Williams convey this camera/male gaze adoration. Of course, the history of the young monarch eventually comes through this edifice of image, delivered with some authority, if not a little too much dramatic emphasis.

Inserted 'talking heads' of historians and specialists, including Juliet Gardiner, add their individual voices to the narrative, though they are hemmed into the corner of the frame as per standard classic documentary style. Williams, however, has the freedom of the frame and is enhanced by a flattering repertoire of shots as she does her pieces to camera.

The concern here is that appearance overwhelms the content. Interestingly, Williams' dominant screen presence was also picked up by a female *Radio Times* reviewer, Jane Rackham:

> Here's a rarity: a history documentary with sparing use of reconstructions. The reason for this radical departure is presumably because of its comely presenter, Kate Williams. The camera lingers on her Pre-Raphaelite locks and delicate features as she breathily enthuses about her topic – which, by the way, is the 'melancholy' early life of Queen Victoria. Fortunately, Williams is also an expressive storyteller with a talent for hyperbole.[18]

As far as representation through archetypes and stereotypes operate in television, programme-makers still adopt a range of characters within deterministic masculine and feminine roles. This form of characterisation can trace its roots in visual culture to art and artists, and a visual heritage that is seen as a cultural legacy.[19] Joan Wallach Scott summarises the essence of attempting to define the role of women in history, by citing the work of Darline Levy, Harriet Applewhite and Mary Johnson questioning women's subordination as invisibility and emancipation as visibility.[20]

Williams, described by the BBC in current television parlance on the *Timewatch* website as 'key talent' rather than presenter, addresses the feminist argument on the visibility of women as she unmasks the young queen's powerful character and through her own screen presence. Paradoxically, it is the way that Williams has been framed as an object that creates visibility for all the wrong reasons.

The proliferation of channels and the ability to download programmes on computers have significantly altered the interface between TV-users and television history. This particular episode of *Timewatch*, for instance, could be seen on the BBC's free to air High Definition channel, on BBC2, as a repeat on BBC1 at two-thirty in the morning and via the BBC's iPlayer. It is no longer simply a question of which is the natural channel for commissioning new history but one of how much value the past holds as it is re-parcelled and sold on as means of re-revisiting the past.

Even *Timewatch*'s reputation or ability to sell on the past is not a guarantee that it will survive a change of course for BBC history. With Laurence Rees leaving as Creative Director of history following his latest series – *World War II: Behind Closed Doors* (BBC2, 2008) – the emphasis is changing to new angles on history not covering the Second World War, with strong presenter-led themed series. *Timewatch* is also expected to lose its own dedicated editor as well as not even having its usual run in the schedules guaranteed to continue.[21] This new direction is led by Martin Davidson in control of BBC specialist factual commissioning, who admits that he is 'looking to bring on the next generation of presenters', and intends to ensure that 'BBC2 will remain the home of history. It always was, only now it will be reinforced.'[22]

The future of BBC history may be assured, but how it is presented may raise some of the issues already covered by Kate Williams' *Timewatch* contribution.

Putting the past into perspective

As the 2008 financial crisis has deepened into a damaging recession, it is worth assessing whether the strategy of using the past as a means of reassurance, as seen in previous troubled decades, is being revived. A survey of scheduled programmes listed in the *Radio Times* on four separate weeks, 26 July – 1 August, 13–19 September, 1–7 November and 22–28 November covered programming during the build-up to the financial market crash on 30 September and the ensuing post-crash turmoil.

Apart from Niall Ferguson's *The Ascent of Money* (C4, 2008) perfectly coinciding with a global loss of faith in the capitalist system, 2008 terrestrial, cable and satellite schedules were woefully thin on original history. From the 1,094 programmes broadcast, 321 were first transmissions, 773 were repeats. Out of the total series and on-offs listed, 331 were devoted to the First and Second World Wars, mostly repeats. At least this re-covering of wartime victories in times of uncertainty does permit a society unsure of its present and future to have a token form of security of sorts.

The repeats in this brief survey amounted to 31 per cent of output with UKTV History, Discovery and the History Channel the worst offenders with a considerable amount of scheduling time made up of constant history loops and streams. UKTV History, a satellite and digital provider, constantly recycles series and one-offs previously transmitted on other channels, predominantly the BBC, which jointly owns the channel through BBC Worldwide in partnership with Virgin Media.

In terms of overall programming, the History Channel had 32 per cent of the share, followed by UKTV History with 28 per cent, and National Geographic claiming 14 per cent. All the BBC's combined output stood at 11 per cent, Discovery at 9 per cent, all of Channel 4's at 2 percent, ITV's at

1 per cent, as was Five's. The others, consisting of UKTV Documentary, Sky Arts 1 and the esoterically named Dave, amounted to 2 per cent in total. Out of UKTV History's 307 programmes aired across those weeks, 59 per cent were made up on the whole of BBC repeats, 9 per cent were new transmissions and 32 per cent revisited the First and Second World Wars.

As an emerging equivalent channel to BBC2 for history, BBC4's programming based on newly commissioned material mixed with archive programmes did have a topical resonance with one-off documentaries themed on commerce with *Pile It High, Sell It Cheap* (BBC4, 2008) and *Shopping for England* (BBC4, 2008), examining the founding of Selfridges and the Woolworths stores.

Of course, it could be coincidence that BBC4 traced the success of the Woolworths chain just as it was about to go into receivership, but it did serve to remind TV-users how the high street as a bastion of British culture and society had evolved and, latterly, dissolved. It is not only on the high street were products have exchange-value, however: TV-users are also products.

Just as for any commercial channel, TV-users for BBC history programmes are a commodity. Unlike commercial television where TV-users are available to the highest bidder in terms of advertising time, what Sut Jhally classes as 'communications-defined time',[23] where 'watching time',[24] equates to programme success, the BBC sells TV-users back to itself for similar targeted programmes, or to sell-on to other BBC services in order to justify licence fee increases.

It is perhaps ironic that both commercial and PSB television in Britain aim to invest in history programming, *time-past* in order to reap and harvest *time-present* as the amount of hours TV-users exchange in front of their televisions in return for programming rewards in the shape of entertainment, knowledge and reaffirmations of nationality.

The evolution of factual history programming in Britain, consistently forms genres and genealogical re-presentation that reinforce national identity. This has embraced technological change within the television industry, encompassing and reflecting significant stages in the history of the moving image on the small screen. Yet, many one-off programmes and multi-part series also come to express how society sees itself. During different decades of production and transmission of factual history programming, peaks of political and ideological activity have acted as primary motive power behind the commissioning and production of factual history across PSB and commercial channels.

Popular factual programming when dealing with taboo subjects, or the untold as in *Yesterday's Witness*, does have a cutting edge quality about it that Steve Humphries has developed as a producer and director of *Timewatch*.

Using oral history and memory, Humphries' six-part series *A Secret World of Sex* (BBC2, 1991) and *The Call of the Sea* (BBC2, 1997) both demystified the past through personal accounts. Channel 4's *Pornography: The Secret History of Civilisation* (C4, 1999), another revelatorily titled six-part series, again highlights how television is not an inhibited or timid medium in choosing content designed to maximise screen appeal.

History has been classed as the 'new rock 'n' roll' by Tom Stearn,[25] and as the 'new gardening' by Andy Harries of Granada Television.[26] Its increasing appearance in peak-time scheduling and the emergence of channels devoted entirely to it demonstrate how popular re-presenting the past on television has become.

Establishing itself as a popular choice for programme-makers and TV-users, factual history was never going to receive a warm reception from the highly partisan and closed community of academic historians. Television is a relative newcomer as a mass-communication vehicle in comparison to the printed word, radio and cinema, never achieving full acceptance as a suitable conveyor of complex serious themes. On the one hand, it provides instant, easy access to the past, capable of recreating events vividly in a highly entertaining visual style. On the other hand, its on-screen navigators tend to draw criticism for the course by which they choose to steer television back into the past, the destinations they rediscover and the way they represent and present these 'Other' times as events streamlined for television.

Recycling themes, events and characters as repeats to bulk out schedule slots and bolster entire channels devoted to history has become an industry convention, with the BBC, ITV, Channel 4 and Five including more than 500 hours of repeats in their 2008 Christmas schedules.[27]

In many ways television operates as an electronic museum and, in line with other museums, holds vast archives – in this case programmes – increasing by the hour, but there is only so much it can display which is influenced by attempting to tap into current social and cultural trends. Television as an electronic museum creates and celebrates heritage by making the past a commercial product through branding programmes and periods of the past with an exchange-value based on the comforting notion of 'our shared, national, heritage'.[28] This then draws TV-users not only into history but also into the channel and programme identity that is used as a portal to the past.

One advantage of television in reissuing the past in revised formats or repeats is that as an industry, it also represents a popular past that it has largely manufactured. The setting aside of special themed evenings celebrating pro-

grammes, studios and individuals from different eras signifies the central role
that television has played in the cultural life of the twentieth century.

It cannot be overlooked how 'media history is part of consumer history
and an important part of twentieth-century history,'[29] with the BBC quick to
assert its right as the nation's broadcaster, providing a three-part retrospective
with *Lord Reith Looks Back* (BBC1, 1967), the third part intriguingly titled 'I
Found the BBC Or the BBC Found me'. The fabric of the BBC was offered in
Lime Grove – 'The Television Years 1950' (BBC2, 1991) and the bond between
nation and institution featured in the four-part *Auntie: The Inside Story of the
BBC* (BBC1, 1997). Channel 4, not to be left out of having a long-established
television heritage of its own, appropriated the output of one of ITV's main
providers, Thames Television, which lost its franchise in 1992.

The resultant 'Vintage Thames Season' in 1995, featured a sit-com *Bless
This House* (ITV, 1971–76) and a crime drama *The Sweeney* (ITV, 1975–78)
amongst other 'classic' programmes. *The Sweeney* can in fact be studied as a
social-cultural history text from the fashions, vehicles, architecture and locations used in the series. The scripts too, can provide a general insight into the
beliefs and values circulating at the time.

Any excursion into the past, particularly in terms of reviewing decades or
even the cultural changes in television advertising, engages TV-users with what
Charlie Brooker terms 'nostalgia bombs',[30] when television encapsulates particular moments in time. The BBC used its own considerable archives to produce
I Love the Seventies (BBC2, 2000), where icons and celebrities from the decade
– Sir Jimmy Saville, Britt Ekland, David Cassidy and Noddy Holder amongst
others – presented each episode themed around one year. The BBC even had
a 'cult' website devoted to the concept and series of *I Love…*, though it is currently in the process of being mothballed.[31]

Popularising the past through emotive memories of soap operas, sit-coms,
commercials and music makes history personal and makes citizenship familiar and understandable. When in-house or bought-in archive clips are woven
together with commentary and the opinions of 'talking heads', the past does
become an economical means of producing entertainment through nostalgia,
a form of factual entertainment, or what commissioning editors deem 'Fact
Ent'.[32]

Compilation series have spawned entire nights of television, usually at
the weekend or on public holidays, themed on clips and commentary. Five
has allowed its TV-users the opportunity to vote for its 'greatest' compilation
series: *Greatest Ever Romantic Movies* (Five, 2007); *Greatest Ever Scary Movies*

(Five, 2006); *Greatest Ever Comedy Movies* (Five, 2006); *Greatest Ever Block-buster Movies* (Five, 2006)

Channel 4's assemblages have included the two-part *100 Greatest TV Characters* (C4, 2001) and the *Greatest Comedy Catchphrases* (C4, 2008), 'featuring some of the funniest clips of the most popular comedy shows of the past 50 years'.[33] Using one of its subsidiary channels targeted at the under thirty-fives, the BBC has Richard Bacon, the sacked presenter of the children's show *Blue Peter* – dismissed over allegations of drug-taking – narrating a strand of compilation series titled *The Most Annoying.* With derisory narration and commentary, the series has singled out *The Most Annoying People* (BBC3, 2008), *The Most Annoying Couples We Love to Hate* (BBC3, 2008) *and The Most Annoying TV…We Love to Hate* (BBC3, 2008). Easy to create, produce and engage with, television in this format is tailoring itself to the *bricolage* experience of computer users who assemble their own cultural references of what national identity stands for from visual clips.

As new technologies produce advanced systems of communication, opportunities for myth creation and stimulation increase and progress. In the case of compilation series, it is a question of gatekeeping in terms of selecting the clips, or if assembled through public voting, attempting to identify which groups of TV-users are determining what is the top hundred, the top fifty, the greatest.

Television forms part of this communication chain where myths are easy to produce. From the oral word to the written, from photography to radio, from cinema to television, to the internet and today's multimedia, intertextualised convergence society, myth is always a component of the communication system.[34] It was inevitable at some stage in factual history programming that this would entail individuals being invited to 'live in the past' and physically re-engage with history and its myths.

The past as reality TV…

There can be no question that technological change brings enormous shifts not only in how society organises itself but also how it sees itself in a linear scheme of progress, which directly affects the production and reception of history.

> This tremendous speed-up in social upheavals repeatedly widens the gap between generations and breaks down traditions … One of the consequences has been considerable contempt for history. It is the contempt of men intoxicated with their own successes, with no time to found any enduring structures on them, for there will be new achievements next day throwing everything once again into the melting pot.[35]

As a result of this 'melting pot' it may be that memory is the only cohesive device that links generations, creating new myths, confirming old ones, so even when each generation may feel more and more physically remote from the past, they retain a route back into it when the present becomes too chaotic, too fast. Ironically, rather than the perceived radical and rebellious 1960s, for some people it is the stability of the 1950s that is seen as the cultural foundation of a decent, civilised British society.[36]

Attempting to recreate these formative periods through innovative frameworks, television can rely too much on technology and dramatisation. This, in turn, allows the imperatives of action and character to dominate, turning history into a reality themed show. No matter how much the makers of Channel 4's *The Edwardian Country House* (C4, 2002) prefer to define the series as a 'social experiment',[37] it displays all the binary modes of characterisation to be found in television dramas. In fact, *Upstairs Downstairs* (ITV, 1971–75) represents its nearest fictional cousin.

Television history experimented in the 1970s with the reality format of 'living history', with *Living in the Past* (BBC2, 1978). Then the most ambitious reality series in terms of duration, it involved fifteen volunteers from different social backgrounds, sacrificing their modern lifestyles to live and work in a recreated Iron Age village for a twelve-month period.

Not without its controversy with scenes of animal slaughter and nudity, the series adopted Paul Watson's 'fly-on-the-wall' documentary style that had been employed to provide a close and personal account of the Wilkins family from Reading in *The Family* (BBC1, 1974). Later living history series, *The 1900 House* (C4, 1999), *The 1940s House* (C4, 2001) and *The Trench* (BBC2, 2002), would accentuate the unreality of the reality by melding Hollywood's dramatic codes and conventions with the unscripted confrontational element of *Big Brother* (C4, 2000–).

Whereas *Living in the Past* created real fission as personal and group dynamics genuinely disintegrated, TV-users now expect performance with their re-enactment of the past for productions of good 'living history'. Individuals carefully selected and screened bring their modern psychological baggage and physical condition, displaying a high level of natural, or prompted, disposition towards a Dickensian character trait for the melodramatic.

One of the latest experiments in living history has seen two series produced by BBC Wales – *Coal House* (BBC1 Wales, 2007) and *Coal House at War* (BBC1 Wales, 2008) – attempting to dispatch chosen Welsh families back in time. The three families in *Coal House*, 'hand-picked to live in a cramped miner's cottage at Stack Square, Blaenavon for four weeks',[38] can hardly be typical of the mining families of the 1920s who had to endure more than a number of weeks hardship in order to live and survive rather than produce good television. Even the year itself, 1927, was hand-picked by the historical consultant, Chris Williams, Professor of Welsh History at Swansea University.

> One issue was what period to set the programme. We decided on 1927 to have the greatest dramatic impact – a year after the general strike and before the pits were nationalised.[39]

The *Coal House* families may have undergone a selection process, including a final day-long test overseen by the army to determine their physical strength and mental robustness for a return to 1927, but the Cartwrights, the Griffithses and the Phillipses were ultimately 'cast' because their family dynamics and personalities would ensure good reality television. In the first episode on the double DVD set where Nicola Reynolds, the series' narrator interviewed each successful selected family, challenges and opposition between past and present are set up to create dramatic expectation. Cerdin Griffiths confessed on camera to being claustrophobic, the Phillips family numbered eight – six children and two adults – and the Cartwrights, with Joe professor of geology and Annabel an astrophysicist and their two daughters, were described by the series' psychologist Philippa Davies as an 'alpha' family.

As demanded of good television, emotive tension, the challenge of adapting to a strange environment, inter-family rivalry, intra-family conflict have all been expertly engineered to deliberately create a misfit between the modern families and their 1927 'set'. The production crew had spent all summer converting three iron-workers' cottages into 'authentic replicas' of the cottages of Welsh working miners towards the end of the 1920s. Reynolds, as presenter of the introductory, behind the scenes, 'episode' – a dramatic convention, unlike the factual 'part' – neatly and gleefully outlines the challenges each family will face in their four-week endurance test as she tours the 'set' and talks to members of the production team.

The height of the coalface seam at Blaentillery No 2 Mine, a working drift mine, is placed against Cerdin Griffiths' claustrophobia, with Reynolds pondering for the sake of a nicely balanced curious face to camera on how Cerdin will cope. During a *Big Brother* style walk around the cramped two-up two-down cottages, Reynolds uses the lack of modern amenities along with issues of privacy to again wonder how the families will endure these staged hardships. Pointedly, the size of accommodation is commented on as a particular challenge for the eight-member Phillips family.

Once the dichotomy of then and now has been established, the TV-users are primed, charged and ready for the arrival of 'our' intrepid families into a 1927 historical zoo. To some degree the series does serve an educational purpose in bringing the past to life, though it does the past an injustice in having it tailored for a social experimentation in how much things have changed between then and now.

Of course, the families endured the hardship; they were selected to do so, as well as entertain. By episode four, we had the Griffiths family unable to master the coal-burning range that provided their only means of heat and cooking. The eight-strong Phillips family had to come to terms with mealtime logistics required to feed small children with the added production drama of no milk being available from the visiting grocer.

Cast as binary opposed outsiders to the other families, the alpha Cartwrights became socially inferior as an injury to Joe's hand while preparing kindling prevented him from working underground and earning a full day's piece rate. When the Griffiths children were struck down with sickness and diarrhoea, the mother provided an informed piece to camera on how much washing of clothes and sheets this would now entail.

The fact of how much backbreaking manual labour women of the period had to complete over eighteen hours never missed a beat in Reynolds' narration throughout the series. With children from two families catching chicken pox, and the bonding of Cerdin Griffiths and Richie Phillips working underground, leaving Joe Cartwright isolated on the surface, a whole range of natural and production-induced crises and dilemmas gave a strong dramatic edge to each thirty-minute episode.

Forsaking the banality of the reality approach in *Coal House* – the families were even cheered *Big Brother* style as they left the square – *Victorian Farm* (BBC2, 2009) is apparently, a 'historical observational documentary'.[40] Not to be confused with Frederick Wiseman's observational style, nor that of direct cinema, the six-part *Victorian Farm is* living history. With a team of professional re-enactors – for that is what they are – consisting of a domestic and social historian Ruth Goodman, alongside archaeologists Peter Ginn and Alex Langlands, they heighten the drama of each challenge by not being 'sure whether they're supposed to be surprised by what they find, or use it to tell us what they know'.[41]

Having already re-enacted together previously in the twelve-part *Tales from the Green Valley* (BBC2, 2005) recreating life on a 1620 farm and the one-off *Tudor Feast at Christmas* (BBC4, 2007), Goodman, Ginn and Langlands spent twelve months living and working as Victorian farmers. Here, as in *Coal House*, the abiding dialogue to emerge from the past was that manual labour is tough and tiring, and as a result, domestic, industrial or rural work took considerably longer.

In the first part of *Victorian Farm*, the problem of chronological compression also arises. A cottage had to be renovated, a new coal-burning range fitted, ploughing and sowing to be done, fruit to be preserved, apples to be pressed for cider, coal to be carted from the canal … and all within sixty-minutes. Specialists who fitted the range brought the coal by canal, and the owner – and his son – of the Acton Scott estate in Shropshire all appeared neatly costumed in order not to spoil the illusion. The common factor in these living history series is that they have a tendency to be nothing more weighty than museum displays brought to life, television equivalents of illustrated histories or 'pop-up' books with the additional benefit of having sound and movement.

It would be nonsense to argue that living history series do not give an insight into the past. Of course they do, but so do books. What differs here is that television assumes control of the imagination and hikes up the dramatic element. So much so that one TV-user commenting on *Coal House at War* on the series' website, thought the 'plots' were 'tremendous' and wanted to 'praise your stars – the whole cast'.[42] Another deemed it a 'superior example of Reality TV'.[43]

One of the few dissenting TV-users thought, 'The families are playing to the camera and it is more like a reality show than a history programme this time around.'[44] The vast majority of the comments congratulated BBC Wales on the production, on its accuracy and showing how people really had lived, 'Well done BBC Wales for telling the historical facts of the last war so accurately in *Coalhouse at War*.'[45]

It is clear from the comments that both series did open a dialogue between past and present, but the series should not be regarded as portraying the actual experiences of a given community at a specific time. The producers and specialist consultants may aim for accuracy and authenticity, parachuting contemporary families into the past, but no matter how much they have been screened, authenticity is a well-crafted illusion.

As a disgruntled TV-user of *Coal House at War* put it, 'they just come over as families of today pretending to be living in that era and still being part of today',[46] which probably sums up the problem of encouraging amateur dramatics on a televisual scale. On the websites for each *Coal House* series, visitors are invited to meet 'the cast',[47] and the popular appeal of the series has been recognised by the release of the 1927 themed *Coal House* on DVD.

Factual television history literally dressed up in an attempt to fabricate the past traduces itself, and its chosen characters, into shallow forms of heritage and nostalgia as the dialogue between the past and present breaks down, leaving only a vapid spectatorship on offer. The damage that reality TV is having on factual history cannot be overlooked or dismissed, as John Humphrys observed in his 2004 MacTaggart Lecture at the Edinburgh International TV Festival.

> I've already said how impressed I was by Schama and Starkey: simple narrative, lots of information delivered intelligently and pretty straight. Now it has to be 'living' history. One of the most respected independents in the business has a great idea for a series based on the relationship between Christianity and Islam and centred on the Crusades. But he says no-one would buy it because it would have to be in a 'living history' format. You know the sort of thing: you get together a bunch of young upper class twits and working class lads, take 'em off to Jerusalem and make 'em relive what it was like to fight the crusades.[48]

Television narratives have to rely on cultural values for making sense of individual and group identities. If that collective identity is plucked from the present and transported into the past, despite attention to detail spent by a production team on dressing the characters and location, there will always be contextual slippage.

Continually changing with cultural trends and developments, television shares the nation's concerns by utilising the screen as a contested space. Factual television history's increasing value as a commodity has inevitably come at a price. Its popularity and dependence on images have constantly drawn it into the debate about high and low cultural forms. In his *TimesOnLine* piece, Bryan Appleyard charts how good history programming has had its legacy corrupted by the mediocre and downright bad.

> The high points of the non-authored tradition were *The Great War* in 1964 and *The World at War*, exactly a decade later. Both shared an absolute commitment to telling us what happened and what it meant, and to giving us some glimpse of what it felt like at the time. The 'at the time' is crucial, because the deep problem of much current historical gimmickry is that it is determined to make the past feel like the present – so we see the Gunpowder Plot as a *Top Gear* stunt gone wrong, Helen of Troy as a feminist *avant la lettre* and Rome as a gigantic sex resort. Ephemeral contemporary attitudes are of absolutely no help in understanding the past; only the profoundly ignorant think otherwise.[49]

One reason why these heritage-framed programmes, *The 1900 House, The Edwardian Country House, The Trench* and *Coal House* do not work is due to the characters becoming artificial barriers between the present and the past. As hand-picked constructs they turn the past into a controlled make-believe fantasy, where the dressing up, chores, activities and detail are historically correct, but the minds and bodies inside the costume are inherently modern and therefore are meaningless false constructs.

This means that past is always going to function as a misfit when it is brought into the present, resulting with a cultural mismatch where 'then' and 'now' are out of synchronisation. The past is then open to abuse as a game space, an imagined 'Other' world that can be activated, populated and managed for the needs of entertainment. Worryingly, a number of susceptible individuals are suffering from what has been classed as 'The Truman Show Syndrome', when they believe that their daily lives form part of a reality show.[50]

Creating this illusion of realism in living history formats imposes a controlling narrative presence and character opposition enforced through editing. This narrative control may not always be evident because the edited realism disguises any sense of artificiality, propelling TV-users into entertaining situations that bring with them a transformative power of their own.

> Editing moves the viewer across times and places, it involves a continual process of opening up and then closing down specific looks at the world, which may, for instance, be a studio world, a dramatic world, or the evidential and expository world of a documentary programme.[51]

Consequently, this referencing of historical characters through constructed realism can conceal any original characters behind myth, superficiality and what TV-users have come to expect from certain historical characters. This, as far as television history is concerned, inhibits each character within precise referential frames that, more often than not, lead to crude or simplistic stereotyping that is assumed to be representing the truth.[52] Another pertinent question that is overlooked when dealing with 'living history' is how far, or to what an extent, mediated and personal memory intrudes into each character's appropriation of a life in the past. In many regards, television history as reality format has reinvented one of its earliest forms, that of oral history.

Notes

1 Douglas Hurd, Home Secretary, House of Commons Hansard debates for 8 February 1989. Vol. 146, Cols. 1007–08 www.publications.parliament.uk/pa/cm198889/cmhansrd/1989-02-08/Debate-4.html.

2 Brian Winston, *Media Technology and Society. A History: From the Telegraph to the Internet* (London: Routledge, 1998), p. 302.

3 Ofcom, 'The television viewer proportion of homes with free and pay television, 2006' www.ofcom.org.uk/research/cm/cmrnr08/tv/.

4 Tara Conlan, 'ITV's Big Switch-Off', *Daily Mail* (5 August 2004), p. 12.

5 Tara Conlan, 'BBC TV Ratings Melt Away to Hit a New Low', *Daily Mail* (5 January 2005), p. 38.

6 *Today's History*, BFI Film and TV Database http://ftvdb.bfi.org.uk/sift/series/14477.

7 Foucault, *Power/Knowledge*, p. 83.

8 Foucault, *Power/Knowledge*, p. 83.

9 Rees, interview with the author.

10 Rees, interview with the author.

11 Alison Graham, 'Secret History: Britain's Boy Soldiers', *RT* (12–18 June 2004), p. 76.

12 Urmee Khan, 'Selina Scott Wins Ageism Battle Over Job With Five', *Daily Telegraph* (6 December 2008), p. 7. See also Anita Singh, 'Ageism Row at BBC as Countryfile Gets a New Presenter', *Daily Telegraph* (10 December 2008), p. 9 and Nicole Martin '"Pretty" Newsreaders Will Be Found Out, says ITV's Austin', *Daily Telegraph* (16 September 2008), p. 3.

13 Guy Debord, *The Society of the Spectacle*, trans. Donald Nicholson-Smith (New York: Zone Books, 1999), p. 15.

14 John Berger, *Ways of Seeing* (London: British Broadcasting Corporation/Penguin, 1972), p. 55.

15 Laura Mulvey, 'Visual pleasure and narrative cinema', in Patricia Erens (ed.), *Issues in Feminist Film Criticism* (Bloomington: Indiana University Press, 1990), p. 33.

16 Mulvey, 'Visual pleasure', p. 33.

17 Mulvey, 'Visual pleasure', p. 33.

18 Jane Rackham, 'Timewatch – Young Victoria', *RT* (18–24 October 2008), p. 56.

19 Berger, *Ways of Seeing*, pp. 45–6.

20 Scott (ed.), *Feminism and History*, p. 2.

21 Maggie Brown, 'The End of an Era', www.guardian.co.uk/media/ 2008/nov/10/bbc-history-programmes.

22 Brown, 'End of an Era'.

23 Sut Jhally, *The Codes of Advertising* (New York: Routledge, 1990), p. 72.

24 Jhally, *Codes of Advertising*, p. 72.

25 Tom Stearn, 'What's wrong with television history?', *History Today*, 52:12 (2002), 26.

26 Sarah Cassidy, 'History Man Starkey in "Golden Handcuffs" Deal', *Independent* (15 February 2002), p. 9.

27 'Christmas TV Has 500 Hours of Repeats', *Independent* (19 December 2008), p. 16.

28 Noakes, 'Making histories', in Evans and Lunn (eds), *War and Memory*, p. 93.

29 Diane Barthel, *Historic Preservation: Collective Memory and Historical Identity* (New Brunswick: Rutgers University Press, 1996), p. 118.

30 Charlie Brooker, *Charlie Brooker's Screenwipe* (transmitted BBC4, 25 November 2008).

31 *I Love the 70s* www.bbc.co.uk/cult/ilove/years/70sindex.shtml.

32 Channel 4 Commissioning, Factual Entertainment www.channel4.com/corporate/ 4producers/commissioning/factualentertainment.html.

33 *Greatest Comedy Catchphrases, RT* (22–28 November 2008), p. 70.

34 Barthes, *Mythologies*, p. 110.

35 Febvre, *New Kind of History*, p. 28.

36 Christopher Hope, 'Bad Parents Have Caused Britain's Decline Since the 1950s, Says MP', *Daily Telegraph* (27 November 2008), p. 12.

37 Juliet Gardiner, 'The Edwardian country house', *History Today*, 52:7 (2002), 18.

38 *Coal House* www.bbc.co.uk/wales/coalhouse/sites/families. The narrator for the series, Nicola Reynolds, does actually say three weeks in the introductory episode on DVD.

39 *Coal House* www.bbc.co.uk/wales/coalhouse/sites/behindthescenes/pages/chriswilliams.shtml.

40 *Victorian Farm* www.bbc.co.uk/programmes/b00gn2bl.

41 James Walton, '19th-Century Nostalgia to Rival Lark Rise to Candleford', *Daily Telegraph* (9 January 2009), p. 30.

42 www.bbc.co.uk/wales/coalhouse2/sites/programmes/?page=4#comments-pager

43 www.bbc.co.uk/wales/coalhouse2/sites/programmes/?page=1#comments-pager

44 www.bbc.co.uk/wales/coalhouse2/sites/programmes/?page=6#comments-pager

45 www.bbc.co.uk/wales/coalhouse2/sites/programmes/?page=6#comments-pager

46 www.bbc.co.uk/wales/coalhouse2/sites/programmes/?page=7#comments-pager

47 *Coal House at War* www.bbc.co.uk/wales/coalhouse2/sites/cast.

48 John Humphrys, 2004 MacTaggart Lecture to the Edinburgh International Television Festival www.mgeitf.co.uk/home/news.aspx/John_Humphrys_Delivers_the_ 2004_MacTagga

49 Bryan Appleyard, 'Report: TV Needs a History Lesson'. http://entertainment.times-online.co.uk/tol/arts_and_entertainment/tv_and_radio/article586608.ece.

50 Tom Leonard, 'Truman Show Syndrome: When Reality TV Takes Over Your World', *Daily Telegraph* (26 November 2008), p. 3.

51 John Corner, *Critical Ideas in Television Studies* (Oxford: Oxford University Press, 1999), pp. 28–9.

52 Mieke Bal, *Narratology: Introduction to the Theory of Narrative* (Toronto: University of Toronto Press, 2nd edn, 1997), pp. 120–1.

5

Truth or drama: documentary history

Genre, for better or worse, has become a formula equated with success or failure across all media industries. Justifying investment in what are held to be successful formats if TV-user figures remain high, television genres are used as evidence of TV-user sophistication, education and preference.

Genre conveniently allows programmes and series to create popular or high-brow levels of expectation in TV-users through their formats. The BBC's *The Historyman* (BBC2, 1989) with its diverse themes, including, 'Sid Bates V.C.', is a less demanding type of five-minute programme, whereas a series such as *Stalin – The Red Tsar?* (ITV, 1978) expects in-depth intellectual interaction from TV-users. In this way, genres function as social barometers, gauging the interests and value that society places in and on itself through the television it consumes.

Factual history, as documentary, positions TV-users according to what they can expect, creating expectation and a sense of reward. Moreover, factual history programming encapsulates cultural concerns, social values, political and economic trends and the competency of TV-users at the time of production. Within genre, consideration to narrative trajectory, causal motivation and the stylistic codes and conventions contained in the type of shot, the use of the frame and the *mise en scène* determine the rules of engagement for TV-users.

Television to some extent has inherited genre from the cinema, its codes and conventions based on difference constructed through 'creative toolboxes' that standardise the production process.[1] Some of these 'creative toolboxes' have become adapted by television factual history programming when they have to function within the constraints of documentary. This permits subtle differences through the way archive footage, voice-overs, dramatic reconstructions and cutaway shots are used.

Difference defines how a programme deals with the past in a specific way and style. 'The Swashbucklers', in *Hollywood and the Stars* (BBC1, 1964), and *The Building of the Bomb* (BBC1, 1965) equally come within the documentary spectrum through their use of archive footage, incidental music and narration, the former by Joseph Cotten, the latter Rene Cutforth. Any similarity, however tenuous this may seem, comes from sharing basic documentary codes and conventions of production; the real difference is the choice and style of both narrators and editing.

Genre is more than an informal agreement with TV-users on how they are to be entertained, educated or informed. Genre underpins television production with benchmark models from which future programmes can be measured – not only by cost but also the continuing use of codes and conventions, including ideological values, that have proved successful and generated TV-user numbers time and time again. The formulistic properties also depend on market forces as well as cultural values, TV-user preferences and social systems at its moment of production.[2] Over a considerable number of years, factual history programming has developed into a variety of formats that exploit the documentary genre.

Television history and the documentary form

Documentary as a genre seems, at first hand, an ideal visual system for dealing with re-presenting events from the past. Within genre frameworks, there are a number of stylistic conventions determining how each documentary is structured, how it projects its narrative and how it articulates a documentary voice. Classic expository documentary, observational *cinéma vérité* and reflexive documentaries comprise the main genre frameworks that TV-users have, over the years, become familiar with, along with their variant formats such as docudrama, docusoaps and fly-on-the-wall.

According to Laurence Rees, any serious reinterpretation of the past for the small screen is organised around three main documentary-related formats.[3] The first involves a classic documentary mix of interviews, voice-over and archive footage capable of handling any topic, whether it is a re-evaluation of anarchy and terrorism in *Baader-Meinhof: In Love with Terror* (BBC4, 2003) or a nostalgic return to steam with *The British Transport Films: A Nation on Film Special* (BBC4, 2008).

The second strand incorporates the presenter as anchor, a screen guide that provides a shared experience. A style perfected by Kenneth Clark in *Civilisation*, Jacob Bronowski's *The Ascent of Man*, John Roberts in *Triumph of the West*

(BBC2, 1985), David Starkey's *Elizabeth*, Simon Schama's *History of Britain* (BBC2, 2000) and Bettany Hughes' *Seven Ages of Britain* (C4, 2003).

The final format, an increasingly popular convention derived from technological innovation led by Hollywood, allows any aspect of the past to be recreated through CGI. This final form has evolved from attempts at being-there realism through reconstruction, as in Mike Figgis' re-enactment of the bloody and violent clash between police and striking miners during the 1984–85 bitter dispute, in *The Battle of Orgreave* (C4, 2002). TV-users now expect great visual spectacle where screen time is reduced to impact, colour and action, and television history cannot ignore these expectations if the market is to continue to develop new forms.

This familiarity bridges any strangeness, creating a structured space complete with a contract that contains prescribed rules for engaging with documentary texts. Documentary is just as much a social construct as drama, carrying with it the fears, concerns, aspirations and ideologies of not only its creators but TV-users also. Viewing patterns and habits inevitably change due to developments in demographic shift, media technologies and the preferences of TV-users.

These social and cultural shifts structure a compendium of effects that significantly alter the intensity, scope and range of television conventions ranged at manufacturing realism. At the same time, these conventions mark out genres and themes that continue to appeal to TV-users. War in its different guises continues to be a constant success in terms of durability and popularity. From some of the examples already examined in previous chapters, not all factual history programming conforms to a documentary framework. Nevertheless, where documentary is the organising format, there is a certain uniformity in its style and presentation techniques when dealing with the past.

Although documentary is regarded as primarily a non-fiction format lacking scripted dialogue, its dilution and transformation into a television hybrid encompassing factual programmes other than news and current affairs means that it is increasingly facing questions on its claims on presenting the truth.[4]

When factual history programmes do don their documentary jackets, it is in an amalgam of documentary styles cut to suit the level of direction. This corresponds to the level of action on the screen, more often than not, based around the 'classic' or 'expository mode', with its off-screen narration connecting events, providing links and giving commentary on the images that manoeuvres TV-users into a preferred position of collusion with the narratorial voice.

Organising each programme's approach through content, presentation, its use of archive footage, cutaways, and interviews, the classic style of documentary has established factual history programmes as vehicles for truth and accuracy. As the name implies, documentary represents a document, a record of events, of people and of places. Documentary provides an insight into the fabric of society, recorded in such a way that it provides a transparent and seamless journey through past events and past lives.

As with all television genres, the versatility of the expository documentary format to provide unbiased realism is misleading. Any realism created is entirely down to the director, producer, editor and researchers. The BBC, never far from controversy nowadays, has admitted to an unbalanced documentary on Baroness Thatcher, amidst claims of more bias as researchers for a documentary to be released after her death actively sought anti-Thatcher contributions.[5] Reality, truth, trust and realism are always going to be in the balance, depending on the agenda of the production team.

As with all television formats and genres, documentary functions by working to a strict formula of tried and tested conventions, primarily as a non-acted format with its mode of storytelling derived from the cinema's biopics. As a drama-based reconstruction of history, the biopic became the ideal vehicle for adaptation into television documentary forms, utilising varying combinations of archive film, reconstructions and a strong chronologically determined narrative.

Institutional practice and governance are part of the customs and traditions of Britain's television industry. These prescriptive traditions and values have a fundamental role in shaping how documentary realism is activated and produced.[6] None of these conventions are fixed, firm and fast, but shift with each prevailing cultural wind and are 'historically determined',[7] enabling the documentary form to become adaptable and versatile.

However, there is still a rigid backbone of stylistic documentary effects, shot composition, framing and editing that really does not change all that much over time. By picking and choosing events and characters as units of representation from the past, producers, writers, researchers, editors and presenters never deviate far from this inherited typology – a visual grammar of the past determined by institutional and professional practice as well as by programme codes and conventions.

The pressures of institutional and professional codes and conventions are wound into the cycle of production.[8] They are a contributing factor in the inherited shot typology and memory of factual history programmes from 1946 onwards, through their 'look' and their method of addressing TV-users. If television presents the past through prescribed shots, a stock library of history, then it also reworks history in an epic storytelling cyclic style that retells the past as a modified version of its previous collectively remembered elements.[9]

Hence each generation of factual programme-makers lay down their own variations on how events from the past should be told and look, remaining firmly within a given look of the past, functioning as a television equivalent of 'theaters of memory'.[10]

By aligning collective memory as the product of a group, or groups, certain forms of memory are located outside the individual so that any recollection is only possible through a collective act of remembering.[11] This collective act includes television and the sharing of programmes, news, events and opinions as the foundations for the 'complex cultural products' that collective memory and oral history represent.[12] In interacting with external memory sources in this way, groups and individuals do create a 'usable past', and this is very much the realm of television history production.[13]

As interactive points of reference, memory and image are bound together, one informs the other, and one substantiates the other and provides shape and structure.[14] Memory in this sense does become at the point or moment of recording – and at the point of telling – a dramatic narrative, though one that is constantly undergoing revision. Editing memories so that they become usable has a direct correlation in the editing of documentary.

Documentary has the power to create what appears to be completely unmediated, unrehearsed, natural realism, as though viewing the events or action unfold at first hand, with no technical codes and conventions intervening between the events and TV-users. In the same way that historians are bound by their social and cultural contexts, so too are factual history programmes. With documentaries having to compete within schedules and across channels, documentary appropriates codes and conventions from other genres in order to appeal to wider groups of TV-users, resulting in the hybrid form of factual entertainment.

On the one hand documentary is 'authorial' in the way in which each programme depends on the creative vision of the production team; on the other hand it is 'dramatic', not in a theatrical sense but in its depiction and use of reality. Here then is the main problem for many history programmes that have no option but to reconstruct the past due to a lack of archive material. Whether it is Egypt during the reign of the Pharaohs, or life in Viking Britain, the visual reality presented on screen is a construct, an imperfect, imagined reality in as far as it sits outside the sphere of actuality, remote from any archive footage.

Documentary style and narrative devices

One of the major drawbacks of applying dramatic narrative techniques to factual events within documentary is that the relationship between programmes and TV-users is altered considerably.[15] The power of dramatic narrative when imposed on factual programming moves the emphasis away from trust to belief, and to the conventions of fiction.

Constructing distractions to guide TV-users from one causal sequence to another limits the amount of questioning of the credibility of the material presented.[16] Essential to the narrative form of documentary are realism, trust and authenticity, achieved through the cutaway emotive shot as secondary narrative indexes reinforcing or refuting a contributor's version of events.

Combining these different visual voices into a natural, apparently transparent narrative comes through the art of editing, the final stage in the production process where realism is shaped to meet the production team's agenda. Production agendas should not necessarily be regarded as malicious, but as an expression of ideological beliefs and values of the production team. In this way, narrative 'truth', the meaning, can be regarded as largely representative.

Narrative is also a convenient system of disclosure in which binary opposition, not only through characters but also through how events are structured, produces dynamic points of interplay. This allows TV-users to make decisions about truth and claims to truth. Narrative in documentary is never innocent or pure unmediated reality; it is always a 'mode of cultural self-expression'[17] that attempts to privilege one view above another.

The power of factual history television, in fact its very popularity and value as a commodity, lies in its ability to assemble three forms of narrative into what I term a consolidated narrative. In this way, narratives form an almost irresistible quest for truth, driven by a desire to understand how and why events unfolded in certain ways. History in itself is narrative presented as units of ordered temporality, a logical way to organise and reassemble the past.[18] When history as narrative is synthesized within narrative codes and conventions of television as a dramatic medium, alongside the oral narrative of eyewitnesses, it formulates a plot, complete with characters, elements of intrigue, mystery and suspense. This combination, which vastly outweighs any simple linear chronological ordering of events, forms the consolidated narrative. When asked what makes a good television programme, Bettany Hughes, David Starkey, Michael Wood, Adam Hart-Davis and Laurence Rees were unequivocal in naming narrative as a principal factor.[19]

Documentary is under the same levels of pressure as all programmes within broadcast schedules to pull in its fair proportion of TV-user share and not only instil loyalty but ensure repeat viewings in terms of series. This has created a move towards dramatisation and reconstruction as it offers the high level of spectacle that characterises much of today's television output.

An increase in style over content can lead only to further problems for factual history programming, as it has for the documentary,[20] compressing dramatic and factual elements into an ever increasingly tighter narrative arc. How much more spectacle and dramatic reconstruction the past can safely take is not clear; the greatest worry is that television history will gradually slip out of its mode of education and informing to concentrate more on entertaining.

Reconstructing the past

Reconstruction is a format where television excels. Television, as well as cinema, produces discourses based on the past that are regarded as special in some way, given a privileged status amongst the flow of other programmes, regardless of genre. Reconstruction has grown out of the need to compete more and more for TV-user share, within competitive scheduling strategies. News coverage, from either professional journalists or 'citizen reporters' armed with mobile telephones capable of recording moving or still images, gives immediate access to dramatic events, creating 'instant history'. In this scenario, the documentary had to progress into a more dynamic format, utilising genre formulas as a secure platform, from which experimentation can take place.

Documentary reconstruction raises a number of pertinent questions. Does it require TV-users to engage with the form and content as fact or fiction? Does it go further than the original event by adding dramatic imagery and simulated events in order to adequately narrate the facts? How are TV-users meant to read the documentary in terms of authenticity?

The primary role of reconstruction is to give TV-users access to events that were unable, for one reason or another, to be recorded as they happened. Immediately the problem is broached of whether this serves as an accurate representation of the past or distorts it. In factual history programming, reconstruction usually contains:

- Eyewitness accounts intercut with related archive footage of the period, which, importantly, is not always actuality footage of the event.
- Secondary accounts by individuals not present during the event, but who claim to have knowledge of what really took place.
- Dramatisation through actors as off-screen narrators, providing voice-over or taking part in full screen performances.

This last method of using actors as off-screen narrators provides a strong emotive edge in Home Box Office's (HBO) *Dear America: Letters Home from Vietnam* (HBO, 1987/BBC2, 1990), hereafter, *Dear America*. In *Dear America*, Martin Sheen heads a raft of Hollywood stars reading soldiers' letters against a backdrop of archive and actuality footage synchronised with contemporary music of the period. The inclusion of tracks by Bob Dylan, the Rolling Stones and Alice Cooper – amongst others – emotionally locks TV-users into the Vietnam period. Add to this a range of well-known actors as 'voices' for the letters, including Robert De Niro, Michael J. Fox, Harvey Keitel, Sean Penn, Kathleen Turner and Robin Williams, and there is a considerable increase in the emotive weight of the documentary.

But this external pressure of powerful music and 'acted voices' tends to collapse *Dear America* in on itself, abandoning any notion of documentary objectivity, becoming instead, a highly motivated dramatic critique of the Vietnam War, functioning as a very efficient form of propaganda. The art of anti-war propaganda directed at investing conflict within the boundaries of national interests and aspects of nationality, can be found in Peter Watkins' *Culloden* (BBC1, 1964). In a powerful ideological statement locked within an emotive dramatic narrative – a theme taken up by *Dear America* – Watkins' imaginative creative skill is focused on bringing history fighting and screaming into the present.

Culloden

Written and directed by Peter Watkins, *Culloden*, a seventy-minute docudrama shot in black and white, employs dramatic reconstruction within the genre conventions of documentary and television news. Watkins, a BBC director, saw 'parallels' between the war in Vietnam and what had taken place on Culloden Moor.[21] Many of the news reportage conventions in *Culloden* are references to the style of television news reports coming out of Vietnam, with reporters interviewing American troops prior to engagements or during actual fire fights. This news-bulletin type of battlefield reportage was included in *Dear America* where, in the midst of a fire fight, a news reporter questions American troops as to whether they believed in the legitimacy of the war live on camera. The device has been adapted and re-worked by Watkins for *Culloden*.

Transmitted on Tuesday 15 December at 8.05–9.15 p.m. on BBC1, the programme depicts the Battle of Culloden Moor on 16 April 1746. As the last battle heralding an end to the Jacobite rebellion, it recreates the defeat of 'Bonnie Prince Charlie' – Prince Charles Edward Stuart's assorted warriors from Highland Clans – by the professional English troops led by the Duke of Cumberland. Determined to break free from the dramatic conventions of melodrama,[22] Watkins rejected professional actors, opting for locally recruited non-professionals, many of them direct descendants of participants in the original battle.[23] Watkins adopted a binary opposed approach to the confrontation, composed of four integrated segments:

1 Introduction of the armies and leaders.
2 Preparation for the battle.
3 The battle.
4 The post-battle slaughter and aftermath.

In the first segment, the opening shot reveals English soldiers appearing over the brow of a hill with a news/current affairs voice-over naming the location as 'Culloden Moor'. The central characters are introduced, forming an impression of documentary immediacy as their experiences, their physical and mental state, and their ranks and position in the Clan system are conveyed in direct comparisons to the English officers and men.

This personalisation organises narrative trajectory, controlling pace, tension and emotive links with TV-users. Opposing participants are asked direct questions from an unseen narrative position behind the camera, heightening the TV-user participant bond.

Here Watkins reveals *Culloden* to be a direct stylistic descendant of the Crown Film Unit's 1941 *Target For Tonight* where the combination of a documentary approach founded on factual evidence is spiced up with dramatic reconstruction. What this creates is a raw newsreel style intended to provoke a charged emotive screen impact. This is a tactic at the core of narrative documentaries,[24] and the emotional intensity of *Culloden* is difficult to ignore. As the title appears on screen, the narration continues with an account of a mishandled battle. The Clan system is detailed and the place of each Scottish commander in the hierarchy is foregrounded, with delivery by the actors in Gaelic to reproduce the illusion of authentic archive material. This anchoring of period, place and people is maintained as the Gaelic is translated, again drawing on the classic style of documentary production.

There is little doubt that *Culloden* stands as an innovative approach to programme-making in 1964. According to screenwriter John McGrath, *Culloden* broke new ground by bringing the Highlander's story in from the margins, concentrating on 'people ignored by history'.[25] Creating popular history by retelling their story in such a way as to attract a large number of TV-users, rather than just academics, is the whole point of television history.[26] By choosing Clan descendants as his cast, Watkins was making not only a 'creative gesture' but also a 'political, and social gesture'.[27] Ken Loach, a British film-maker from the same generation and realist creative school as Watkins, sees television not as Watkins does as a medium for 'sharing experience', for correcting social and political inequality, but as a 'political medium which is used to manipulate consciousness',[28] a factor Watkins ultimately brought to play with *Culloden*.

Where dramatisation inside the genre framework of documentary seems to ultimately break down to betray its fictional roots comes when the documentary format cannot contain the dramatic slippage, fracturing any possibility of each element working in unison. This arises when the script is created by a writer who has a political, ideological or historical view to impart, combining fictional dramatic codes and conventions in shot selection, editing and characterisation with classic documentary techniques. To some extent, this surfaces in Watkins' lining up of the opposing forces in the second segment, preparing for battle when the weakness of the Highland forces becomes a narrative counterpoint to the strength of the English, heightening the dramatic tension.

An overview of the battlefield is provided by an omniscient narrator, describing how the moor provided ideal terrain for the English. This is followed by short scenes setting up causality as opposing troops are questioned by this omniscient voice or implied documentary-maker, preparing TV-users for an impending personal bloody battle. Reasserting its documentary narrative arc, a survey of the English equipment and manpower takes place. Accompanied by voice-over, these knowledge-based details and insights are told over a close-up of a Clansman's face revealing fear, trepidation and dread.

Heightening Watkins' interpretation of a one-sided battle, the English officers and soldiers also become personalities. Individually identified and named, along with their background, experience and pay, they counteract the individual personalities from their Highland enemy. Enforcing the sense that this is an unfair struggle, the equipment of the English is scrutinised in detail, with the type of musket, weight of the ball and its distance set against the outdated pistols used by the Clans. Seemingly adding substance to a sense of actuality, truth and trust, an eyewitness to the battle arrives on-screen in the form of Andrew Henderson, introduced as a 'Whig historian ... biographer of Cumberland ... eyewitness to the battle,' replete with a handy sketch map of the battle lines, telescope and assistant.

Watkins is perhaps symbolically overstating a point here, that historians do not always make ideal eyewitnesses or report events faithfully, as Henderson's point of view of battlefield events is never presented in supporting shots. Continuing his binary divisions along a highly dramatic narrative line, Watkins is at pains to emphasise how the Clans were divided, keen to settle their own disputes. Rival Clans are juxtaposed with the views of the English troops on their Highland opposition, deeming the Clans as 'savages'. In contrast to the pathetic half-starved Highlanders, the English are portrayed as hardbitten fighters, but at least, they explain, they are fed by Cumberland. Maintaining the portentous anticipation of a massacre, the bickering between the Clans on where to stand on the line reveals an inherent social fracturing within the Highlanders' strategy.

Information on which position provides status and respect is integrated between short biographical portraits of the leadership of both camps, sufficiently spiced by relevant experience, judiciously weighed and assessed. As the battle nears, the final irony is that it is a family versus family encounter, with members of Clan families fighting for the English. 'Charles Edward Stuart's war is a civil war', notes the narrator flatly.

There is no doubt that Watkins has created a 'reality' through the documentary build-up to the battle. Even when viewing *Culloden* almost half a century after its initial screening, the programme still demonstrates gripping television. This is primarily due to the reality of the battle sequences and the butchery afterwards, but the true strength of *Culloden* comes through the personalisation of opposing combatants in true classic documentary style. The battle scenes, punctuated by a precise chronological timeline, prosaically articulated by the narrator, accelerate the narrative through tragedy after tragedy, allowing the starkness to speak for itself.

The dramatic personae of Watkins' documentary represent an acted realism, a constructed realistic impression and interpretation of the men and the battle they fought. In turn, this forms a cathartic bond with TV-users, creating a relationship of 'participant-observer'.[29] In this sense, one of the gratifying elements of *Culloden* comes in its assemblage of information as an untold story, and is one of the key motivators that entice TV-users to watch in the first place.

Dealing visually with history, as *Culloden* successfully does through dramatic and emotive scenes, is not fact faithfully re-represented or recreated but an interpretation of fact. This is particularly true when Charles Stuart takes his leave of Culloden Moor, his departure caustically noted by the narrator as abandoning his army to save himself, taking the remaining war fund with him.

Attempting to justify the documentary's expository style amidst the detritus of the battle, English troops are interviewed, to be asked, rather mundanely, 'How do you feel?' Here, as with all scenes in *Culloden*, the 'expository' mode utilises a direct mode of address to the TV-users through voice-over narration or presenter as narrator/interviewer. Narration too in documentary is never free from an ideological agenda, and in *Culloden* the narration, as in all documentaries, pre-positions TV-users as to how they should engage with the action, which side to take, which to believe in.

There is a demonstrable indicator of Watkins' intentions and sympathies as director and writer when the narrator describes how Cumberland's victory ensures security for English financial interests. A curt summary of the slaughter as necessary for trade to be safeguarded in the future, tips his documentary scales towards English exploitation as a capitalist means to an end. Because the expository mode relies so heavily on recreating everyday events, there is a clear danger that reinterpretation of events can lead to stereotyping and distortion for the sake of screen effect.[30] In *Culloden,* this represents raw portraits of national characteristics.

One scene that functions as a means of ensuring that the Duke of Cumberland represents the stereotypical English 'butcher' moves seamlessly between shots of Clansmen being methodically slaughtered on the battlefield as Cumberland dines with his officers, described without emotion by the narrator. *Culloden* never shrinks from reconstructing events from 1746 that reveal battle and carnage with the frankness of a news report, such as the brutality of the English and their lowland Scot allies when fleeing Clansmen and innocent men, women and children are cut-down as Cumberland's men make their way to Carlisle.

Despite its flaws, *Culloden* does re-present the past with a naïve honesty that Simon Schama regards as the closest a programme has come to 'embodying the prime time manners of contemporary news debate'.[31] Though for Schama some elements of what he terms as 'fly-on-the-moor reality reporting',[32] may have dated, he still believes the programme broke new ground in 'de-romanticising the rebellion',[33] with the programme clearly capturing the bloody futility of battle.

By recreating history as an unknown factor,[34] rather than the known, through a creative or different interpretation for example, Watkins heightened the tension of what the outcome would bring. This enabled him to engage with TV-users through motivated dramatic conventions that asked them to suspend their belief in the past. In this way, *Culloden* becomes a fixed point in historiography, forming collective memories, particularly for the battle's descendants.

It is these memories that are as poignant as the Clan grave markers on Culloden Moor.

For TV-users to suspend their belief in a known past, a programme must rely on an ever-increasing scale of dramatic spectacle – a technique that whets the appetite of TV-users, so they hold their attention through well documented events in a way they could not anticipate. This clearly has serious implications for a distortion of the past in order to create an enthralling time capsule for TV-users, one that purports to be based on the truth, but uses that truth for its own ends.

One scene in the final segment does tend to suggest that creative embellishment has taken place when the execution squads finish off the Highland wounded, a dramatic point-of-view shot from a wounded Clansman focuses directly up into the face of an English soldier, hammering home a sense of needless slaughter. The unsettling camera angle for the point-of-view shot actually places the TV-user as participant-observer, in the role of victim.

It is this dramatic spectacle that marks *Culloden* out for Schama as a formative moment in historical filmmaking. That its methods of shock through brutality became an influence in re-presenting Schama's own version of *Culloden* and its inane killing in his *History of Britain* (BBC2, 2000), provides a further example of how a spiral of influence re-circulates key moments from the past based on collective memory.[35]

Reconstructions in varying forms existed before Watkins formed the generic style of docudramas with *Culloden*. From studio bound re-enactments in *The Trial of Madeleine Smith*, and part four of *Buried Treasure* – 'The Proud Princess' – containing a full reconstruction of the Sutton Hoo boat,[36] scope and ambitions expanded. Street scenes were reconstructed through different historic periods in *City of York* (BBC, 1957), and *Man and the Vikings* (BBC, 1961) consisted of a filmed reconstruction of Viking raids on the Isle of Man.

Just as eyewitness testimony went on to become a valorised requisite in many factual history programmes, the dramatic reconstruction has increased in production terms as factual history one-off documentaries and series have had to compete with diverse other factual and fictional programme genres.

To some extent, all factual history programmes are reconstructions, though the term is increasingly reserved for dramatic re-enactments. Reconstruction in this sense can be classed at its best in *Culloden*. As factual history programmes are not renowned for having lavish budgets, the use of dramatic reconstructions to enhance the screen-driven narratives of presenters can, as Schama acknowledges, do little justice to mimicking filmic conventions and effects. The result can often be that: 'taped reconstructions, imprisoned in documentary budgets, make the line between plausibility and giggles perilously fine'.[37]

Reconstructions for historian and presenter Michael Wood reinforce problems of accuracy, and he argues vehemently that it is impossible to use modern people to portray the past.[38] Reconstructions can help TV-users to imagine what the past was like he insists, but reconstructions can also hinder. The problem for Wood is that commissioners cannot sanction television history programmes without reconstructions. If reconstructions are to be included, they must, according to Wood, attempt to be as faithful to the period as possible, including the use of language, movement, dress and behaviour.

He does point out that historians do re-evaluate the past, and this can create the same problems as a reconstruction, resulting in an attempt to define the past from the present. As Wood asserts, television history can influence the way individuals assess their own lives in comparison to what they have learnt about cultures and individuals in the past.[39]

Bamber Gascoigne reveals an equally pensive approval of reconstructions, regarding them as 'certainly not necessary, and in [his] view an embarrassing cop-out',[40] and going on to compare his own thirteen-part series, *The Christians*, with contemporary practices:

> My own old-fashioned preference is for the old style where the only options were paintings, objects, buildings, landscape, real-life scenes that would have happened anyway, and pieces to camera. I remember in particular, for *The Christians*, my delight at finding enough variety in images of the Trinity to carry the early disputes on the subject. But it has to be said that the present convention means that a great many more subjects, lacking perhaps in any source of illustration, can be tackled.[41]

Melvyn Bragg is also quite forthright on dramatic reconstructions, arguing that it is merely an excuse for factual directors to become drama directors, though they inevitably fall short of their objectives.[42] Bettany Hughes is equally adamant that reconstructions are not necessary in an accurate portrayal of the past.[43] The result often results in a waste of screen time in attempting to provide a vivid accurate picture of the past. For all that emerges is a reconstruction that unsubtly hammers a point home because of budget limitations. Where reconstruction has demonstrated its worth in casting light on history's dark spots is when dramatic techniques support or question eyewitness testimony, confirming or denying which voice may be a true voice of the past.

Documentary and oral history: a true voice of the past?

If the descendants of the Clansmen and woman who fell on Culloden Moor had inherited 'race memories',[44] suppressed voices of nation and nationality, they were consumed beneath the directorial voice of Watkins, whose agenda on Bonnie Prince Charlie as romantic hero differed from theirs.[45] Documentary in this sense is a form that normally privileges the eyewitness, the personal testimony over other 'voices' in a preferred hierarchy.

Popular history, including factual history programmes, involves a predominance in relying on eyewitness accounts as a central organising code. Shaped by genre conventions, a selective narrative is constructed and 'told' by an on-screen presenter functioning as guide/gatekeeper or from an omniscient voice-over narrator.

Constructed of events, facts, people, locations, buildings, artefacts and dates, the past becomes the raw material for factual programming that invites narrative style and order to be imposed either through the individual as eyewitness or the camera as witness in archive footage or stills. Eyewitness tends to imply the reliability and accuracy of someone who has direct experience of an event. In the same way, the evidence from a still or moving camera is perceived as a reliable record of what actually took place.

The notion that the recording of events gives them their own self-referential system of objectivity and self-evident facts is a fallacy. Any act of recording is subjective, and the camera-produced image is no different when fixing the meaning of a given event. This it does by providing it with a '*representational legitimacy*'[46] through the illusion that the camera never lies when in fact it blatantly can and does.

How television production legitimises its constructed reality is achieved through anchoring the moment. By locking the images into a moving narrative so tightly, there is little opportunity available for questioning their validity or authenticity except through the experience and in-depth knowledge that a good number of TV-users do not possess. What comes into play here, for both factual history programming and academic history, is the issue of what did and what did not occur.

The problems of attempting to construct the past through those 'who were there' are clearly shown by Arthur Marwick's objection to eyewitnesses as being fallible,[47] perhaps too far removed in temporality from the original event. Yet this distancing between then and now should not, Trevor Lummis believes, negate the validity of recollection or recall, as memory does not operate 'sequentially' and older memories can be clearer than recent memories.[48]

Oral history is rooted in collective and personal memory, two forms of remembrance and forgetting open to corruption and modification. This in itself holds 'many traps for the unwary',[49] but its direct connection with then and now, the correlation of 'objective and subjective', is an essential feature of perception. Treated with the same veracity and rigorous methods of validation as other sources, oral history should not be ruled out as a means of reaching a valid understanding of the past.[50]

Reconnecting with the past collectively is no bad thing as it offers another avenue for historical investigation. An increase in recording and preserving of oral histories for posterity is in fact, regarded by some historians as a legitimate form of understanding the past.[51] Oral history as a public narrative of memory has no clearer voice or genealogical roots than *The Great War*, perhaps one series above all others representing this objective and subjective dichotomy. Oral tradition is in fact governed by performance, with each enactment conditioned by social and cultural normative rules, together with TV-user expectations.

Popular history, formed around ritualised ceremony together with television's own rituals, creates a shared understanding of the past. National, local, regional and personal identities and power relationships gathered through collective memory act as defining narrative devices in so many factual programmes. The BBC's early endeavours in oral history, most notably in its ten-part series *First Hand* presented by Peter West, developed a format that married directly experienced accounts to archive film.

In part ten, 'Edward VII', transmitted on 20 December 1957 at 9.30–10.00 p.m., the format of using archive footage as an opening montage to contextualise the period is a technique that *All Our Yesterdays* (ITV, 1960–73/87–89) and *People's Century* also employed. This laying down of significant national events and achievements alongside memories is evident from my condensed outline of *First Hand's* 'Edward VII' camera script.[52] (see table opposite)

Another form of first-hand experiences that represent national characteristics is present in *Arena's* 'Chelsea Hotel' (BBC2, 1981) as individual and collective identities are traced and indexed through the hotel itself. The building serves as the locus for memories of its former and current guests, retold by guests themselves, or in the case of the Irish poet, Brendan Behan, by the hotel manager, Stanley Bard. Memories are unlocked from the hotel as the camera follows a guide and his party through the hotel where, at seemingly random locations, the film cuts from the guided tour to staff and guests as memories are released. This releasing of memories, their power and their trace energy that form collective memories has equivalence to Roland Barthes' concept of

First Hand – Edward VII (BBC, 1957)

Vision	Sound
Film of Victoria's funeral	PETER WEST: Queen Victoria died in 1901 …
Coronation film	Happy crowds celebrated the coronation of a King …
Daily Mail	The popular newspaper was born in 1896 …
Still of Marconi	Marconi's success in 1901 in sending …
Film of an ancient car	Then there was the motor car …
Wright brothers' flight	More daring still was the aeroplane…
Indian film	India was the brightest jewel in the Imperial crown …
Canada arch	But already the Dominion of Canada expressed a new idea of Empire …
Sporting events	Sport was becoming increasingly popular …
Bicycling	Victorian prejudice still kept women out of most sports…
Henley	Henley was one of the many occasions …
Still of garden parties	Throughout the summer, the families who had met at Henley …
Still of destitute family	It was an age of great luxury, but also of extreme poverty …
Interviews with various Edwardians of all types	Descriptions of their memories of Edwardian life

'*punctum*' and '*studium*',[53] whereby images hold different levels of meaning that require triggers for release.

Barthes cites two elements as constituting natural photographic content – the '*studium*', the denotative level, the basic facts, compared with strong emotive effects generated by an unexpected aspect of the content, the '*punctum*' the connotative level. Both '*punctum*' and '*studium*' work in a corollary to produce a new level of meaning.[54] 'The *studium* is ultimately always coded, the *punctum* is not',[55] suggesting that at the connotative level there is the possibility for images to hold depths of meaning according to the TV-user's experience, knowledge and bands of personal memory.

The gloomy soulless corridors of the Chelsea Hotel may be exactly that for some TV-users, though others may have personal memories that are triggered by the deep structural '*punctum*', initiating a move from the collective 'open' '*studium*' to personal remembering. The low angle shots down corridors is also reminiscent of Stanley Kubrick's *The Shining* (Hawk Films/Warner Brothers, 1980), opening as wide a range of memories as possible.

In this way, it is the power of the image that forms an initial impression or attraction, a process not dissimilar to how the power of original events in memory formation produces a lasting trace that meshes with the '*studium*' operating as the general content within the frame that attracts initial interest. This is followed by the second stage of interpretation caused by the mood and emotive power within the frame, its '*punctum*' reopening or reactivating a trace 'wound', a long-term personal or collective memory scar. These scars are created by a highly charged exceptional point of interaction between the TV-user and image in a particular way. They fuse and form a contract made on the TV-user's first-hand direct experience, or second-hand mediated experience from similar texts.[56]

The power of these contracts comes through being in a position to 'look back' from the present, identifying with a scene or particularly with an individual who, at that moment of photographic recording, is unaware how their future will unfold, replayed as a memory and meaning lost and a memory and meaning found. This is graphically underlined in a sequence in *Dear America* where a still photograph of American troops is held in shot as a letter is read describing the death of a best friend in action. As the death is recounted, the focus is pulled gradually in on a single face. The voice-over continues during a cut to an archive footage sequence of dead and wounded being brought in, before cutting back to the still photograph, the zooming-in distorting it from youth to a skeletal representation of death.

The '*punctum*' as far as Barthes was concerned is beyond the rational and beyond the scope of language; this is how it creates its impression, its vitality, its impact.[57] Even without direct experience of events, the difference between 'then and now' can still motivate. In John Betjeman's *Metro-Land* (BBC1, 1973) a dual distance of 'then and know' exists in every sequence as Betjeman's fixed point of production in 1973 is a transitional fulcrum from 1973 back to the 1920s and 1930s, and forward from 1973 to this present, the 'here and now'.

The triggering of the '*punctum*' can be equally effective without narration as in *Chelsea Hotel*. Here, as a form of 'structuring absence',[58] the memory tour around an iconic New York bohemian resting place appears impromptu, unstaged and entirely natural. *Chelsea Hotel*, however, has been seamlessly structured without on-screen intervention to emphasise the visibility of the subjects, as are all other factual history documentaries, when deciding who is suitable as a voice from the past.

Who makes it onto our screen, however, is not left to chance, as in many documentaries the subjects are carefully selected, ensuring they meet and fill production-led values for good television. Emphasising how individuals and groups are denied legitimate access to their own past, John Tosh sets out the argument against oral history from an academic historian's point of view. 'It is naïve to suppose that the testimony represents a pure distillation of past experience, for in an interview each party is affected by the other.'[59] For television in general, particularly in the production of factual programming, the visibility and screen duration of the interviewee is tightly controlled, through constantly cutting back to the interviewer as the dominant and controlling presence.

One significant problem of including eyewitness accounts, however, is that they can be quickly consumed within a programme's array of voices such as voice-over, competing viewpoints and the visual spectacle. Added as a counter-weight, eyewitness testimony forms a sense of legitimacy as programmes strive to blend fictional codes and conventions with the factual. With so many dramatic elements employed in factual history programming, the distinction between fact and fiction is going to become unsustainable to a point where their boundaries break down and the fictional becomes a reference point for the factual.

> Most interestingly of all from the perspective of the use of television as an aid to teaching history, a 1996 BBC television documentary on the revisionist view of the Western Front, *Haig: The Unknown Solider*, used scenes from *Blackadder Goes Forth* intercut with the commentary of historians in order to establish the stereotype before subjecting it to scrutiny.[60]

The influence of fiction formed through collective memories on factual programming is evident here, and as Patrick Hutton acknowledges, 'imagination and memory are virtually interchangeable, because each is defined by its capacity to form images in which past, present and future are intimately joined'.[61] But imagination is not invited to roam freely by television's codes and conventions as it attempts complete exposition. Television history articulates the past through framing, shot selection, composition and editing that place the visual emphasis on the individual account as a dominating screen presence.

Of course any use of oral testimonies carries an inherent number of dangers, not only that the survivors will have enhanced, modified or fictionalised their account but also that national cultural values will have intervened in the production of memory. Not only are memories edited, but individuals have the capacity to lie, often quite deliberately for a variety of reasons when it involves their own past coming under scrutiny. Constructing memories for consumption can involve conducting a 'life-review',[62] a process of memory retrieval made more palatable as time elapses between original formation and memories released as part of sharing experiences.

In some cases, the act of sharing is redundant because the experience sits outside collective experience and shared memories. This is particularly evident when perceived shame or guilt is attached to memories, as those of Allied prisoners of war returning home after 1945.[63]

If the oral tradition is regarded as an unofficial discourse, its lack of validity arising because it comprises vocal sources and not document sources means it runs the risk of being treated circumspectly by some historians.[64] Interviewees are not merely individuals who recount their story to a camera, answering questions from an off-screen director; they also comply with TV-user expectations of how eyewitnesses must behave, adopting their own on-screen personas that bring with it a predefined set of conventions of what a personal narrative must contain, what must be left out.

Programme-makers do, however, rely on oral history as a starting point for building the past into factual history programmes, and as Laurence Rees insists, oral accounts must be as scrupulously checked and treated, as all other sources ought to be, with due scepticism.[65] Despite the distaste for oral history of some academic historians, others, including Raphael Samuel, regard it as a valuable means of connecting past and present. In his *East End Underworld: Chapters in the Life of Arthur Harding* (Routledge and Kegan Paul, 1981), Samuel provides a clear example of how individuals and individuality do have a role to play in interpreting the past by allowing historians access to their personal stories.

This accessing of the past through individuality and personal narrative is a factor that television producers will continue to employ, embedding eyewitness testimony into factual history programming because the medium maximises the relationship of intimacy between TV-users and interviewees. It amplifies the life experience of the interviewee, personalising events, creating a simplified emotive back-story that is more effective than facts alone. The dimensional aspect of television is important here, with the screen size reinforcing intimacy through framing and a shot typology of medium shots and close-ups that extenuates personality.[66]

Television, as documentary-maker Roger Bolton points out, does not handle complexity well, not through any major technical implication, but because of an inherited mindset within the industry.

> It is hard to avoid simplifying and there are sirens to be heard calling the producer away from the difficult and the complex. 'Television can't cope with ideas, it's for story-telling, for facts not issues.' I have heard this siren song from the mouths of most distinguished broadcasting figures.[67]

Television may be highly original and creative when budgets allow, testing the boundaries of television as Watkins did with *Culloden*, but discovering the truth from eyewitnesses will also involve collective popular memory, a framework that factual television history has utilised and refined over the years.

Notes

1 Jane Feuer, 'Genre study and television', in Robert C. Allen (ed.), *Channels of Discourse Reassembled* (Routledge, 2nd edn, 1992), p. 142.

2 Fiske, *Television Culture*, p. 112.

3 Rees, interview with the author.

4 Michael Sean Gillard and Laurie Flynn, 'Channel 4 in New Documentary Fake Row', www.guardian.co.uk/uk/1999/mar/23/8

5 Nicole Martin, 'Wales Documentary Was Biased Against Thatcher, Admits BBC', *Daily Telegraph* (14 November 2008), p. 8.

6 Richard Kilborn and John Izod, *An Introduction to Television Documentary* (Manchester: Manchester University Press, 1997), p. 30.

7 Kilborn and Izod, *Television Documentary*, pp. 30–1.

8 Denis McQuail, *Mass Communication Theory* (London: Sage Publications, 3rd edn, 1994), p. 212.

9 Patrick H. Hutton, *History as an Art of Memory* (Hanover: University Press of New England, 1993), p. 18.

10 Julia A. Thomas, 'Photography, national identity, and the "cataract of times". Wartime images and the case of Japan', in Lorey and Beezley (eds), *Genocide, Collective Violence, and Popular Memory*, p. 242.

11 Halbwachs, *On Collective Memory*, p. 38.

12 Popular Memory Group, 'Popular memory: theory, politics, method', in Richard Johnson, Gregor McLennan, Bill Schwarz, and David Sutton (eds), *Making Histories: Studies in History Writing and Politics* (Minneapolis: University of Minnesota Press, 1982), p. 241.

13 Anna Green and Kathleen Troup, *The Houses of History: A Critical Reader in Twentieth-Century History and Theory* (Manchester: Manchester University Press, 1999), p. 234.

14 Vico, *Ancient Wisdom of the Italians*, p. 95.

15 Corner, *Critical Ideas in Television Studies*, p. 49.

16 Corner, *Critical Ideas in Television Studies*, p. 49.

17 Bal, *Narratology*, p. xi.

18 Alex Callinicos, *Theories and Narratives, Reflections on the Philosophy of History* (Cambridge: Polity Press, 1995), p. 49.

19 Bettany Hughes, written responses to the author's questionnaire (31 February 2005); David Starkey in an interview with the author, The Department of History, Lancaster University (14 July 2004); Adam Hart-Davis, written responses to the author's questionnaire (14 May 2004); Rees, interview with the author.

20 Corner, *Critical Ideas in Television Studies*, p. 57.

21 Kirsty Wark, *The Making of Culloden* (transmitted BBC4, 3 July 2006).

22 Wark, *Making of Culloden*.

23 Wark, *Making of Culloden*.

24 James Chapman, *The British at War: Cinema, State and Propaganda 1939–1945* (London: I.B. Taurus, 1998), p. 129.

25 John McGrath, *Making Reel History* (transmitted BBC Scotland/BBC1, 15 April 1996).

26 McGrath, *Making Reel History*.

27 Peter Watkins, *Making Reel History*.

28 Ken Loach, *Making Reel History*.

29 Peter, C. Rollins, '*Victory at Sea*, cold war epic in television's historical fictions', in Edgerton and Rollins (eds), *Television Histories*, p. 111.

30 Kilborn and Izod, *Television Documentary*, p. 61.

31 Simon Schama, 'Television and the trouble with history', in Cannadine (ed.), *History and the Media*, p. 28.

32 Schama, 'Television and the trouble with history', p. 28.

33 Schama, 'Television and the trouble with history', p. 28.

34 Schama, 'Television and the trouble with history', p. 29.

35 Schama, 'Television and the trouble with history', p. 26.

36 WAC, T32/96/3, T32/96/2, T32/96/1, T32/96/17, undated.

37 Schama, 'Television and the trouble with history', p. 30.

38 Michael Wood, telephone interview with the author (27 April 2004).

39 Wood, telephone interview.

40 Bamber Gascoigne, written responses to the author's questionnaire (16 December 2004).

41 Gascoigne, written responses.

42 Melvyn Bragg, 'The adventure of making *The Adventure of English*', in Cannadine (ed.), *History and the Media*, p. 85.

43 Hughes, written responses.

44 Michael Bradsell, film editor, *Making Reel History*.

45 Bradsell, *Making Reel History*.

46 Hamilton, 'Representing the Social', p. 87.

47 Marwick, *Nature of History*, p. 235.

48 Lummis, *Listening to History*, p. 121.

49 Paul Thompson, *The Voice of the Past* (Oxford: Oxford University Press, 2nd edn, 1988), p. 135.

50 Thompson, *Voice of the Past*, p. 135.

51 Jacques Le Goff, *History and Memory*, trans. Steven Rendall and Elizabeth Claman (New York: Columbia University Press, 1992), p. 96.

52 WAC Teli-D421-37-1781, copy of the camera script – *First Hand*, 'Edward VII', BBC Television (transmitted BBC, 20 December 1957).

53 Roland Barthes, trans. Richard Howard, *Camera Lucida: Reflections on Photography* (London: Jonathan Cape, 1982), pp. 26–7.

54 Barthes, *Camera Lucida*, pp. 26–27.

55 Barthes, *Camera Lucida*, p. 51.

56 Barthes, *Camera Lucida*, pp. 26–8.

57 Barthes, *Camera Lucida*, p. 51.

58 Kilborn and Izod, *Television Documentary*, p. 203.

59 Tosh, *Pursuit of History*, p. 303.

60 Stephen Badsey, 'Blackadder goes forth and the "two western fronts" debate', in Graham Roberts and Phillip M. Taylor (eds), *The Historian, Television and Television History* (Luton: University of Luton Press, 2001), p. 114.

61 Hutton, *History as an Art of Memory*, p. 17.

62 Thompson, *Voice of the Past*, pp. 116–17.

63 John Nichol and Tony Rennel, *The Last Escape: The Untold Story of Allied Prisoners of War in Germany 1944–45* (London: Viking, 2002), pp. xvii–xix and p. 31.

64 Michel Foucault, *Discipline and Punish: The Birth of the Prison*, trans. Alan Sheridan (London: Penguin, 1991), pp. 95–6.

65 Rees, interview with the author.

66 Corner, *Critical Ideas in Television Studies*, p. 26.

67 Roger Bolton, 'The problems of making political television: A practitioner's perspective', in Tim O'Sullivan and Yvonne Jewkes (eds), *The Media Studies Reader* (London: Arnold, 1997), pp. 261–2.

6

Characterising the past

TV-users have come to expect television realism to be aligned as closely as possible to their own world of reality. When their world does not include coming under fire in a trench, being engaged in a dogfight from the cockpit of a Spitfire or cowering in the background as a courtier of Henry VIII, television narratives offer an opportunity to experience these reassembled 'realities'.

Documentary and its representation of individuals are weighted down by the twin burdens of television codes and conventions in presenting reality pre-scribed by the expectations of TV-users. Realism in this sense becomes the antithesis of what it sets out to portray; it becomes non-natural, non-real. It functions as an enacted drama where individuals in front of the camera adopt an archetypal persona, assuming this is what the camera requires. Documentary can never be real, as its subjects misread the terms and conditions of the reality required and become untrained performers, acting out modes of behaviour assembled from collective memories.[1]

Television's presence in the home; its multiplacement within a domestic environment as a seemingly freely available source of news and entertainment, elevates its content beyond that of a consumer product contract that exists with each physical visit to the cinema. Television constructs a relationship built on trust and 'social ritual' formalised decade after decade.[2] It is a very special ritual, however, that can trace its roots to the spectacle and drama that have always combined pre-Christian rituals, dance, games and ceremonies with a dominant ideology – religion for instance – where the formal and informal provide a communal experience in the form of a celebration.[3]

Within television's function as social ritual, its position of authority and power is invested with a symbolic presence in the form of an all-seeing, all-knowing guide that connects the TV-users with the world within a world through the screen. For John Fiske and John Hartley, this ritualised, totemic guide is equivalent to a bardic figure through which the television message and language used are channelled and controlled.[4]

Factual history programming, with its codes and conventions within its predominantly documentary genre system based on telling stories of the past, is highly suited to Fiske and Hartley's concept of the bardic role. Television as a bardic medium relates narratives that not only establish the place of the past in the present but also confirm and reinforce how the past has led to, and supports, the cultural and social values of nation and national characteristics inherent in society in its present form.

In this way, the television as bard naturalises past and present, dissolving one into another through its visual content and scripted story. This enforces narrative ellipses, distorting any complexities, ambiguities and differing views and versions of past events. It irons out the bumps and hollows of the past into a smooth, clear linear and delineated chronological link between 'then and now'.

An example of this can be seen in Denis Mitchell's *Morning in the Streets* as it attempts to portray everyday working-class realism in Liverpool. In Granada Television's *A Tribute to Denis Mitchell* (C4, 1990), a celebration of the documentary film-maker's career shortly after his death in 1990, Sir Denis Forman, Chairman of Granada Television 1974–87, describes Mitchell as: 'One of the great documentary film-makers of all time',[5] before pinpointing Mitchell's ability to maximise his raw material:

> Denis Mitchell could make people talk and not only could he make people talk, he could pick the right people to put on the screen, he had a wonderful connoisseur's judgment as to who would come off as a subject for a film.[6]

Forman also observes how *Morning in the Streets*, first made for radio as a mix of music and voices, demonstrated how Mitchell 'had a wonderful ear for the human voice'.[7] The short sequence analysed below aptly illustrates Mitchell's 'connoisseur's judgment' and his 'ear for the human voice'. Shot in black in white, Mitchell's thirty-four minute film conveys an immediate sense of gritty realism that would mark out the 1950s as the period of the 'Angry Young Man', as novelists, playwrights and film-makers strove to emphasise working-class heritage and culture within the wider realms of British society.

It is not only Mitchell's ear that is acutely tuned to capturing the essence of a community, but his documentary-maker's eye too has a gift for turning realism into a powerful visual statement that Karel Reisz's *Saturday Night and Sunday Morning* (Woodfall Film Productions, 1960) and Lindsay Anderson's *This Sporting Life* (Independent Artists, 1963) replicated.

In the opening of this sequence, Mitchell has the camera track back from right to left along a row of terrace houses, framing them diagonally, accompanied by the haunting bars of the *Last Post*. Over this, an off-screen female subject's voice-over commences a personal story 'well anyhow, I tell you he had a few hours sleep and they all went home and they adjourned to a singing room here'. A dissolve connects place and time, the street, with the female subject, with an interior shot of her in a living room/kitchen, where Mitchell allows a close-up of her face, emotionless, poignantly not speaking, to underscore her character and her story.

As this lingering close-up continues, the subject's off-screen voice reveals how her husband left for France during the First World War. She is framed in what has become a conventional documentary subject's position, right of screen, looking down and away through the bottom left of the screen into the past, into her own memories. Her natural voice, its hesitancy, inflection and delivery create an overwhelming sense of impending tragedy: 'well anyhow they went and took bottles of beer with them to the station.' Dissolving back to the tracking shots down the street, the voice-over proceeds as patiently as the camera 'and he said now Mary, he said if you have a little girl call it Margaret, and if it's a little boy call it Stephen. I said all right, so he kissed us and he went away.' Another dissolve from the street creates a transition to a close-up of her hands. Grasped in a tight knot in her lap, they symbolise a moment of pain, a great personal loss: 'and we never seen him after, he was killed at … I got noted to say that he was killed, seems he was killed on the 12th March, at Neuve Chapelle, so there you are.'

Single voices are not enough for Mitchell as he cuts back to the street, employing a low camera angle, just above the front doorstep to juxtapose a voice-over actuality recording of a Remembrance Day commentary. 'The wind stirs the leaves and the flags at the Cenotaph as slowly these tributes grow at the very foot of the Cenotaph.' This commentary, an official voice, is juxtaposed with the camera tracking back, a slow traverse along the doorstep to focus in on three toy soldiers lying on the step as though wounded or killed, on their backs as the actuality voice-over from the Cenotaph continues 'there are many wreaths to be laid this morning'. Here, in this short sequence, Mitchell is deliberately confronting and challenging an officially constructed myth of nation, the celebration of nation-state values and the price of victory. The doorstep becomes Mitchell's cenotaph, the toy soldiers symbolic of innocence and a generation sacrificed and lost.

Mitchell's *Morning in the Streets* is one of the first documentaries that provided factual history programmes with a direct, conversational eyewitness format as people of Liverpool allow their voices and their memory-centred stories to appear as natural as possible in actual recollections and as unobtrusive voice-overs that form their own powerful narrative arc.

What Mitchell has achieved in creating these highly personal encounters with the past is to highlight Michel Foucault's concept of 'subjugated knowledges'.[8] Formed by hidden structures within multiple discourses, they disguise systems of power and knowledge, those seemingly too trivial in terms of social status and value to be considered in their own right. These were, Foucault observed, 'confined to the margins of knowledge'.[9]

In a similar way that the power of the storyteller in the past was to hold the audience's attention, so too does television. It also continues the storytelling tradition of emphasising aspects of the narrative that served as a sliding scale of moral imperatives, as codes of behaviour, confirming an individual's place in society and culture. Television-constructed narratives mix real and imagined collective experiences together, equally suppressing or minimising any dissenting voices within the story that may have questioned dominant ideology at work.

Deciding which subject/character attributes are emphasised is a well-established documentary convention that rests as much on the film-maker's technical and creative skills as on their ideological beliefs. In this way, personal values and beliefs are forms of ideology that circulate within other streams of ideology that evolve within a society at a specific time, reinforcing aspects of nationality.

Travelling back and forth through history via television can be quite solitary, but when undertaken within a real or imagined sense of community where television is accepted as an everyday ritual, it demonstrates television's bardic ability to unite individuals through 'culture's felt need for a common centre, to which the television message always refers'.[10] In this way, television as a medium produces the ritual, and the programme the ceremony, providing TV-users with the implicitly understood knowledge that they are part of a wider disconnected community.

Morning in the Streets' success at providing powerful *puncta* is because it works as a revelatory narrative, epitomising concepts of northern characteristics. These operate as counter-cultural avatars for the dominant middle-class national characteristics of its time. Other series also articulate individuality as a motivating factor in national development, arriving on screen already classified, in this case, as encapsulating 'greatness' as part of the nation's moral fibre.

Great Captains (BBC1, 1960), *Great Britons* (BBC1, 1978), *Late Great Britons* (BBC1, 1988) and *Great Britons* (BBC2, 2002) typify how television makes assumptions on what being a national hero or figure represents.

Great Britain and its great characters

Great Captains (BBC, 1960–61)

Part 1	Oliver Cromwell
Part 2	The Duke of Marlborough
Part 3	Admiral Lord Nelson
Part 4	The Duke of Wellington

Great Britons (BBC1, 1978)

Part 1	Horatio Nelson
Part 2	Thomas Cook and his Son
Part 3	Florence Nightingale
Part 4	Robert Burns
Part 5	David Lloyd George
Part 6	The Duke of Marlborough

Late Great Britons (BBC1, 1988)

Part 1	King Henry VIII
Part 2	Queen Victoria
Part 3	Winston Churchill
Part 4	Charles Darwin
Part 5	Robert Walpole
Part 6	Oliver Cromwell

Great Britons (BBC2, 2002): Appearance in order of public votes*

1	Winston Churchill	28.1%
2.	Isambard Kingdom Brunel	24.6%
3	Diana Princess of Wales	13.9%
4	Charles Darwin	6.9%
5	William Shakespeare	6.8%
6	Isaac Newton	5.2%
7	Queen Elizabeth I	4.4%
8	John Lennon	4.2%
9	Horatio Nelson	3.0%
10	Oliver Cromwell	2.8%

---

*Percentages calculated from total of 1,622,248 votes.
Source: BBC, *Great Britons.*[11]

Living up to its alternative ethos as usual, Channel 4 spent an evening reducing reputations to the specious scrutiny of 'commentators' after a public vote had decided on the 100 worst Britons:

Not so great Britons

100 Worst Britons We Love to Hate (C4, 2003):
Positions decided by online votes from the general public

1 Tony Blair
2 Jordan – (Katie Price)
3 Margaret Thatcher
4 Jade Goody
5 Martin Bashir
6 Gareth Gates
7 Alex Ferguson
8 'H' from Steps
9 Geri Halliwell
10 The Queen

Source: C4 Television.[12]

Dealing with one of Britain's most enduring figures, in the third part of *Great Britons* – 'Florence Nightingale', transmitted 8 August 1978 – Philippa Stewart, the biographer of Nightingale, aimed to prove that Nightingale was more 'human, more abrasive and far more pitiable than ever the myth allowed'.[13] The visual symbols in the opening establishing shot and title sequence could not enforce concepts of nation and nationality any harder. The programme and series' intro sequence,[14] described below, metaphorically wraps Nightingale into the nation-state, joining her with other national heroes and their associative greatness.

Great Britons – Part 4, 'Florence Nightingale' (BBC1, 1978)

Programme intro sequence

Establishing Shot
WS HOUSES OF PARLIAMENT & BIG BEN
PAN right across Westminster Bridge & River to St Thomas' Hospital…

Series' title sequence

Furl of Union Jack wipes left to reveal
GREAT BRITONS
Furl wipes left–right and as it does so reveals
picture of Nelson
– ditto – revealing Lloyd George
– ditto – revealing Robert Burns
– ditto – revealing Thomas Cook
– ditto – revealing Marlborough
– ditto – revealing Florence Nightingale

To be fair, Stewart does provide an in-depth portrait of Nightingale, including her formative years, love for her female cousin, Marianne Nicholson,[15] and Nightingale's attempts to confront social constraints and prejudices. Yet somehow by weighting Nightingale down as an example of a national hero, the programme barely scratches the surface of a complex woman, making much of the anguish, resentment and bitterness she held towards her family for their disapproval of her ambitions to become a nurse. What it does do, to a certain degree, is reinvigorate the 'legend of the Lady of the Lamp' as a model for Britishness, its spirit of reform and iron-willed determination when faced with adversity.[16]

If Nightingale is an enigma, protected by myth, the front cover of *Radio Times* 31 May – 6 June 2008, offered a bold proclamation: 'THE LADY WITH THE LAMP. Why "almost everything you know about Florence Nightingale is wrong"… including *that* lamp!' Although a drama, *Florence Nightingale* (BBC1, 2008) was apparently formed around Nightingale's own words in her letters and diary and, according to director/writer Norman Stone, Nightingale was 'the victim of the nastiest piece of spin doctoring in political history'.[17]

Stone's drama does nothing to shake free the myth surrounding Nightingale but enhances it by turning Nightingale into a political victim. Stone may have 'lived, slept, breathed, read and studied almost everything there is to know about the founder of modern nursing' for eighteen months,[18] but the programme has been constructed and directed to provide good television not a probing factual insight. With a 'lumpen script … that reminded me of something BBC Schools might have shown in the 1970s',[19] the programme appeared to be shot and lit so that it adhered to what has become a contemporary television high-definition house style. It is a production style where no effort is made to distinguish one programme from another through framing and shot typology, effectively blurring the boundaries between then and now, which does nothing to give a sense of place or time, or of Nightingale herself.

Nightingale, like so many British national heroes, somehow has to rise from personal weakness or character flaws to become a supreme example of national characteristics; a factor bardic television is suited to articulating. It rationalises ideological myths and makes them appear natural and inevitable,[20] so that in *Morning in the Streets*, the personal narratives are the *puncta* that are actively involved in confronting part of the northern working-class myth. This production of myths through a bardic voice is perhaps one of the dominant strengths of television as a dynamic amplifier of citizenship. When citizenship is amplified by television, its assumptions, values and ideologies are rarely challenged, unless through the work of counter-view programme-makers and the views of TV-users.

In this way, bardic television is always moving on just as the travelling storyteller moved on in the past, from location to location, from one narrative to another. Arthur Marwick argued that programmes never provide TV-users with an opportunity to assess the validity of their claims,[21] though this is nigh on impossible, except where channel websites carry over the programme's themes and offer a dedicated arena for further discussion – what are known as multiplatform approaches or projects. The internet does allow for additional, supplementary debates on factual history series that imitate to some extent the accumulation of argument and evidence in academic history. Yet, somehow, this still seems unsatisfactory, for the creation and the construction and management of websites only succeeds, to me at least, to push historical facts around and around an electronic universe of authentic and unauthentic evidence.

In this electronic past without barriers, it collides, collapses, collects influences from here and there to give a verifiable account, but also leaves a trail of unanswered questions, frustrating inaccuracies and in some cases, total fabrication.

An area of concern regarding sources, particularly how sources are produced, centres on the reasons for production and the influences that those sources place on an accurate interpretation of the past. Analysing the craft of the historian, Jacques Le Goff is quite clear that selecting sources is rarely straightforward and that it is rare for any source to be innocent or free from ideological imperatives.[22] Evaluating documents, in fact, is hardly ever credited in factual history programming. Passages are quoted, sources examined with barely a hint of alternative views, counter-claims, and arguments.

So much television history appears designed to be taken at face value, as though belief and trust in the presenters/narrative/characters/narrator is assumed from the outset and is implicit. For academic historians, being taken at face value and being trusted are not a given right or a privileged formality. In the immediacy of storytelling as a bardic television discourse, factual history programming does create a central process of historiography as being one of demystification as a search for the truth.[23]

Of course, the bardic nature of television does not operate in isolation over and above other codes and conventions. Its utterances are part of the framing, the shot typology, the editing, presenting and narrative flow, ascribing rather than describing what it means to be British. This categorisation of nationality relies on what Roland Barthes describes as myth functioning as a 'type of speech,'[24] a highly structured form of discourse conversion. Myth simply does not work on one level, but draws together all related and interconnected concepts that reinforce the principal core of the dominant myth from other media formats and forms. In this way, individual experience, individual memory and collective memory fuse fragments of other television programmes, novels, magazines, newspapers, radio, music and the internet into a consolidated, mythologised whole. At the centre of this consolidated myth are cyclical and interdependent strands of nation and nationality.

Television's reliance on archetypes and stereotypes through production values based on cost effectiveness, particularly where television history budgets are concerned, amplifies representations of class awareness in the general scheme of nation and nationality.

Neither history memory nor myth can ever be static. Reworked through documentaries, current affairs and dramatic reconstructions, the individuals, incidents, triumphs and disasters represent what Carl Jung identified as 'forms without content'.[25] These are, in effect, the basic, pre-made formula for programme-makers creating the formulistic narrative arcs of factual history programming.

In many ways, the oral or 'bardic' form of articulation is ideal for television as it offers immediate history without preamble, without on-screen explanation. It is a style of history, however, that Vico describes as 'an ideal eternal history traversed in time by the histories of all nations'.[26] It is this cyclic production of the past that depends on collective memory as its point of reference, though not as a rigid locked form of memory but in the context that Vico alludes to as *memoria* or the imagination that is capable of taking a fixed point in the past and expanding or modifying it.[27]

As historical evidence, established through the oral tradition and displaced by communication technology through the centuries, memory does require a visual stimulus based on perception.[28] This involves a method of visually sorting, accumulating and filtering: skills that television teaches us from an early age.

Archetypes, stereotypes and representation

Without characters, a term I apply to define the subjects or interviewees of documentaries, television history would struggle to create any form of personal link or relationship for the TV-users between past and present. Characters, as well as being regarded as stereotypes, can also be assessed from the Jungian per-spective of archetypes. This position touches on the notion of inherited values as well as memories that have their foundations in the unconscious.[29]

There are, of course, similarities between stereotypes and archetypes, but these are only surface detail; the real difference lies in their deep structural formation.[30] Indeed, archetypes have been a continuous issue of contention for critics concerned to identify how characters function within given narrative trajectories.

Following Aristotle's lead, Northrop Frye puts forward a basic formula for works of fiction that is based on the hero's 'power of action', constructed around five fields of action and interaction. The first involves a 'superior in *kind*' hero based on myth and outside the usual confines of narrative themes, drawn mainly from religious sources. The second is 'superior in *degree* to other men and to his environment', marking the character as a representation of romance, 'whose actions are marvellous but who is himself identified as a human being'. This trope of characters is a central feature of, and essential to, legend.[31]

One such popular character for history makers – Robin Hood – first appeared in *Up to Date* (BBC, 1956) – Part 5, 'Robin Hood'. Since then, TV-users have been taken on regular fictional and factual forays into Sherwood Forest in search of this 'legend'.

- Factual Robin Hood

  Up to Date (BBC, 1956) – Part 5, Robin Hood
  Fact and Fiction (BBC1, 1971) – Part 3, Robin Hood
  Living Legends (BBC1, 1979) – Part 3, Robin Hood
  Fact or Fiction (C4, 2003) – Robin Hood
  Historyonics (BBC1, 2004) – Robin Hood

- Fictional Robin Hood

  Robin Hood (BBC, 1953)
  The Adventures of Robin Hood (ITV, 1955–59)
  A Challenge for Robin Hood (Hammer Films, 1967)
  The Legend of Robin Hood (BBC1, 1975)
  Robin of Sherwood (ITV, 1984–86)
  Robin Hood Junior (BBC1, 1989)
  Robin Hood: Prince of Thieves (Warner Brothers, 1991)
  Robin Hood (BBC1, 2006–09)

For his quest of this myth-shrouded figure, Magnus Magnusson in *Living Legends* (BBC1, 1979) – Part 3, 'Robin Hood' – orchestrated an 'investigation' to discover if Robin Hood did 'ever exist as a real person around whom legends then developed',[32] tracing a Robin and Marion to 'French pastourelles of the 12th and 13th centuries'.[33] This highlights Frye's point that archetypes have a shared universal core that is adapted by different societies who need these 'superior in *degree*' characters at strategic points in the formation of a collective concept of national characteristics.

The third type of action, for Frye, involves the hero as being 'superior in degree to other men but not to his natural environment' when the character functions as a leader, 'the hero of the *high mimetic* mode, of most epic and tragedy'.[34]

> Tragedy in the central or high mimetic sense, the fiction of the fall of a leader (he has to fall because that is the only way in which a leader can be isolated from his society), mingles the heroic with the ironic.[35]

There is little difficulty in assessing how this archetypal trope of the tragic hero has populated factual history production in the lives, loves and deaths of the monarchy at home and overseas.

- *You Are There* (BBC, 1954)

  Part 2 'The End of Mary Queen of Scots'
  Part 4 'Trial of Charles I'

- *Royal Heritage* (BBC1, 1977)

  Part 3 'Charles I'
  Part 4 'The Stuarts Restored'
  Part 5 'The First Three Georges'
  Part 9 'Edward VII and the House of Windsor'

- *Timewatch*

  'Wartime Roles of the Duke and Duchess of Windsor' (BBC2, 1983)
  'Loved and Hated King: Richard III' (BBC2, 1986)
  'The Nine-Day Queen: A Most Dangerous Woman' (BBC2, 1987)
  'Fateful Century: Mary Queen of Scots/Anne Boleyn' (BBC2, 1987)

Of course there is one political dynasty that Frye's archetype of the tragic hero applies equally well to – that of the Kennedys, covered in a variety of biographical portraits:

- *The Age of Kennedy* – 'Man and President' (BBC1, 1967)
- *The Death of Kennedy* (BBC2, 1967)
- *J. F. K. – The Childhood Years* (BBC1, 1967)
- *Power from Beyond* – Part 2, 'John F. and Robert Kennedy' (ITV, 1968)
- *That Day in Dallas: LBJ Speaks* – 'Tragedy and Transition' (BBC1, 1970)

The fourth class of characters for Frye is a type lacking superiority to both the environment and other characters, suggesting a mere mortal. These are what Frye deems to be 'one of us', locked into the '*low mimetic* mode, of most comedy and realistic fiction'.[36]

The final, fifth category of character mode involves the 'inferior' hero whose actions are regulated by the '*ironic* mode'[37] and perhaps no one other than Robert Falcon Scott, CVO, RN, meets this criterion quite so well, as discussed later in the chapter. Archetypes for Frye are not limited to character tropes but embody cyclic or recurring genre themes that connect texts and discourses to form interrelated spheres of meaning.[38] When linked to genres, archetypes function as motifs for a particular text, as well as for the figurative conventions of the genre itself that depend on TV-user understanding, knowledge and experience to relate each link in the symbolic chain.[39]

Although Frye regards Jungian collective unconsciousness an unnecessary burden on literary criticism,[40] he acknowledges that archetypes do display universality in order for them to function and make sense.[41] By far the most significant and recurring genre convention in factual history programmes resembles Frye's 'mythos of summer'.[42] This consists of a journey governed by the conventions of a dramatic quest,[43] embracing conflict, struggle and discovery that investigations of the past construct as detective mysteries or incomplete puzzles. It involves the presenter/narrator acting as a symbolic questor working for and on behalf of TV-users in a constant search for fulfilment. The quest as an enticement is, in many cases, pledged by the titles of a variety of one-offs and series typified by the following selected examples:

• *Secret Mission* (BBC, 1948)
• *A Quest for Charlotte [Brontë]* (BBC, 1955)
• *Desert Search* (BBC, 1961)
• *Expedition* (ITV, 1962)
• *Discovering London* (ITV, 1969)
• *Secrets of the Deep* (ITV, 1970)
• *In Search Of...* (BBC2, 1980)
• *In Search of Paradise* (C4, 1983)
• *In Search of the Trojan War* (BBC2, 1985)
• *In Search of the Real Dracula* (ITV, 1986)
• *In Search of Our Ancestors* (BBC2, 1994)
• *Quest for the Ark* (C4, 1995)
• *Time Travellers* (Discovery, 1995)
• *Secrets of the Ancient Egyptians* (Discovery, 2002)
• *Wreck Detectives* (C4, 2004)
• *In Search of Myths & Heroes* (BBC2, 2005)
• *Riddle of the Romanovs* (Five, 2008)

Tracing how different genres have evolved from cultural practices, Frye states that there is a deep structural unified framework that informs all creative practice founded on 'ritual, myth and folk tale'.[44] Creative vision stems from these universal archetypes that become transformed and written into culture in such a way that they not only make sense but also provide a link between other texts, other images and the present. This then is the basis for the inherited collective memory, not only for TV-users, but also for the programme-makers.

> In today's visually orientated world, powerful images – even images of images – are circulated in an eternal cycle, gaining increased acceptance through repetition … Thus history becomes an endless loop, in which repeated images validate and reconfirm one another.[45]

This of course can lead to an inherited collective memory of shot typologies and framing devices that serve to strengthen a cyclical re-presentation of nation-state values as self-referential; formed and reformed over time as Schama's *History of Britain* did with *Culloden*.

Genres are quite capable, then, of generating another distinctive form of factual history programming hermeneutics that originates from universal types, motifs and inherited visual codes and conventions. At the core of this universality lies Jung's theory of the 'collective unconscious.'[46] Emphasising that meaning is arbitrary, Jung explains that language and classificatory systems overwrite and impose meaning on archetypes in order to make them conventional, more able to fit into social and cultural patterns without having the need to explain their historical origin.[47]

The universal nature of the archetypes can be seen through the inherited use of locations, framing, themes and binary oppositions present in factual history programming. This visual and ideological inheritance recycles 'motifs',[48] or outline frameworks, that societies adapt for their own needs. Behind every stereotype, therefore, is an inherited archetype, and it is through the abundance of images encountered in everyday life where stereotypes dominate that archetypes disappear into the background.

Collective memory, founded and formed through visual imagery, is happy to displace archetypes as it operates on the surface, in opposition to individual memory that occupies a deep structural position.[49] Archetypes, according to Jung, are constituted through myth structures in the collective unconscious, providing a ready framework for ideological adaptation when they enter the public domain, included in stories or as the basis for cultural beliefs and social values.[50]

Any creative production of a narrative, factual or fictional, draws on these archetypes. Stereotypes therefore can never be replaced; they are a constant, modified for the age in which they are used.[51] Archetypes are a bridge between the past and the present, which is why they have to be constantly modified as society moves on. Each new generation has to reinvent the archetypes in order for it to meet and fit in with its own cultural patterns of ideological values.[52] It is inappropriate, Antony Easthope believes, to assume that ideology operates as some sort of monolithic structure that automatically reinforces the economic values and beliefs of society. Ideology is far more informal and disorganised, it is modified not only by the economic and political climate sanctioned by controlling groups but also by individuals and groups who have to live and work within ideological spheres, modifying them to suit their own personal needs.[53]

Archetypes, stereotypes and myth

Archetypes, stereotypes and myth are companions. At a base level, archetypes contain the skeletal framework for the construction of stereotypes that myth requires to substantiate and circulate common ideals that bolster concepts of nationality. One of the main core units of nationality, an integral factor in projecting the values of a nation-state, is through settlement and opening up new frontiers as an expression of nation-state expansion and cultural ownership of the 'Other'.

How different archetypes and stereotypes hold symbolic value for one generation is evident in the innocuous biographical portrait of Cecil Rhodes in the 1950s, *Cecil Rhodes – A Centenary Review* (BBC, 1953). Colonisation and expansionism as a model of pioneering spirit may have survived into the liberalising 1960s with *The Real West* (BBC, 1961) or *Adventure* – 'Trail to Dawson City' (BBC, 1962), but any notion of pride in colonisation had been tempered by the 1970s.

In a decade where national pride was disintegrating, the rights and plight of indigenous people *Now the Buffalo's Gone* (ITV, 1971) for example, demonstrated that as Britain suffered a loss of confidence, the nature of ethnic roots, equality and national rights clouded by stereotypes and myth were being re-examined. The more challenging and critical the present became, the more the past was opened up to critical re-evaluation. *A Touch of Churchill, a Touch of Hitler* – 'The Life of Cecil Rhodes' (BBC2, 1971) reveals how revision by the next generation results in myth displacement.

Archetypes and stereotypes when working in conjunction with myth formation needlessly simplify, modify and tailor the past according to whichever group assembles it to suit their own social cultural preferences and values. This re-editing of the past as a reaction to perceived modifications in official memory is the antithesis of academic history.[54] Re-editing attempts to overturn one set of archetypal characterisations and myths by popularising and prioritising new simplified myths that draw their strength from their visual power; an act of privileging visual myths through television's emotive narrative arcs.[55]

Any appeal to the emotions comes directly through the subjects or character positions within factual history programming. Characters, therefore, are the principal motivators of narrative progression and have special qualities depending on the type of narrative they operate within, being identified either as generalised 'actants' or more specific 'acteurs' from which action stems in a cause-and-effect fashion.[56] In *Culloden,* the Clansmen operate as 'actants', secondary subsidiary characters, whilst Bonnie Prince Charlie functions as a principal 'acteur'. It is those value-laden representations, or modified archetypes, that tend to occur frequently in factual history programming when dealing with adventure and exploration.

These modified archetypes include the hero figures represented in *Adventure* – 'Scott's Last Journey' (BBC, 1962) – and *The World About Us* – 'Some Very Gallant Gentlemen: The Irony of Fate' (BBC2, 1972). Timed to mark the anniversary of Scott's fateful expedition, the attempt by *The World About Us* programme-makers to re-evaluate the mystery surrounding Scott was transmitted on 19 March 1972. As the *Radio Times* stated, 'Exactly 60 years ago tonight Captain Scott took his last painful steps across Antarctica.'[57] In many ways, Robert Falcon Scott epitomised the dogged, resolute British explorer, 'the Englishman who conquered the South Pole and who died as fine death as any man has had the honour to die'.[58] Any arguments to the fact that he was considered by some, as early as 1920, to be an 'incompetent bungler',[59] were consumed by a dominant myth system. Despite his failings, this myth system re-circulated the impression that Scott was a legendary hero. His decision to man-haul to the South Pole rather than take dog-teams the full distance, as Roald Amundsen did, produces a solid representational trope of what it means to be English and play a noble sporting game even if the outcome is death.[60]

By becoming the first men to reach the South Pole and beating Scott to what was seen as another prize for the nation, the Norwegian team were regarded as somehow underhand, displaying the characteristics that set foreigners apart from the English. Here, Apsley Cherry-Garrard, a member of the 1910–13 expedition, sums up his view of Amundsen.

I have not attempted to disguise how we felt towards him when, after leading us to believe that he had equipped the *Fram* for an Arctic journey, and sailed for the north, he suddenly made his dash for the south. Nothing makes a more unpleasant impression than a feint.[61]

It is this individual duel between Scott and Amundsen that drives Central Television's seven-part drama *The Last Place on Earth* (ITV, 1985). It is a drama based on fact that exposes Scott's flaws, emphasising them as a means of proving his inability to lead a successful bid for the Pole. That Scott did have weaknesses is no secret. Cherry-Garrard, one of the search party that found the bodies of Scott, Wilson and Bowers – Seaman Evans had died at the bottom of the Beardmore glacier and Oates had deliberately walked out into a storm – makes no attempt at building Scott into some mythical Colossus.

And not withstanding the immense fits of depression which attacked him, Scott was the strongest combination of a strong mind in a strong body that I have ever known. And this because he was so weak! Naturally so peevish, highly strung, irritable, depressed and moody.[62]

Although it comes within the drama genre, *The Last Place on Earth*, scripted by Trevor Griffiths, based on Roland Huntford's book *Scott and Amundsen: Last Place on Earth* (Pan, 1979), is worth examining for a number of related points. Firstly, the series may be officially classed as drama based on fact,[63] highlighting questions on the accuracy of docudramas and reconstructions, their point of crossover and influence on each other. As Lord Kennet, the son of Scott's widow Kathleen and her second husband, in his letter to *The Times* on *The Last Place on Earth* points out:

It is true many of the things said and shown are in the historical record. But some contradict the record, and some others are invented … I suggested that a clear statement, 'this is fictional drama', should appear with each episode. These criticisms and suggestions have, I understand, been rejected out of hand.[64]

Secondly, reconstructions labelled either as drama or more misleadingly as documentary create a grey area of interpretation and validity. They also raise the problem of representation. That some historical characters, such as Scott, are already enshrined as archetypal heroes for certain generations – 'For more than 70 years, Captain Robert Falcon Scott CVO, RN, has occupied privileged quarters in the hearts and minds of the British'[65] – means that, like any historical fact, they are open to revision and reinterpretation as different generations utilise the past.

The problem here is that this re-evaluation by Huntford, a journalist before he specialised in polar exploration biographies, and Griffiths, a screenwriter, is the work of writers and not historians. For Lord Kennet, Griffiths' aims are highly transparent in *The Last Place on Earth*. 'It thus seems to combine fiction and a political critique of history.'[66]

For a series constructed at an 'estimated cost of £7 million' it seems an awful lot of money to justify Griffiths' attempts to redress what Huntford had exposed as 'British Imperial mythography', a collective attempt to deride the Norwegian's triumph.[67] Though for one critic, Griffiths' determination to undermine Scott so completely created a distorted view of Scott's final expedition.

> And further claims are made in Trevor Griffiths' script that Mrs Scott was the source of the steel without which her husband's spine might have become bent into a U-shape. Indeed, if one accepts Mr Griffiths' prognosis, it might not be too fanciful to ask oneself whether the outcome of the race to the Pole might not have been very different if Mrs Scott, and not her husband, had been in charge.[68]

Certainly, the series can be dismissed as drama, though the danger here is that because of its subject matter – the questionable issue of it being based on fact – *The Last Place on Earth* and its characterisation become absorbed into the canon of factual history programming that have dealt with Scott. Quite apart from the series not serving as a critique of Scott's bravery, nor the men who died with him, Griffiths' refraction twists historical events to serve his own ideological beliefs of the present.

As Griffiths admitted, the series was a reaction to the political climate surrounding 1985, particularly official propaganda and news reporting. Griffiths, keen to draw parallels between then and now, deconstructed Scott as an example of official nation-state propaganda, claiming: 'it seems important to look at how a myth of glorious and heroic failure was constructed in that way'.[69] Scott and his expedition become representational indexes of nation and nationality that Griffiths feels hidebound to warp in order to make his own ideological statement on government policy during the 1980s.

> We are living with a government that constantly exhorts us to return to the great Imperial traditions of this nation, and to embrace not just the rhetoric but the practices of the Victorians and the Edwardians. So the series looks at the characteristics of the age, at the class differences and at nationalism.[70]

For Scott and other national characters, myth is a self-perpetuating system projecting representational traits and actions far beyond the factual boundaries of events that actually took place. The base level of events is continually transformed into myths through each new layer of collective memory added, as appears to have been the case with Scott the man and his final expedition, creating an entirely false case of representation.

For myths to remain constantly in circulation they must not only contain elements of personal narrative, a core of a good story, but they must also 'confirm' and fit with other myths.[71] This suggests why so many genres of factual history programming cover the same themes, the same people, leaving aside events which would make less popular stories a risk commissioning executives are less likely to commit a budget to.

Myth as history arranges events into a convenient snapshot of the past, articulated through archetypal characters. For Jung, archetypes stem from a universality of traits common to all cultures and assemble meaning through 'historical categories that reach back into the mists of time'.[72] Barthes, however, denies the existence of 'eternal' myths,[73] concentrating on myth as a product of an image rather than a concept that somehow predates the image.

Myth refuses to be pinned down because it is not composed of ordinary language, but as discourses that are modified, made available for revision, rein-ventions and rewriting. They are constantly moving the nucleus of the myth with each new transcription, so that it becomes a cultural paradox. Ethereal and permanent, myths are a construct of collective memories that are also the products of national tradition.

Disguising its origins as it moves through generations, myth is easily rein-vested with further cultural and social powers because it is adapted to the dis-courses of its day – a process that Barthes describes thus: 'Myth is not defined by the object of its message, but by the way in which it utters this message.'[74] This factor is true of the factual and fictional accounts of Scott, as it is of other biographical personal profiles in factual history programming.

Within these character representations there are traces of archetypes, their personalities demonstrating 'attributive proposition'[75] that forwards certain character traits when required by the narrative and hides others when not needed.

Stereotypes work because of difference, of separating out like from like on the grounds of social values and any perceived threat from new or modified values. As tropes of difference, stereotypes function as immediate forms of clas-sificatory systems, which makes them an ideal 'type' base for television, as time is short in both narrative and screen time and they offer a simplifying code for narrative construction.[76] Stereotypes in their on-screen manifestations are the socialised articulation of archetypes and the 'mythical'.[77]

Narratives of equality and inequality are, for Michel Foucault, confirma-tion of how society is responsible for producing discursive practices. Of course, isolating discourses of power is difficult because they are enmeshed so closely with cultural and social institutions. They are within the individual and within the family, so that all aspects of daily life produce discourses that are designed to regulate in one way or another.[78] Discursive practices for Foucault consist of systems of power that place certain individuals into privileged positions of control.

From this position of power and privilege, they have the ability to pre-scribe social and cultural values as being normal, abnormal or deviant through a closely structured classificatory regime of choice and exclusion.[79] Natalie Zemon Davis goes straight to the crux of the matter of some women being singled out as being more worthy than others and, therefore, having a signifi-cant place and role in a masculine view of history:

> Some studies were seriously researched; others mixed the mythical with the real. But all of them had a polemical purpose: to disclose the range of female capac-ity, to provide exemplars, to argue from what some women had done to what women could do, if given the chance and education. Indeed, a certain part of women's history today is still in the tradition of Women Worthies.[80]

Stereotypes that underwrite national identity have been a part of English culture for centuries,[81] and television factual history programming seems in no immediate hurry of replacing this televisual convention. Up until the 1960s and 1970s, the depiction of 'women worthies' in factual history programming was sporadic, except for women connected with the monarchy. Gradually through the 1960s and 1970s, more programmes began to concentrate on the roles and achievements of women in history, with for example *Solo* (BBC2, 1970) featuring Eileen Atkins as Mary Kingsley, a critic of Colonialism follow-ing her explorations in Africa.

Other series too, in particular *Times Remembered* and *Yesterday's Witness,* attempted to look beyond the great and the good and provide recognition to the role woman had played in creating a national identity. Unfortunately, much of television history in 2009 still presents a straightforward choice of archetypes as central characters drawn out in stereotypical surface detail for the sake of immediacy and clarity.

Notes

1 John Fiske and John Hartley, *Reading Television* (London: Routledge, 1989), p. 66.
2 Fiske and Hartley, *Reading Television*, p. 85.
3 Sophocles, *The Theban Plays*, trans. E. F. Watling (Harmondsworth: Penguin Books, 1986), pp. 8–9.

4 Fiske and Hartley, *Reading Television*, p. 85.

5 Sir Denis Forman, *A Tribute to Denis Mitchell*, Granada Television (transmitted C4, 6 December 1990).

6 Forman, *Denis Mitchell*.

7 Forman, *Denis Mitchell*.

8 Foucault, *Power/Knowledge*, p. 82.

9 Foucault, *Power/Knowledge,* p. 83.

10 Fiske and Hartley, *Reading Television*, p. 86.

11 *Great Britons* www.bbc.co.uk/pressoffice/pressreleases/stories/2002/11_november/25/greatbritons_final.shtml.

12 *100 Worst Britons We Love to Hate* www.channel4.com/entertainment/tv/microsites/G/greatest/britons/results.html.

13 Martin Muncaster, narrator, WAC, script, 5145/1621, p. 2. *Great Britons*, Part 4, 'Florence Nightingale', BBC Television (transmitted BBC1, 8 August 1978).

14 Nightingale, pp. 1 and 3.

15 Nightingale, p. 12.

16 Nightingale, p. 30.

17 Stephen Armstrong, 'Ode to a Nightingale', *RT* (31 May–6 June 2008), p. 13.

18 Armstrong, 'Ode to a Nightingale', p. 13.

19 Alison Graham, 'Florence Nightingale', *RT* (31 May–6 June 2008), p. 68

20 Fiske and Hartley, *Reading Television*, p. 87.

21 Marwick, *New Nature of History*, p. 234.

22 Le Goff, *History and Memory*, pp. 183–4.

23 Le Goff, *History and Memory*, p. 184.

24 Barthes, *Mythologies*, p. 109.

25 Carl Gustav Jung, *The Archetypes and the Collective Unconscious*, trans. R .F. C. Hull (London: Routledge, 2nd edn, 1968), p. 48.

26 Vico, *New Science*, p. 57, para. 114.

27 Vico, *New Science*, p. 264, para. 699.

28 Thompson, *Voice of the Past*, pp. 109–13.

29 Jung, *Archetypes and the Collective Unconscious*, p. 282.

30 Jung, *Archetypes and the Collective Unconscious*, p. 38.

31 Northrop Frye, *Anatomy of Criticism* (Princeton, New Jersey: Princeton University Press, 1971), pp. 33–4.

32 WAC, script, 4147/7325, p. 2. *Living Legends*, Part 3, 'Robin Hood', BBC Television (transmitted BBC1, 10 May 1979 BBC1).

33 Robin Hood, p. 5.

34 Frye, *Anatomy of Criticism*, p. 34.

35 Frye, *Anatomy of Criticism*, p. 37.

36 Frye, *Anatomy of Criticism*, p. 34.

37 Frye, *Anatomy of Criticism*, p. 34.

38 Frye, *Anatomy of Criticism*, p. 99.

39 Frye, *Anatomy of Criticism*, p. 102.

40 Frye, *Anatomy of Criticism*, p. 112.

41 Frye, *Anatomy of Criticism*, p. 118.

42 Frye, *Anatomy of Criticism*, p. 186.

43 Frye, *Anatomy of Criticism*, pp. 186–7.

44 Northrop Frye, 'The archetypes of literature', in David Lodge (ed.), *20th Century Literary Criticism* (London: Longman, 1972), p. 426.

45 John Whiteclay Chambers II and David Culbert, *World War II Film and History* (New York: Oxford University Press, 1996), p. 158.

46 Jung, *Archetypes and the Collective Unconscious*, pp. 3–4.

47 Jung, *Archetypes and the Collective Unconscious*, pp. 32–3.

48 Jung, *Archetypes and the Collective Unconscious*, p. 42.

49 Jung, *Archetypes and the Collective Unconscious*, p. 43.

50 Jung, *Archetypes and the Collective Unconscious*, pp. 152–3.

51 Jung, *Archetypes and the Collective Unconscious*, p. 153.

52 Jung, *Archetypes and the Collective Unconscious*, p. 157.

53 Antony Easthope, *Poetry as Discourse* (London: Methuen, 1983), p. 20.

54 Richards, 'Popular memory and the construction of English history', p. 30.

55 Richards, 'Popular memory and the construction of English history', p. 30.

56 Shlomith Rimmon-Kenan, *Narrative Fiction: Contemporary Poetics* (London: Methuen, 1983), p. 34.

57 *The World About Us*, *RT* (18–24 March 1972) p. 27.

58 Apsley Cherry-Garrard, *The Worst Journey in the World: Antarctica 1910–1913* (London: Pimlico, 2003), p. 206.

59 Susan Solomon, *The Coldest March: Scott's Fatal Antarctic Expedition* (New Haven: Yale University Press, 2001), pp. xv–xvi.

60 Solomon, *Coldest March*, p. 22.

61 Cherry-Garrard, *Worst Journey in the World*, pp. 562–3.

62 Cherry-Garrard, *Worst Journey in the World*, p. 206.

63 Lord Kennet, Letters to the Editor, 'Scott and Reality', *The Times* (18 February 1985) p. 13.

64 Kennet, Letters to the Editor, p. 13.

65 John Wyver, 'Hero Caught in an Icy Blast', *The Times* (11 February 1985), p. 12.

66 Kennet, Letters to the Editor, p. 13.

67 Wyver, 'Hero Caught in an Icy Blast', p. 12.

68 Peter Davalle, 'Today's Television and Radio Programmes: Choice', *The Times* (20 February 1985), p. 29.

69 Wyver, 'Hero Caught in an Icy Blast', p. 12.

70 Wyver, 'Hero Caught in an Icy Blast', p. 12.

71 Samuel Hynes, 'Personal narratives and commemoration', in Winter and Sivan (eds), *War and Remembrance*, p. 207.

72 Jung, *Archetypes and the Collective Unconscious*, pp. 32–3.

73 Barthes, *Mythologies*, p. 110

74 Barthes, *Mythologies*, p. 109.

75 Rimmon-Kenan, *Narrative Fiction*, p. 37.

76 Tessa Perkins, 'Rethinking stereotypes', in O'Sullivan and Jewkes (eds), *The Media Studies Reader*, p. 78.

77 Roland Barthes, *Image, Music, Text*, trans. Stephen Heath (London: Fontana Press, 1977), p. 165.

78 Michel Foucault, 'Systems of thought', in *Language, Counter-Memory, Practice. Selected Essays and Interviews with Michel Foucault,* ed. F. Bouchard (Ithaca: Cornell University Press, 1980), p. 200.

79 Foucault, 'Systems of thought', p. 199.

80 Natalie Zemon Davis, '"Women's history" in transition: The European case', in Scott (ed.), *Feminism and History*, p. 79.

81 Samuel, *Island Stories*, p. 10.

7

Britain as a warrior nation

War is always going to be a defining moment for any nation, setting out its political, military and national credentials for the entire world to see. British military history as a subject can be traced back to the eighteenth century and the campaigns of Marlborough, further established through British exploits in the Napoleonic wars, North America and India.[1] As any viewer of factual history programming in the United Kingdom can testify, Britain is no stranger to war on a national and international scale, having fought two world wars, reluctantly embarking on the second within twenty-one years of the first's ending.

As a symbolic, if not literal, 'island fortress', taking-up arms in a 'just' cause is well established as part of the tapestry of England/Britain as a proud nation-state. It is a theme recognised by factual programme-makers in parts one and two of the seven-part series *Invasion Road* (ITV, 1979) featuring 'The Last Invasion…?' and the mythical, misleading 'Island Fortress' itself. Woven through each period of battles and wars pre-dating the 1914–18 'war to end all wars' are the golden threads of leaders and warriors who depict a striking picture of valour, self-sacrifice and courage – Boudicca, Harold II, Richard the Lionheart, Henry V, Drake, Cromwell, Charles I, Wellington, Nelson and Gordon.

Trapped between these shimmering threads are other military encounters that shine a little less fervently – Richard III's defeat at Bosworth, William III's victory at the Battle of the Boyne, and defeats suffered in the Zulu, Boer and Crimean wars. Military and political reputations also fade and catch the light of scrutiny for reasons not conjoined with victory but with the quality of leadership, loss of life, motivations and personal reasons that deploy British armed forces overseas and specify rules of engagement. Some of the most reactionary and revisionist condemnations have been directed at General Haig, the most recent, Tony Blair and George Bush.

In Britain compiling the history of skirmishes, attacks, victories and defeats on land and sea was left to military men with abundant time on their hands and not seen as an area of notable historical study or attention in its own right.[2] The First and Second World Wars, however, would shatter this approach as campaigns had to be explored through their social and cultural context, not merely reportage of battlefield exploits.[3] Conflict of any nature creates a rupture in the flow of everyday activity; when it revolves around political decisions and military action it acts as a significant point of refraction. It focuses attention not only on theatres of war and conflict but also on the circumstances that led to military intervention in the first place.

The tradition of Britain as a warrior nation that fights for what it believes is right is a defining and formative element of national character. With the Second World War particularly eulogised and mythologised as a shared endeavour, a period when everyone pulled together, it is no surprise that references and stories about this period still feature heavily on the media agenda.

In *Hitler and Churchill: Secrets of Leadership* (Weidenfeld and Nicolson, 2003), Andrew Roberts explains how he did a random survey of stories directly connected to events in 1939–45, or those forming a reference for contemporary events. The results of his two-week survey led Roberts to conclude: 'The Second World War was thus continuing to make headlines, almost on a daily basis, even over half a century.'[4] Roberts believes this prioritising of the Second World War, 'especially the year between June 1940 and June 1941, goes to the very heart of Britain's self-perception as a nation'.[5] The grip of the Second World War still remains a benchmark of national identity and character that creeps into reporting the past and the present in 2009: 'Suicides dropped after terrorist attacks thanks to Blitz spirit', and 'Nazi doctor and the mystery of "twins town".'[6] Memory too, in the case of wartime childhood experiences, is also firmly embedded into the Second World War in ITV's *Evacuees Reunited* (ITV1, 2008).

War, then, becomes an integral facilitator in understanding who we are and how we developed – a factor that factual history commissioning and production has not been slow to exploit, demonstrating a voracious appetite for war on a large and small scale. Proven as a successful format, the genre of war and conflict has been heavily commissioned because it works so well. This was demonstrated by *The Great War*, which appealed to TV-users through its content and format that still provides the backbone for many one-off programmes and series.

Factual history programming themed on war had, up until the 1960s, followed the expository mode of documentary production with programmes both imported and produced in-house. It is safe to say that a TV-user base was already firmly established before the arrival of *The Great War* in 1964, with 163 programmes, or 21 per cent of the scheduling, derived from war and conflict between 1950 and 1959.[7]

Programmes and series featuring war and conflict are popular, and their steady rise in terms of output can be explained, Roger Smither believes, because of its competitive cost when compared to other options of filling a screen for a specific amount of time.[8] Frank Rosier, Secretary of the Portsmouth Branch of the Normandy Veterans Association, while agreeing that war should be an integral element of history, does believe that far too little history is 'recorded about us the people', and says that 'we seem only to get recorded as to how well we fight in wars'.[9]

There is little doubt that history has become increasingly profitable for British television as a commodity, though the new approach to history at the BBC seems ready to abandon the Second World War as a commodity entirely.

> In the future both money and focus are to be moved away from the second world war [*sic*], the Nazis and the Holocaust. 'It is time for a change. The well has run dry. We are looking to put the spotlight on other areas,' says Martin Davidson, the BBC's commissioner of specialist factual output.[10]

Time will tell if a fresh direction away from the Second World War will be endorsed by TV-users, but programmes featuring military history do represent significant developments in factual television history in this country. The themes of war and conflict continue to circulate collective memories of nation and nationality as indexical units of Britishness modified, conditioned or shaped by the tradition of Britain as a fighting nation.

War, memory and revision

Immediately following the Second World War as the BBC began to resume transmission in 1946, albeit on a limited scale, the foundations of history programming were being laid. These included retrospective documentary insights on how the war was won with documentaries commemorating the allied victory. It was not to be until the 1950s and 1960s that programmes dealing with war and conflict started to diversify. During the mid- to late 1960s, war became a source of social and cultural conflict as a different generation questioned the validity of war as a political tool.

As vehement anti-Vietnam War protests gathered pace in the United States and Britain, culminating in the Grosvenor Square demonstrations outside the American Embassy in London, television history makers had no qualms in bringing distant campaigns to the living room. This was at a time when a major link with the armed forces was finally broken with the ending of National Service in November 1960.[11]

If Peter Watkins' remarkably brutal and original take on battle and its aftermath in *Culloden* was meant to mirror American policy in Vietnam, resolute military leadership provided a solid strata of British fortitude as a national characteristic in television history portraits of Cromwell, Marlborough, Nelson and Wellington. Whilst the main impetus of programme making was to be formed around the Second World War, the basis for modern armed conflict in a more horrific guise would create a defining moment in factual history programme making in the 1960s.

For a generation at odds with the perceived codes of the establishment, the 1960s marked a period of social and cultural rebellion that had an uncanny resonance with the social and cultural changes accelerated by the First World War. Military history programming in the 1960s showed no sign of losing its appetite for military action, with factual history programming on war and conflict revealing a marked increase, rising from 163 in the decade 1950–59 to 366 in 1960–69.[12] Heightened East–West tensions found an altogether different form of warfare occupying current affairs, news coverage and factual programming in the 1960s. These examined government policy and strategies with programmes such as *World War* – 'The Cold War Starts' and 'The Cold War Spreads' (ITV, 1966). But during the mid-1960s, a technological war that had been bogged down by trench conflict, by political and military belligerence, would become the focus for a series that reinterpreted war through living memory.

In his 1930, 'Original Preface to the Real War', Basil Liddell Hart declared that documents alone cannot be relied on as absolute historical evidence, being 'too superficial' and the 'unwitting hand of "mythology"'.[13] The answer, Liddell Hart insisted, was that personal direct experience of events or those from other witnesses is the only way of 'testing' official accounts for their accuracy.[14] This was to be an ethos that informed and shaped the 26-part *The Great War* that is best remembered as a turning point in factual television history production.

The Great War is credited by Jeremy Isaacs with creating an immense impact in history produced for television, by refraining from what he terms as the 'insouciant gung-ho of US series like *Victory at Sea* (BBC, 1952), or Jack le Vien's *Churchill: The Valiant Years* (BBC, 1961).[15]

Attempting to understand, analyse and explain a conflict that caused so much devastation and brought with it a fundamental change in society was not the sole preserve of the BBC. Three years before the launch of BBC2 in 1964 and the first episode of *The Great War*, ITV screened Alan (A. J. P.) Taylor's *First World War* (ITV, 1961), a six-part series of thirty-minute programmes beginning on 27 February and running until 3 April, chronologically schemed around each year of the war.

Other one-off programmes forayed into the First World War using emotive and personal stories, beginning with *Fifty Fathoms Deep* – 'The Story of the Lusitania' (BBC, 1962). Attempting to lift away some of the myth surrounding the tracks of T. E. Lawrence was *Adventure* – 'Desert Journey Tracing the Guerrilla Action of Lawrence of Arabia' (BBC, 1962), complemented by a biographical portrait *T. E. Lawrence* 1888–1935 (BBC, 1962). Abrupt and ironical in its title, ITV transmitted *14–18* (ITV, 1963) – 'It Was the War to End All Wars'. Though far from setting the record straight, television was only just beginning to address the Great War in detail. Even the *Sunday Story* series, utilising its storytelling format, turned to the personal wartime profile with a four-part biography of Edith Cavell (BBC1, 1964), as part of its regular five-minute Sunday slot.

The Great War series is not only a product of its time technically, when filmed in 1914–18 and produced by the BBC in 1964, but creatively, a marriage of chance and opportunity. This stemmed not out of a visionary desire to embark on a groundbreaking series but from the ethos and working practices of the *Tonight* team, led by Alasdair Milne. *Tonight* (BBC, 1957–65/BBC1, 1975–79) was a topical magazine series put together on a minimal budget and constantly looking for free or inexpensive footage around which it could structure its programmes.[16] The anniversary of the First World War was approaching, the team knew the Imperial War Museum was a source of inexpensive footage, and the *Tonight* programme launched an appeal for veterans on-air,[17] as the collaborative project got underway.

Critics of the series may have good reason to question the use of archive footage in the series,[18] or to raise issues on aspects of distortion and manipulation by reversing film footage. This should not come as a surprise. Television producers are always going to be primarily concerned with the 'look'; everything else that follows is, by convention, secondary. This was a philosophy that Tony Essex, joint producer of the series knew only too well. Achieving a desired 'look' was an element of television production that Correlli Barnett, a historian and scriptwriter on the series, had to accept:

Tony's wish, totally understandably, was to make great television, he wanted to produce things which were going to have a great impact on the viewer and he saw the historians as the servants of this process.[19]

Television thrives on drama, conflict, suspense and surprise; elements carefully structured to command attention. One of the strongest features of the series was how it took these elements, combined them with oral history and transformed the brutality of war into a powerful visual voice. This was achieved by interweaving eyewitness accounts, the narration by Sir Michael Redgrave and archive footage in what has now become a standard documentary format.

Personal narratives when intertwined with warfare create a privileged position, that here is something memorable and culturally important to be told. For Roland Barthes, not only does this equate with the concept of constructing a sense of having been there, but through archive footage, photographs and personal testimony it also becomes a position of sharing, a socially defined moment of 'being there'.[20] But being there, actually living through trench warfare and having to recall it for television, does bring the reliability of memory into question, as Julia Cave, eyewitness researcher on the series points out:

> The nature of memory was very interesting because I think that most people remember several incidents very, very clearly which may come to haunt them over the years. But probably, their total memory of the whole war would not exist, it's fragmented.[21]

Again the intimacy of the shot typology offered by television is well suited to narratives that revolve around causal effect, dramatic opposition and closure wound into the testimony of eyewitness as seen in *The Great War*.[22] *The Great War* is very much concerned with 'personal dramas', as the opening title sequence makes abundantly clear.

Its combination of evocative stills move from a silhouetted soldier standing over a grave and marker cross, down into a trench over a skeletal corpse, to a British soldier staring at the camera – each frame bringing him closer – then out through the frame. Its effect is to construct a very personal position structured through eye contact for TV-users, creating a position of shared, or an offer of sharing, experiences. Throughout the sequence, the highly emotive, personal toll of war is rhythmically matched by the melancholy music performed by the BBC Northern Orchestra conducted by George Hurst, gradually reaching a nerve-shattering crescendo of timpani drums.

The necessity of television to construct a smooth, unobtrusive and easy-to-follow narrative, however emotive and charged the memories may be, will always take precedence. Barry Toovey, supervising film editor for the series, admits the priority of the programme-makers when he discusses the reversing of film footage:

> We tried to have all the British and French troops pointing left to right and the Germans right to left so it would match in with the maps of the Western Front. And so, we had to decide which to flop over, that's why if you look carefully there are quite a lot of left-handed soldiers.[23]

Manipulation in this way calls into question the camera's role as an accurate recording device of history when archive footage is used as aesthetic motivating narrative devices. Such editing offers numerous opportunities for imposing personal perspectives when documentary has its narrative ordered by editing rather than through a storyboard or script in fictional formats.[24]

There is good reason why *The Great War* series is regarded as an important milestone in how television can very adeptly deal with such an important aspect of the past, sustaining its primary function of creating good, entertaining television whilst at the same time giving TV-users access to history they may never before have encountered by meshing archive footage with oral history.[25]

Opposition between archive footage of events and personal recollections, the remembering of the actual event by those caught up in it as eyewitnesses, tends to be amplified when war is the subject area. As Henry Rousso points out when analysing the *Vichy Syndrome*, it is the 'distance' between events and 'subjective' recollections, that cause friction and disparity.[26] The military historian John Keegan also points to issues of perception in the heat of battle when 'Truth is highly subjective. What's happening to one person at one moment is not what's happening to another person at the same moment a few yards from them, all soldiers say that.'[27]

The Great War is a record of how images scar the memory; some of these cicatrices may disappear over time, some remain fresh and livid. It is when these powerful memories become oral testimony, that they bestow on factual history programme-makers a stamp of approval that the past they have reconstructed is indeed, accurate. There is always, however, the nagging doubt that oral history and memory are unstable and unknown qualities capable of floating free of their period anchors to function as symbolic myths. Without reliable anchors, they act as mausoleums for a given age, open to exploitation by 'nostalgia-merchants'[28] rather than being professionally handled by historians and dedicated programme-makers.

Perhaps smarting from the critical acclaim and reception of the BBC's *The Great War*, ITV took the opportunity to air Columbia Broadcasting System's (CBS) 1964 *World War 1* from January to July 1973 in regular Monday late-evening time slots of thirty-minutes. Not to be outflanked by their commercial rivals, BBC1 ran a full repeat showing of *The Great War* from August 1974 until March 1975, before changing tack to reflect a growing feminist campaign for equality, independence and acceptance with a return to the First World War in an expanded two-part *What Did You Do in The Great War Mummy?* (BBC1, 1976), first shown in 1974.

The oral connection with war continued in the six-part *Yesterday's Witness: Women at War* (BBC2, 1977), denoting how feminism had emerged from war, long held to be a masculine preserve, and tilted the balance of social and cultural values. War as a popular theme and commodity may not have decreased in dealing with the Second World War, but by 1980 the pull of 1914–18 campaigns had diminished somewhat for programme makers.

Battles by instalments

As collective memories of the First World War were being overwritten by memories of events between 1939 and 1945, the BBC's post-war resumption of television ensured that memories still powerfully and painfully strong would not wither for a lack of stimulus.

The BBC, not afraid to add to a collective memory of victory from any angle they could, steadily began to weave the Second World War into the fabric of nation and nationality. Presenting history as a means of disclosing a secret or as a 'new' aspect of a well-known narrative is a strategy that attracts TV-users. As many post-war TV-users had experience of war first-hand, the BBC retold and reinforced the narrative of victory as one composed of ingenuity. *The War Underwater*, broadcast in 1946, featured a 'visit to the special diving tank, to a well-known submarine engineering works. Viewers see demonstrations of two of the war's great underwater surprises, the Frogman and the two-man torpedo.'[29]

The untold secrets of how the war was won were also revealed to TV-users in *Secret Mission*, telling the story of the sabotage attempts on Norway's heavy water production during the war.[30] The BBC as a self-appointed guardian of national achievement continued the commemorative theme into the 1950s with *Burma Victory* (BAFPU, 1945/BBC, 1953), followed by *The True Glory 1939–1945 War* – 'The Western Front' (BBC, 1954), originally released in 1945.

Unlike the cinema, where narratives are produced as a single, inclusive unit, television is designed as an episodic medium around the seasonality and timing of the schedules. Multi-part series are therefore an ideal vehicle for present-ing events that cover a wide chronological time frame. It was in the 1950s when the British TV-users were introduced to war packaged as a dedicated series, neatly arranged in chronological boxes, complete with omniscient sombre narration and narrative trajectories forming neatly binary opposed self-contained stories.

These elements, narrative devices Charles Dickens perfected in his monthly serialised novels where 'every instalment had to come to a climax of suspense [because] action and excitement must be maintained at all costs',[31] form the core of series such as America's National Broadcasting Corporation's (NBC) twenty-six episode *Victory at Sea*. The series was ambitious to say the least, directed by M. Clay Adams and written by Richard F. Hanser and Henry Salomon who also produced the series. The original score was composed by Richard Rodgers and the footage edited by Isaac Kleinerman.[32]

Assembled from 'over 50,000,000 feet of official film from ten different governments and 26 separate governmental agencies all over the world'[33] and narrated by Leonard Graves, the series has become a commemorative mile-stone in constructing American popular memory and culture.[34]

The philosophy behind the series was quite simple; to record history as it happened. However, this also raises significant problems as this recording is also controlled by a number of subjective positions.[35] According to Peter C. Rollins, the series was put together in the best tradition of propaganda films, with the aim of proselytising the belief in America as a righteous, morally just and courageous country prepared to fight to defend notions of freedom.[36] *Victory at Sea* may have attempted to embed core values of American concepts of nationality into a collective memory,[37] though the problem with propa-ganda, as a foundation for collective memory, is that some individuals will obstinately view events rather differently than others.

Caught between America and Russia flexing its muscles in the early 1950s, Britain and its government led by Winston Churchill could already feel the icy stirrings of the Cold War. Any factual history series attempting to establish ideological points was, however innocuous its aims, likely to heighten inter-national friction. Not apparently predisposed to adding its weight to Cold War political manoeuvring, the BBC inadvertently did just that when it decided to broadcast *Victory at Sea* in 1952.

After the Prime Minister Winston Churchill had viewed three episodes sup-plied by NBC in advance at his family home of Chartwell in Kent,[38] he was in high dudgeon at what he had seen with the result that he had 'gone up in smoke'.[39] What caused Churchill to ignite was the American bias in the series, and this led to a flurry of letters between Downing Street and the BBC. In a letter to B. E. Nicholls, CVO, CBE, the BBC Director of Home Broadcasting, Churchill's joint Principal Private Secretary, Jock Colville, had no doubts that international relations could be strained and 'produce anti-American feeling among the viewers'.[40] Colville made it abundantly clear how delicate the balance of power was at that point, and warned Nicholls that the series may

> prejudice the feelings of our people to the United States at a time when it is of such importance that the opposite should be the case. Really the Politburo themselves could not have selected films better suited to their purpose![41]

In his reply on the day following the transmission of the first episode on 27 October 1952, Nicholls pointed out that the series was a 'free gift' and the BBC would do everything in its power to 'keep the perspective clear for viewers'.[42] This included permitting the series to be 'vetted', with the offer of dropping one of the contentious episodes covering D-Day from the BBC's transmission.[43] The BBC accepted Churchill's offer of the services of General Pownall and Commodore Allen, 'who have assisted me in the writing of my war histories',[44] to carry out the vetting. Churchill's ire stemmed from the narration in an episode dealing with the U-boat war: it 'talks of our "feeble and pathetic" defence, but we did practically the whole work',[45] the Prime Minister wrote. The American slant on D-Day in another episode fared little better from Britain's wartime Prime Minister, with Churchill quite indignant at what he took to be biased American propaganda.

> The third, the Landing on D-Day, gives the impression that only Americans took part in this, with occasional British units. In fact, however, we landed almost as many Divisions as they, did four-fifths of the transportation and naval bombardment, and quite a good share of the air.[46]

Responding to the charge of bias, Sir Alexander Cadogan, Chairman of the BBC Board of Governors, pledged to the Prime Minister that the services of Pownall and Allen would be used to provide 'advice on the proper presentation of the films on the British Television Service'.[47] As a result of Churchill's fury and BBC compromise, the series was saved from heavy censorship and was broadcast in full.

Before the intervention of the Prime Minister, the BBC had made an attempt to readdress American subjectivity and bias by carrying an introduction by the naval historian Professor Michael Lewis in each episode, reaffirming the British contribution.[48] Just how far these 'introductions' were shaped by the advice and guidance of Pownall and Allen is difficult to tell.

As with all actuality sequences of military action in factual history programmes depicting war on television, *Victory at Sea* allowed TV-users to experience battle without encountering direct danger or death. Without the slightest risk, TV-users could also take part in front line engagements in *Epic Battles* (BBC, 1958) following the European action in Stalingrad, the Battle for Cassino or the equally bitter 'fight to the death' at Kohima in Burma,[49] ably guided and narrated by Sir Brian Horrocks. Armchair strategists could assess military tactics and the resulting engagements in *Command in Battle* (BBC, 1958) expertly steered through the battles of Alamein and Moreth, the invasion of Sicily and Italy, Normandy, the winter of 1944 and the German surrender on Lüneburg Heath by Field-Marshal Montgomery.

It might be no coincidence that an increase in factual history programming dedicated to reviving memories of victory in the Second World War was being broadcast following the major military campaigns in Korea 1950–53, and during the Suez Crisis of 1956. Whether this was a coincidence in scheduling on the one hand, or a subtle reinforcing of a collective memory framed and formed by the strength of British spirit in the face of adversity on the other, it is difficult to tell. For whatever reasons these types of memories were being recirculated, it firmly reinforced Britain as a nation with a strong military past.

Steering clear of damaging international relations, the fledgling ITV network's programming on the Second World War featured the role of women in Associated Rediffusion's six-part *Secret Mission* (ITV, 1956), a docudrama written by Robert Barr, reconstructing the work of six female Special Operations Executive agents and concentrating on the personal nature of warfare.

For many TV-users in the 1950s, this concept of personal sacrifice would be familiar from British wartime propaganda films such as *In Which We Serve* (1942) and *Went the Day Well* (1942), which extolled the very same message. This reinforcement and commemoration of past events as totemic markers in national development generates varying levels of collective memories on what it is to be British. Factual history war programmes from the 1950s do tend to be bold declarative statements on this British military ideal, with titles such as *Men of Action* (BBC, 1959), making no apologies for what the call of war requires, spotlighting in part one the unconventional visionary behind the Special Air Service Regiment (SAS), Colonel David Stirling.

Changing attitudes towards war during the 1960s and 1970s saw factual history programming devoted to peeling away the gloss of victory in order to pose some pertinent, and in some cases long overdue, questions. Some programme-makers were no longer satisfied with a personal biography; their objective was to create accountability such as in *Who Raised His Voice Against It?* – 'German Opposition to Hitler 1939–1945' (BBC1, 1968). Likewise, the *Tuesday Documentary: In the Name of France* – 'From Defeat to Resistance 1940–44' (BBC1, 1969), and *Late Night Line-Up* – 'I am English, I was German. But Above All I Was There' (BBC2, 1969), focused on the dilemma of dual nationality at a time of war.

How far investigations into accountability went remained dependent largely on the public profile of the subject concerned, with the twelve-part *Mountbatten* – 'A Television History of the Life and Times of Lord Mountbatten' delivering a flattering biography.

In an era when science and technology did seem capable of creating a brave new world, and television eagerly covered the Apollo 11 and 12 attempts at a moon landing in 1969, factual history programming turned to military technology. A two-part investigation into Royal Navy weapons development in *Secret War* (BBC, 1961), written and narrated by Gerald Pawle, was followed by *The Secret War* – 'A Challenge to Invention' (BBC, 1962). And there was an *All Our Yesterdays* 1968 tribute to the ingenuity and genius in 'Barnes Wallis and the Bouncing Bomb'.

Concerns over an entirely different type of bomb also dominated the 1960s as Cold War tensions intensified following the Cuban Missile Crisis in October 1962, with *Ten Seconds that Shook the World* (BBC, 1964), *The Building of the Bomb* (BBC1, 1965) and *Too Near The Sun* – 'The history of the super-bomb' (BBC1, 1966). The topicality of these programmes using the past to explain the present highlights the international tension at the time. They were screened when there was genuine concern that another world war fought with nuclear weapons was not a question of *if*, but *when?* In 1968 tension rose again when it was believed American forces were prepared to use nuclear weapons to relieve the U.S. Marine Corps' 77-day siege at Khe Sanh, though General Earle Wheeler, Chairman of the Joints Chief of Staff, denied it.[50]

A strong element of revisionism, begun in the late 1960s, flowed through into the 1970s with, for example, *On Trial: Marshal Pétain* – 'A Matter of Honour' (BBC1, 1970), translated and narrated by Stuart Hood, which examined the legal proceedings that brought Pétain to trial on charges of betrayal. A determination to revise strategic military campaigns became evident with the title of the first part of *Sons of the Blood: The Great Boer War, 1899–1902* – 'We Went There to Take Their Country From Them ...' (BBC2, 1972).

The first stirrings of doubt that Imperial aspirations were not quite as straightforward as they had once seemed also surfaced in the 1970s. Learning Corporation of America's *Western Civilisation* – 'The Crusades: Saints and Sinners' (ITV, 1975) suggested that a previously unshaken belief in conquest and war had finally begun to run out of valedictory steam. Questioning the morality of holy wars through 'the motivation of some of its leading figures',[51] the parallel between 'Saints and Sinners' and America's reliance on military intervention – its M16 rifle diplomacy – on foreign soil may not have been lost on British TV-users.

If the past was having any bearing on 1970s Britain, spiralling into industrial anarchy, the Second World War became an ideal platform from which codes of behaviour, lessons in morality and responsibility could be understood. *Personal Choice* – 'Albert Speer' (BBC1, 1970) allowed Michael Charlton access to Hitler's former armament minister, and *Tuesday Documentary: The Strange Case of Rudolf Hess* (BBC1, 1970) attempted to solve a mystery concerning loyalty and duplicity. Equally intent on opening old wounds, *The Issue Should be Avoided* (BBC2, 1971) focused on the Katyn Forest Massacre of 1940 in Poland, whilst *The Sorrow and the Pity* (BBC2, 1971, first shown in France as *Le Chagrin et la pitié*, 1969), became the first documentary to deal with issues of French collaboration with Germans during the Second World War.

Eyewitness accounts also formed the structure for the major series of the 1970s, in Thames Television's twenty-six-part *The World at War* (ITV, 1973– 74), which adopted and adapted *The Great War's* mechanism of archive footage, interviewees, and voice-over narration, in this case Laurence Olivier. Once more, the opening titles sought to emphasise war on a personal basis with poignant stills held in focus before being consumed by the flames of war.

Of course the danger of relying on too many eyewitness accounts is that they are often selected for the sheer emotive power of their testimony. It is this, argues James Chapman, that can turn oral history into nothing more than dramatic stories for television.[52] Given so much control of interviewees, it is hardly surprising that eyewitnesses in turn become commodities 'not on their own terms but on those of the documentarists',[53] becoming components to be inserted at crucial narrative peaks as points of validation.

James Chapman is in no doubt that each programme in *The World at War* series had a pre-defined agenda in terms of what it intended to say about the war.[54] This type of biased production agenda, which influences how programmes adhere to social and cultural values of certain individuals, has little or no bearing on the events themselves, or on contextual anchoring in their own periods.

War as a media event

In the midst of battle, the chaos, the destruction and personal suffering, there is that voyeuristic element of spectacle. Battles visually captured on canvas, on photographic plates, on film and videotape can repel and appeal at the same time. War artists and camera crews operating with or without official sanction have been prepared to risk their lives to document and report armed conflict.

This may account why the BBC offered two series assessing the risks that war cameramen and war artists faced in *Images of War: The Cameramen 1939–45* (BBC2, 1981) and *Images of War: The Artists 1939–45* (BBC2, 1983). Opening new thematic avenues for connecting with personal war experiences can only draw from a limited source after all, as the number of surviving veterans diminishes.

Perhaps attempting to break a cycle of repetitive themes on a standard canon of events, a ready stock of Second World War documentaries was capitalised on by Channel 4 in 1984 with its thirteen-part *The British at War* (C4, 1984), introduced by Leslie Halliwell. Repeating films already broadcast by the BBC and ITV, the series pooled official short documentary and propaganda films into a Thursday mid-afternoon autumn and winter schedule block running from 2.30 to 4.30 p.m., an early strategy of block programming later refined by specialised history channels.

The relatively neglected post-1945 area for programme-makers began to significantly increase during the 1980s, partly through Channel 4's programming that examined the Vietnam War in detail. A co-production between Britain's Central Independent Television, America's WGBH (Boston) and France's Antenne 2, the twelve-part *Vietnam* (C4, 1983) began to highlight a war that had no part in Britain's national psyche. This was followed a year later by a twenty-six part series *Vietnam: The Ten Thousand Day War* (C4, 1984); a Cineworld Production, from the company responsible for *American Caesar* (C4, 1984), a biography of General Douglas MacArthur, and *The American Century* (C4, 1986). Through the 1990s and 2000s, the main emphasis has remained for the most part around the First and Second World Wars. A number of presenters have created a 'military history' profile across terrestrial, cable and satellite channels as they delved into victories and defeats.

These include Richard Holmes' *War Walks* (BBC2, 1996–97) and *Battlefields* (BBC2, 2001), the former covering combat from Agincourt to the Blitz, the latter, a selection of Second World War key events – 'El Alamein', 'Cassino', 'Bomber', and 'Arnhem'. Laurence Rees' British Academy of Film and Television Arts (BAFTA) winning series on the Third Reich, *Nazis: A Warning from History* (BBC2, 1997) would be followed by *Auschwitz: The Nazis and the 'Final Solution'* (BBC2, 2005).

Peter and Dan Snow's *20th Century Battlefields* (BBC2, 2006–07) represented an eclectic choice of destinations by the father and son team, and Al Murray, a stand-up comedian, turned historian for Discovery's *Al Murray's Road to Berlin* in 2004 in a ten-stage tour of the Allied advance to the Nazi capital. Five's history series have also returned to the action of 1939–45 and have been fronted by Nigel Spivey with *Heroes of World War II* (Five, 2003–4) and Major Gordon Corrigan, MBE, with one of his series focusing on *Daring Raids of World War II* (Five, 2004).

As much as the Second World War themes and events circulating in the 1990s and 2000s keep the myth of a unified nation fresh and topical, they came into their own during the 1980s. If the war in Vietnam had no collective memory anchors for British TV-users, the Falklands War, lasting from 2 April to 14 June 1982, would evoke much comparison of Britain's past and then present military reputation. Factual programming concerning military history appears almost to have been scheduled to fit in with the South Atlantic campaign, as outlined in the table opposite.

The repeated six-part *Seapower* provided a valuable and timely insight into naval strategy, vessels and fighting capability during wartime, though BBC2's *Forty Minutes* may have picked an inopportune time to put together a documentary on the British mutiny at Salerno, Italy, in 1943. There could be no confusion or accusations of anti-military sentiment with *Arrival of the Water Carrier for Mesopotamia* – 'The Birth and Development of the Tank', or the clash of Austria and Germany in *Empires at War*.

In an almost prophetic piece of scheduling, Ludovic Kennedy's repeated *The U-Boat War* was broadcast exactly a month before the sinking of the Argentine cruiser the *General Belgrano* by a Royal Navy submarine, HMS *Conqueror*. Deceit ran at the core of *The Trial of Alger Hiss*, whilst military invasion and empire building made a very succinct appearance in *The History Makers* – 'Napoleon', as did *Going Back* – 'A Return to Vietnam', where four American veterans returned to former battlefields. The last factual war and conflict themed programme to be screened during the Falklands War, a repeated *Man Alive* on Raoul Wallenberg, carried a very symbolic reminder of the British deaths in the Falklands conflict in its title 'Missing Hero'.

A purely dramatic fictional four-part series on one of the Royal Navy's most symbolic figures, Admiral Nelson, featured in *I Remember Nelson: Recollections of a Hero's Life*, written by Hugh Whitemore and broadcast just as the Royal

War and conflict scheduling and the Falklands War, 1982

2 January	*Images of War: The Cameramen 1939–45*, Parts 1–6*
10 February	*Surrender* (ITV, 1982) – 'The Fall of Singapore in February 1942'
13 February	*Spain* (BBC2, 1982) – 'A Return to the Battlefields'
16 February	*Seapower* (BBC2, 1982) – Parts 1–6*
25 February	*Forty Minutes* (BBC2, 1982) – 'Mutiny': British mutiny in Italy in 1943
18 March	*Arrival of the Water Carrier for Mesopotamia* (BBC2, 1982)*
19 March	Argentinian flag flying on South Georgia
19 March	*Empires at War* (BBC2, 1982)
1 April	*The U-Boat War* (BBC 2, 1982)*
2 April	Falklands invaded by Argentine Forces
3 April	South Georgia taken by Argentine Forces; Royal Marines captured
5 April	British Royal Navy Task Force leaves for the South Atlantic
6–30 April	Diplomatic negotiations attempt to find a peaceful solution
10 April	*The Trial of Alger Hiss* (BBC2, 1982)
14 April	*The History Makers* (ITV, 1982) – 'Napoleon'
14 April	*I Remember Nelson: Recollections of a Hero's Life* – Parts 1–4 (ITV, 1982)
25 April	Argentine submarine *Santa Fe* damaged and South Georgia recaptured
28 April	*Going Back* (ITV, 1982) – 'A Return to Vietnam'
1 May	British Forces launch first attack
2 May	Argentine cruiser *General Belgrano* sunk by a Royal Naval nuclear submarine, *HMS Conqueror*
21 May	British land at San Carlos in preparation for land-based operations
6 June	*Man Alive* (BBC2, 1982) – 'Missing Hero: Raoul Wallenberg'*

*Repeat.

Navy Task Force began engaging the Argentinians. Its final episode 'Battle', which should have gone out on 5 May, the day of the first British attack, was postponed until 18 October 1982.

As a ceremony of thanksgiving was being planned for 26 July 1982 in St Paul's Cathedral, two months ahead of the victory parade on 12 October, a contemporary history of the Falklands War was being broadcast by the BBC in an eight-part documentary compiled from news footage – *Task Force South: The Battle for the Falklands* (BBC1, 1982). The war in Vietnam may have been the first war to become a television war, but the Falklands conflict would prove to be a heavily censored and controlled war for British TV-users.

The Ministry of Defence (MoD) and the government did not appear to want the British public to experience any of the damaging coverage that helped turn the American public against the Vietnam War. Sir Max Hastings, a correspondent with the naval task force and ground forces, is unequivocal in how the war was controlled, asserting: 'The Falklands war was the most controversially reported of Britain's conflicts since 1945.'[55] As Julian Barnes observed, the 'Falklands war would turn out to be the worst-reported war since the Crimean', firmly blaming the MoD:

> While our armed forces defeated the Argentineans, the Ministry of Defence was putting to rout the British media ... When relations between the press and the navy on board the Hermes were at their worst, Michael Nicholson of [Independent Television News] ITN and Peter Archer of the Press Association prefaced their bulletins with the rider that they were being censored. This fact was itself censored. In the age of image, the Falklands war remained image-free for much of its length – no British pictures for 54 of the 74 days the conflict lasted – and image-weak thereafter. Don McCullin, our greatest living war photographer, was refused accreditation.[56]

It would take five, ten and twenty years before critical documentaries questioned why the war was fought and how the war was won in any detail in *First Tuesday* – 'The Untold Story' (ITV, 1987), followed by the four-part *The Falklands War* (C4, 1992). The twentieth anniversary brought a critical polemical review – *Falklands: When Britain Went to War* (C4, 2002) and *Simon's Heroes* (BBC1, 2002) painfully retold the war from a soldier's perspective.

Any direct or collective memory traces connected to war tend to have very emotive and powerful effects that individuals, groups and governments deem worthy of commemoration. Not only that, but when contemporary events have to be anchored and explained, as happened with the Falklands War, a collective appropriation of British spirit, character and unity is brought into play. The mood in the House of Commons during an emergency Saturday morning debate on 3 April 1982, after confirmation that the Argentinians had indeed occupied the Falkland Islands, offers a pertinent example. During tense non-partisan exchanges between Members of the House and the Government Front Bench, the Tory MP for Surbiton, Sir Nigel Fisher, requiring an explanation for Britain's 'humiliation', declared: 'The truth is that we have been preempted, as we were in Norway by the Germans in 1940, and that led to the fall of Mr. Chamberlain's Government.'[57]

The Labour MP for Battersea North, Douglas Jay, went even further in condemning the Foreign and Commonwealth Office over the handling of the crisis, proposing, 'The whole story will inevitably lead some people to think that the Foreign Office is a bit too much saturated with the spirit of appeasement.'[58]

Discussing an increase in the study of commemoration in the 1980s pioneered by Maurice Agulhon on commemorative images and political identity,[59] Patrick Hutton details how image appropriation and transformation can instigate a new level of meaning unconnected with original images as well as forming new related collective memories of particular images.[60] It is not difficult to understate the implications present in this argument for the treatment of the past in television history programming when visual evidence is interwoven into a documentary where there is already an established paradigm in operation as to how history should 'look' from previous factual programmes and fictional films.

When established framing techniques, shot typologies, eyewitness accounts, illustrations, paintings, photographs and archive film are cut together, it is their juxtaposition in a carefully scripted narrative flow that produces what Sergei Eisenstein deemed the 'montage of attractions'.[61] Because of an association of unexpected shots colliding together in a sequence, they produce a visual emotive hammer blow for the TV-users – what might indeed be termed as montage of shock. Invariably this sequence modifies the original meaning of the images, thereby setting up new frames of reference for a collective memory that not merely informs future usage of the image but mystifies its origins in the past.

This can be seen in a short early sequence from *Falklands: When Britain Went To War*. In the sequence, David Nichols, Editor in Chief of ITN, explains how he cited the German use of images in the Second World War to Margaret Thatcher as reasons why ITN journalists should accompany the Task Force during the Falklands War. What follows next is a rapid montage sequence of the kind developed and advocated by Eisenstein.

The montage fragments in this sequence consist of Second World War icons – a statue of Montgomery, the MoD building, its nameplate and 10 Downing Street – over which has been added the sound of gunfire. Intended as a postmodern pastiche that symbolised the 'war' between journalists and the MoD during the early days of the Falklands conflict, the speed of the juxtaposition is demonstrative of semiotic excess of the type that has become a staple filament in pop music videos. TV-users unable to identify the significance of these Second World War icons individually would have few doubts of their meaning after the montage, whereby their significance would be increased and foregrounded as essential elements of war past and present.

The implicit suggestion of the montage, appreciated by TV-users with positive memories of the Second World War, would become attached to the Falklands War and, in doing so, reinforce and revalidate the myths of heroism and national identity drawn from the Second World War. This in turn recycles and reissues the myth of British solidarity, fighting spirit and resolve nurtured from personal experiences or inherited family memories from 1939–45.

As a formative arch underpinning national identity, major military endeavours, achievements, victories and defeats become the genesis of memory formation for different periods of British history that tend to be viewed and remembered collectively as defining moments. The Falklands War is no exception; its inherited references to the Second World War bind then and now together firmly as undisputed characteristics of a nation and its people.

Of course, the implications for factual history programmes are foregrounded here by possibilities of misappropriation. This happens when one or more images – collective memories also – of an event, person, place or action becomes disassociated with its origins and historical context. In this way, images are often appropriated for exploitation as part of advertising campaigns, in programmes, books and the internet.

Appropriation, or *bricolage*, displaces an event or character from their chronological time frame. It also provides ready made cut-and-paste opportunities to reorganise the past into a convenient format in order to support ideological concepts of nation and nationality, of here and now. Above all, it is a process that invests new myths with roots whose origins are hard to precisely define.

The extent to which those in the armed forces and civilians have directly experienced warfare in the twentieth and twenty-first centuries ensures that memories are long-term, passed from family member to family member as well as being disseminated by the media. With the advances of news reporting allowing for almost instant, live coverage, warfare is no longer remote or distanced, but another form of television drama that creates its own direct and indirect experiences and memories.

With British armed forces now withdrawn from Iraq, and set for a war of attrition in Afghanistan, it is the internet that is bypassing the MoD's policy on accredited reporting from 'embedded' camera crews, reporters and photographers. In a striking parallel to the format of *Dear America*, battle footage synched with emotive music is uploaded directly onto YouTube.

In future, the study of factual history will have to take into account the instant history created for the internet. This is perhaps the latest technological addition to a '"master code" of stories about how we in the twentieth century got to be where we are',[62] and continue to progress in the twenty-first century. This concept of a 'master code' certainly ties in with Jung's concept of universal archetypes and Frye's belief in archetypes as an orchestrating mechanism for narratives. It also applies equally well to narratives and themes covered by factual history programming.

Notes

1 Michael Howard, 'What is military history…?', in Gardiner (ed.), *What Is History Today*, p. 4.

2 Howard, 'What is military history…?', p. 5.

3 Howard, 'What is military history…?', p. 5.

4 Andrew Roberts, *Hitler and Churchill: Secrets of Leadership* (London: Weidenfeld & Nicolson, 2003), p. xxx.

5 Roberts, *Hitler and Churchill*, p. xxx.

6 'Suicides Dropped After Terrorist Attack Thanks to Blitz Spirit', *Daily Telegraph* (6 January 2009), p. 8. Nick Evans, 'Nazi Doctor and the Mystery of "Twins Town"', *Daily Telegraph* (22 January 2009), p. 1.

7 Data from the *RT et al.*

8 Roger Smither, 'Why is so much television history about war?', in Cannadine (ed.), *History and the Media*, p. 61.

9 Frank Rosier, Secretary, The Normandy Veterans Association, Portsmouth Branch, in a letter to the author (30 November 2004).

10 Brown, 'The End of an Era', guardian.co.uk

11 'No More Men to Be Called Up', *The Times* (19 November 1960), p. 8.

12 Data from the *RT et al.*

13 Basil Liddell Hart, *History of the First World War* (London: Book Club Associates, 1973), p. 10.

14 Liddell Hart, *History of the First World War*, p. 10.

15 Jeremy Isaacs, 'All Our Yesterdays', in Cannadine (ed.), *History and the Media*, pp. 37–8.

16 Sir Anthony Jay, *That Was the Great War That Was* (transmitted BBC2, 22 February 2003).

17 Nick Fraser, narrator, *That Was the Great War That Was*.

18 John. A. Ramsden, '*The Great War*: the making of the series', *Historical Journal of Film, Radio and Television*, 22:1 (2002), 7–19.

19 Correlli Barnett, *That Was the Great War That Was* (transmitted BBC2, 22 February 2003).

20 Barthes, *Image, Music, Text*, p. 45.

21 Julia Cave, *That Was the Great War That Was* (transmitted BBC2, 22 February 2003).

22 Gary R. Edgerton, 'Television as historian: A different kind of history altogether', in Edgerton and Rollins (eds), *Television Histories*, pp. 2–3.

23 Barry Toovey, *That Was the Great War That Was* (transmitted BBC2, 22 February 2003).

24 Kilborn and Izod, *Television Documentary*, p. 89.

25 Briggs, *History of Broadcasting*, p. 414.

26 Henry Rousso, *The Vichy Syndrome, History and Memory in France since 1944*, trans. Arthur Goldhammer (Cambridge, Mass.: Harvard University Press, 1991), p. 102.

27 John Keegan, *That Was the Great War That Was* (transmitted BBC2, 22 February 2003).

28 Le Goff, *History and Memory*, p. 95.

29 *The War Underwater*, *RT* (17–23 November 1946), p. 35.

30 *Secret Mission, RT* (10–16 October 1948), p. 26.

31 Walter Allen, *The English Novel: A Short Critical History* (Harmondsworth: Penguin Books, 1984), p. 160.

32 WAC T6/290, undated, National Broadcasting Corporation (NBC) Fact Sheet on *Victory at Sea*, pp. 1–2.

33 NBC Fact Sheet on *Victory at Sea*, p. 3.

34 Peter C. Rollins, 'Victory at Sea, cold war epic in television's historical fictions', in Edgerton and Rollins (eds.), *Television Histories*, p. 103.

35 Rollins, 'Victory at Sea', p. 105.

36 Rollins, 'Victory at Sea', pp. 117–18.

37 Rollins, 'Victory at Sea', pp. 117–18.

38 WAC T6/290, memo from George Barnes, Director of BBC Television, to Cecil McGivern, Controller of Television Programmes, 28 October 1952.

39 WAC T6/290, memo from Barnes to McGivern.

40 WAC T6/290, letter from Jock Colville to B.E. Nicolls, 27 October 1952.

41 WAC T6/290, letter from Colville to Nicolls.

42 WAC T6/290, letter from B.E. Nicolls to Jock Colville, 28 October 1952.

43 WAC T6/290, letter from Nicolls to Colville.

44 WAC T6/290, letter from Winston Churchill to Sir Alexander Cadogan, Chairman of the BBC Board of Governors, 29 October 1952.

45 WAC T6/290, letter from Churchill to Cadogan.

46 WAC T6/290, letter from Churchill to Cadogan.

47 WAC T6/290, letter from Sir Alexander Cadogan to Winston Churchill 31 October 1952.

48 WAC T6/290, Phillip Dorté, Head of BBC Television Films, advance publicity copy for an article for the *Radio Times*, 13 October 1952, p. 4.

49 Barrie Pitt (ed.), *The Military History of World War II* (London: Chancellor Press, 1994), p. 263.

50 General Earle Wheeler, Chairman of the Joints Chief of Staff appearing in news footage in *Dear America: Letters Home From Vietnam* (transmitted Home Box Office, 1987/ BBC2, 1990).

51 *Western Civilisation – Saints and Sinners*, BFI, Film and Television Database, http://ftvdb.bfi.org.uk/sift/title/179201.

52 James Chapman, '*The World at War:* Television, documentary, history', in Roberts and Taylor (eds), *The Historian, Television and Television History*, p. 138.

53 Kilborn and Izod, *Television Documentary*, p. 203.

54 Chapman, '*World at War*', p. 140.

55 Max Hastings and Simon Jenkins, *The Battle for the Falklands* (London: Pan Books, 1997), p. 374.

56 Julian Barnes, 'The Worst Reported War Since the Crimean', www.guardian.co.uk/ Archive/Article/0,4273,4362424,00.html.

57 House of Commons Hansard debates for 3 April 1982. Vol. 21, Cols. 632–68 http://hansard.millbanksystems.com/commons/1982/apr/03/falkland-islands.

58 Hansard debates for 3 April 1982.

59 Hutton, *History as an Art of Memory*, pp. 2–3.

60 Hutton, *History as an Art of Memory*, pp. 2–3.

61 Sergei Eisenstein, 'The Montage of Film Attractions', in Richard Taylor (ed.), *The Eisenstein Reader* (London: British Film Institute, 1998), p. 36.

62 Jay Winter, 'Kinship and remembrance in the aftermath of the Great War', in Winter and Sivan (eds.), *War and Remembrance*, pp. 42–3.

8

Presenting the past

As a visual medium, television can be considered as an electronic version of the Bayeux tapestry, operating as a 'work of art and as an historical document' recording contemporary events.[1] Television also operates in similar vein to the *Hortus Deliciarum* manuscript, produced as so many manuscripts were, to 'inform, to provide an aid to understanding and an aid to memory'.[2] In the same way that medieval manuscripts enjoined 'text-and-picture' to illustrate events,[3] inform a target audience and communicate an ideological array of values, television functions in exactly the same way. It conforms to the same set of communication conventions reliant on the input of different individuals performing specific roles. Perhaps one of the most significant relationships in terms of this communication system is that between the historian/presenter and the production team.

Pressure and influence are always applied and governed by a sphere of inter-reliance. In the case of factual history programming, this includes researchers, writers, producers, directors, camera operators and sound engineers. The fusing of individual agendas institutes a combination of personal, peer and professional pressure that can have a cumulative effect on a programme.

Television is by its nature a team-focused mode of production – what David Starkey identifies as a 'co-operative medium that has to have a synergy between the director, the producer and the presenter, and indeed the cameraman'.[4] Bringing history to the page or television screen is no longer an individual feat of communication or will. Putting a factual history programme together successfully is far from being a simple production line assembly routine. An assembly line comparison takes little or no consideration of the psychological, professional, social and cultural pressures inherent in television production. Any form of mass-mediated communication achieves its primary objectives of reaching its perceived users by adhering to parameters set by the industry and the individuals working within it. A successful form of communication – which television undoubtedly is – also requires one ingredient that cannot be manufactured or created, that of appeal and user approval.

Whether acting as part of a television history production team or TV-user, each individual is always located in a total communication system dominated by a wide range of stimuli, some natural, but the majority of them mediated, commercially produced image-based texts. Any relationship between a text and its users occurs at a mutual, interactive 'meeting place', where:

> Mass communication becomes an act of invitation and sharing realities (or irrealities, depending on the medium). The more tempting the invitation, the more likely the reader or viewer is to accept it.[5]

This aspect of communication practice is bound tightly together with the notion of a dependency between particular forms of communication and their defining codes and conventions. Just as television has its codes and conventions, so do professional historians as 'incentives' that denote career status and recognition.[6] Clearly all these codes and conventions result in the past being 'told' in highly selective, distinct styles moving all the while towards producing preferred readings of the past.

One of the principal modes of engaging with TV-users adopted and practised by factual history presenters is the standard television convention of the 'piece to camera'. As a carefully crafted direct form of address to the camera, and through the lens, to the TV-user, this creates a relationship of familiarity, of friendship that allows the presenter to function as a personal guide. Once this relationship between presenter and TV-user has been created, it is cemented together by respect for authorial integrity and knowledge. It may also be bound together by the TV-user's appreciation of celebrity/personality status gained in another form of television or media-centred branch of communication/entertainment. In both cases, the presenter is the dominant force in the relationship and their view of an event is presented as to be beyond question.

In television history, as in academic history, the relationship between the presenter and the mode of presentation – storytelling, use of locations and archive footage – constructs and reconstructs the past. As Keith Jenkins observes, 'history relies on someone else's eyes and voice; we see through an interpreter who stands between past events and our readings of them'.[7]

As a point of focus, a secondary unit of articulation is gained through the use of location. When this is fused with a vibrant, enthusiastic screen presence and the ability to be a compelling storyteller, television 'historians' – not necessarily academic historians – have the freedom to reconstruct the past. Formalising

these components within each historian's inimitable style has significant parallels with Macaulay's intention of producing history as a drama with consecu-
tive acts complete with plots.[8] Although many producers and commissioning
executives clearly feel that the visual content of a programme is all-important,
Jeremy Isaacs believes that television history can be achieved without 'visual
aids', but not without the contribution of a historian.[9]

Regardless of screen captions that may introduce a presenter as a historian,
only a few names are regarded as true television historians operating within
their specialist subject areas. This can lead to the omission of contributions
that non-historians have made in front of the camera. Tom Stearn, like many
other critics, simply collapses the ecology of presenters into a perilously brief
genealogy that runs from A. J. P. Taylor to David Starkey and Simon Schama,
acknowledging Richard Holmes *en route*, and deriding the lack of academic
specialists fronting programmes.

> Today, however, there is a disquieting trend: presenters are apparently chosen
> because they are telegenic dishy dons, trendy in denim and leather, and they
> pronounce on subjects far from their own expertise. Yet there is really no sub-
> stitute for the enthusiastic expert who really knows and really cares – and the
> viewers can tell.[10]

What Stearn is ignoring in this biased mischief-making is that television,
just as society does, inexorably moves on. Factual television history production not only has to satisfy the needs of one generation, it has to ensure that
it evolves programme formats and styles that encourage and engage with new
TV-users. What Stearn may not take into consideration is that TV-users possess
different expectations and, more importantly, a range of attention spans that
may not be satisfied with Sister Wendy static in a gallery expounding on a
painting – however knowledgeable she proves to be.[11] Nor for that matter, are
they content to have 'the camera lingering on an authentic 18th-century painting while the historian explains it as a historical source',[12] despite how much
insight, expertise, and enthusiasm a historian may bring. TV-users who took
part in a BBC research survey on presenters, did not entirely agree with Stearn
on the merits of Sister Wendy.

> Her mannerisms were found irritating and she was perceived as being unpro-
> fessional and 'not authoritative'. Some felt her novelty value had worn off but
> others saw her as an 'endearing riveting amateur'.[13]

Exactly how many 'dishy dons in denim and leather' it needs to create a
'disquieting trend', Stearn never admits to, though Laurence Rees, Creative
Director of BBC History, believes this type of view represents a 'wholly mis-

informed criticism' by people who do not watch a lot of television history.[14] In fact, some of the criticism aimed at factual history programming, such as Stearn's, does appear to reflect a personal preference gained from engaging with a highly selective and prescriptive range of programmes.

As much as Stephen Badsey, a military historian and Reader in Conflict Studies at the University of Wolverhampton, may want all history programmes to be the work of historians,[15] television is not merely narrative-driven, it is also presence-driven. From the results of my TV-user research, it seems that TV-users of factual history would prefer anyone to guide them into the past as long as they can bring that past effortlessly into the present. In some cases, presenters were not regarded as essential by 11 per cent of TV-users, though 26 per cent did indicate that presenters were quite essential.[16]

From all the group survey responses regarding the desired attributes of presenters, the top three preferred qualities were the ability to make complex issues understandable at 44 per cent, enthusiasm at 42 per cent and specialist knowledge at 33 per cent. Having a solid reputation as a historian was considered important by only 12 per cent, with academic qualifications deemed necessary by just 7 per cent.[17]

Presentation, either on or off-screen, has been an integral feature of factual history on television from its nascent appearance in 1946. Factual history programming has tended to be a hybrid, combining the vision of key members of the documentary film movement – John Grierson, Paul Rotha, Alberto Cavalcanti and Humphrey Jennings – with the entertaining spectacle of the cinematic biopic. It is this endeavour to attain the difficult balance between giving a factual, authoritative educational base and providing a stimulating visual experience that entertains and informs that has endured.

This success has been created by on-screen historians and non-historians alike, voice-over narrators, some well known, others less so. Production-led creativity, technology, insight and, above all, an understanding that history on television can aspire to, and reach, academic standards, have played their part in creating some exceptional series. But first and foremost, history in all its variant forms on the small screen, must conform to the demands of television.

The ecology of presentation reveals how on-screen presenters doing their piece to camera at historic locations have become an intrinsic unit of active location work present throughout the development of factual history programming. The question of whether presenters are bona fide historians or not appears to be covert criticism masked behind questions of validity, research and evidence that detract from the great many series and non-academic presenters who have, in their own way, created genre footprints still visible today.

New formats, new presenters

Naturally, academic historians feel themselves eminently qualified to present history on television. Producers too may accept that historians have a part to play in programme-making, though from the evidence of major series so far produced since 1946, this does not automatically guarantee a historian a place in front of the camera.

For the early non-historians recruited to present the past, a background in factual television and/or print journalism coupled with a screen presence capable of imparting knowledge and authority provided an established route set by Richard Dimbleby in 1949 with *London Town*. With Dimbleby setting the style of effortlessly conveying facts in a narrative designed to entertain, other early presenters added their own inimitable characteristics. Brian Horrocks, Wynford Vaughan-Thomas, John Betjeman, James Cameron, Brian Inglis, Malcolm Muggeridge, Robert Kee, Ludovic Kennedy, Magnus Magnusson, Rene Cutforth, Alistair Cooke and Arthur Negus systematically transformed the factual series into a vehicle that proved it was eminently capable of carrying a considerable amount of material as Fact Ent.

It is a format that has the advantage of not only engaging with TV-users through a logical framework that employs powerful emotive triggers but also ensuring that the narrative has an enduring effect, a factor recognised as an integral component of propaganda as the combination of the rational with the irrational.[18] The success of some on-screen historians rests with their ability to provide a factual core of information within an emotive casing. Revealing a trace of his Icelandic roots, Magnus Magnusson had a steely, almost detached mode of delivering his pieces to camera that verged on the confrontational, of offering a challenge to TV-users to pay the past the respect that it deserved.

The overwhelming impression of Magnusson is of a stickler for detail, of someone who has taken the trouble to do his research and, as a result, expects complete engagement from TV-users. On screen, Magnusson came across as a likeable but rather severe headmaster, who somehow might have the power to notice if anyone was not paying attention or had slipped out of their living room, and who was eminently capable of delivering a severe ticking off on their return.

Trained as a journalist, Magnusson's ability to reduce his material into a condensed form was ideal preparation for the demands of factual history programming that went beyond the bounds of *Chronicle*. In 1977, he demonstrated his passion for attempting to reconcile myth with reality, in *B.C. Archaeology of the Bible Lands* (BBC2, 1977), a twelve-part series, and the ten-part *Vikings!* (BBC2, 1980). Magnusson was equally at home and adept at exploding popular myth as he went about getting to the roots of well known characters in *Living Legends*, and it is this effortless versatility and passionate engagement with his chosen subject that allowed Magnusson to present the past so professionally.

From the late 1970s, however, there has been a fundamental shift from the old school of Vaughan-Thomas, Muggeridge, Fyfe Robertson and Macdonald Hastings, to a much more pronouncedly lighter style of presentation, done, on the whole, by celebrities. Whereas John Betjeman developed familiarity as a household name, beginning a cult of personality-as-presenter for factual history programmes, many celebrity presenters have little to offer other than their own screen persona. Betjeman, for instance, brought an idiosyncratic appeal to his passion for architecture as he toured and discussed stately homes with Arthur Negus in *Pride of Place* (BBC1, 1966) or recalled the age of steam in *Let's Imagine* – 'A Branch Line Railway' (BBC, 1963), screened the same year that Beeching's Report recommended a drastic closure plan for the branch line network.

Betjeman's secondary career as a television presenter, cementing his poet's imagination around a lifelong appreciation and knowledge of architecture, enabled him to face the camera with respected authority. Betjeman's determination, his passion for a building, an architectural style, a way of living long gone or slowly disappearing, is a powerful yet understated force in his style of presenting. This subtle ability to make the screen his own may account for a BBC cataloguer's despair when reviewing original footage of Betjeman at work. Cataloguing an edition of the *Contrasts* arts magazine series presumably for use as potential stock library footage, 'Marble Arch to Edgware Road' broadcast on 31 January 1968, the cataloguer dourly notes 'JOHN BETJEMAN on an historical journey along the Edgware Road (he is in almost every shot).'[19]

Given that Betjeman could demonstrate a proven career provenance in architecture that flowed naturally into his history programmes, there only appears a tenuous link between fictional detective work and the real thing when Stratford Johns and Frank Windsor attempt to unravel the Jack the Ripper case. Presented by two of the BBC's most successful fictional detectives, Chief Superintendent Charlie Barlow (Stratford Johns) and Chief Superintendent John Watt (Frank Windsor) from *Z-Cars* (BBC1, 1962–78) and *Softly, Softly: Task Force* (BBC1, 1969–76) it brought a quirky introduction to the celebrity/personality crossover from fiction to fact. The fictional detectives reinvestigating the Whitechapel murders of 1888 not only combined their own mythical powers of detection with the mythical elusiveness of the Ripper but pooled the whole historical narrative into fact, fantasy and fiction.

Extending his role as a BBC film critic and reviewer, Barry Norman's biopic series *Hollywood Greats* (BBC1, 1977) and *The British Greats* (BBC1, 1980) anchored and developed his investigation on what made a star into his normal sphere of presentation. This type of natural extension also saw James Burke's seven-year run as a presenter on the science and technology series *Tomorrow's World* (BBC1, 1965–2003) flow into his ten-part investigation into the history of technology in *James Burke's Connections*. These spheres of mutual inclusion attracting regular TV-users of *Tomorrow's World* maximised *Connections'* chance of success, allowing it a 7.20–8.10 p.m. Tuesday slot, which would do no harm in either promoting or encouraging sales from the accompanying book from a series that generated healthy ratings of 7.9 million.[20]

Renowned for his intellectual chairmanship of Granada's *University Challenge* (ITV, 1962–87), Bamber Gascoigne aptly demonstrated his interest in history by writing and presenting *The Christians, Victorian Values* (ITV, 1987), *Man and Music* (C4, 1987–89) and *The Great Moghuls* (C4, 1990). Some series presented by celebrities did not share Gascoigne's in-depth academic rigour. Donald Sinden, an actor, presented *Discovering English Churches* (BBC2, 1979), and Gordon Honeycombe, an ITN newsreader, took history into the personal forum with *Family History*. Fred Housego, taxi-driver and winner of the 1980 BBC's *Mastermind*, investigated different towns and cities with *History on Your Doorstep* (BBC2, 1982), and Graeme Garden, a writer and comedian, brought his inimitable style to *A Sense of the Past* (ITV, 1983/86). All of them may have tried their hand at giving the past a fresh edge, though for many would be historians, their first series was also their last.

Bringing her current affairs weight from the BBC's *Newsnight* (BBC2, 1980–), Kirsty Wark used her sharp journalistic skills to probe questions of heritage in *One Foot in the Past* (BBC2, 1993–2000). As well as narrating four episodes of *Timewatch*, Wark also chaired a *Timewatch* studio discussion on Andrew Roberts' investigation into British rule in India (BBC2, 1998). Capitalising on her Scottish background, Wark examined Scottish politics and architecture in *A Restless Nation* (BBC1, 1991) and *Building a Nation* (BBC2, 1999). Wark's own production company, Wark Clements & Co (no longer in operation) set up with her husband John Clements, created both of the series she presented on Scottish development for the BBC.

Given a prestigious Sunday evening peak time transmission, a scheduling strategy previously enjoyed by Kenneth Clark's *Civilisation* and Alistair

Cooke's *America* (BBC2, 1972), Ronald Harwood's *All the World's a Stage* (BBC2, 1984), a thirteen-part historical exploration of drama and the theatre, failed to live up to its co-production budget and brought the playwright mixed reviews.[21] Understanding the advantages and limitations of television as a vehicle for history is evident in the way that Tony Robinson has evolved from playing 'Baldrick', Rowan Atkinson's foil in the historical comedy series *Black-adder* (BBC1, 1983–89), to presenting the archaeological series *Time Team*.

Creating a new angle on how history can be attractive to TV-users has seen Robinson host *History Hunters* (C4, 1998) employing a similar two-day 'challenge' scenario as *Time Team*, featuring enthusiastic local historians attempting to discover more about their local past. Once this niche market has been established, the convergence between Robinson as celebrity actor and Robinson as a respected 'face' for archaeology/history is accelerated.

In turn, this formulates a brand persona complete with added brand value that places a prestige on Robinson as a presentation commodity, differentiating him from other branded presenters. It also sustains Channel 4's reputation as a manufacturer of original history programming, thereby ensuring loyalty, and persuading new TV-users to sample the format.

As soon as a presenter is established as a successful brand through the recommissioning of series, any new formats are securely anchored through the presenter-as-brand formula, complete with associated meanings,[22] by placing more prominence on the brand and not the product. Hence, *Tony Robinson's Romans* (C4, 2003), *Tony Robinson's Titanic Adventure* (C4, 2006), a one-off documentary charting Robinson's trip to the site of the wreck, and *Tony Robinson's Crime and Punishment* (C4, 2008) bear this proprietorial stamp. Yet further new series or one-offs are often referred to as 'Tony Robinson's…', clearly marking this reproduction of the past as being founded on the quality and success of Robinson as a brand, the production company involved and the channel.

The Worst Jobs in History (C4, 2006) format, covering a wide range of occupations, had Robinson back in character as he re-enacts working lives and working practices from the past. This return to historical characters creates tension between Robinson's *Time Team* contemporary 'factual' persona and the dramatic foolishness and irreverence of Baldrick. No matter how gruelling the jobs, how authentically reconstructed, Robinson 'dressed' as various historical characters threatens the factual experience because expectations of him in costume are forever bound with Baldrick. Two of the reviews of his recent series *Crime and Punishment* highlight this dichotomy.

> There is a wonderfully Baldrickian moment during the opening episode of Channel 4's new four-part history series [...] This, of course, is what Tony Robinson does best: making supposedly dry and dusty subjects sound fresh and funny.[23]

Sam Wollaston in the *Guardian* comes to a similar conclusion:

> Tony Robinson is a man who never looks happier than when he's rummaging around in the past, especially if there's muck involved. It all probably stems from having once been Baldrick [...] He's a nice guide, steering an amiable course between scholarly and silly.[24]

There is a danger, however, that this transference of one media-friendly persona for another in an attempt to lock two different career paths together, can, far from building a trusted brand like Robinson, diminish or devalue the product on offer. Rory McGrath's celebrity status as a comedian and comedy writer has not achieved the same brand value as Robinson, or managed to build a sustainable channel platform. Moving from the BBC Knowledge channel with the *History Fix* (1999–2000) and *History Quest* (2000), to ITV and *Killer Queens* (ITV1, 2002) and to the Discovery Channel with the ten-part *Bloody Britain* (2003), McGrath has not found the same loyal niche market of TV-users as Robinson.

McGrath's brand of history is a direct visual parallel to Terry Deary's *Horrible Histories,* a series of history books aimed primarily at young readers, with cartoon-style illustrations by Martin Brown. Of course, broadening the appeal of television history has its merits, forming a basic structure that McGrath has exploited in his investigative series *History Fix*, whilst using *Bloody Britain* as Nick Knowles did with *Historyonics* and Terry Jones' *Medieval Lives* (BBC2, 2004), as a format for injecting their own style of humour into the past.

Both McGrath and Knowles make assertive claims that history can be boring, in McGrath's case during his adolescence 'When I was at school my heart would sink when our teacher entered the room for double history. Such a boring subject.'[25] As a new personality/historian/presenter, Knowles arrogantly declared that nothing produced as television history over the last three decades has served television or history well, not even Simon Schama's *History of Britain.*

> *Historyonics* – the brainchild of Nick Knowles – takes a far from conventional approach to retelling past events. 'If you've watched programmes by the likes of Simon Schama you've probably fallen asleep,' argues Knowles. 'History programming for the last 30 years has been so boring – it's like someone teaching it at school. What I wanted to do was make something you could really laugh

at and learn something along the way.' Howls of derision are likely from some academics over Historyonics – but Nick Knowles welcomes the prospect. 'I'm really hoping I get some flak from those pompous old windbags who've made history the boring subject it is on TV,' the man better known for fronting *DIY SOS* says with relish.[26]

More used to having paint rather than egg on his face, Knowles may have attempted to apply the soap and sit-com conventions of masking or inserting serious issues beneath comic material. However for the television critic *of The Daily Telegraph*, Stephen Pile, *Historyonics* was 'a dire programme … this was history as pantomime for the supposedly pig ignorant children of our island',[27] and Knowles' dumbing-down of history found no favours with Charlie Courtauld *of The Independent on Sunday*:

> It was embarrassing rather than funny. Nick Knowles, familiar from *DIY SOS*, did his usual bish-bash-botch paint job, only this time it was the Battle of Hastings which took the beating rather than somebody's poor kitchen … It was very much in the vein of Terry Jones' Medieval Lives; but crasser and less jolly … truth in history matters – and this show preferred entertainment to fact. As a result, it was neither funny nor historically interesting.[28]

If Knowles had taken an unexpected, but not undeserved, critical pummelling by the pens of broadsheet reviewers, one might have thought that *The Daily Star* could have been rather more generous. Yet Simon Edge found that Knowles' attempt to prop up his lame series by having a historian on hand to verify historical facts was far worse than the half-witted comedy, stretching credulity to beyond breaking point: 'What really cracked me up was Prof Ronald Hutton MA (Cantab) DPhil (Oxon) who was there to convince us that it was serious history. That may have been a spoof too far.'[29] James Walton reviewing the weekend's television for the *Daily Telegraph*, found it 'rather brilliant', though perhaps this was from its innovative use of Motorhead's *Ace of Spades* as a backing track for the Battle of Hastings 'dramatised in scenes that owed something to Monty Python and the works of Ernie Wise, but primarily drew on panto'.[30]

In all three series – *Bloody Britain*, *Medieval Lives* and *Historyonics*, the convergence of celebrity personas into a serious documentary branded presenter requires the assistance of academic historians to supply validity – on or off screen – as a recognised mode of presenting the 'truth'.

Terry Jones sets himself this near impossible task with *Gladiators* – 'The Brutal Truth' (BBC2, 2000) and his two-part documentary *Hidden Histories* (BBC2, 2003), dealing with Egypt and Rome as a means of exposing the 'truth'. A medieval specialist from Oxford, Henrietta Leyser, worked as a consultant on Terry Jones' *Medieval Lives*, whilst McGrath's 'bouncy enthusiasm' on his reconstruction of life during the Battle of Trafalgar,[31] in part four of his *Bloody Britain*, had no doubt been extensively researched to provide factual accuracy. This left McGrath the serious business of demonstrating the effects of the cat o' nine tails on a dead pig. Framed and shot as a scribe checking facts, Ronald Hutton provided *Historyonics* and Knowles with more credibility than it deserved.

This mode of celebrity presenter marks a paradigm shift away from perceived authority figures with extensive experience in an appropriate field, such as Lieutenant General Sir Brian Horrocks, or from those with charisma and a screen presence that made investigating the past a natural adjunct to their craft as journalists and writers.

There can be no doubt that presentation in the late 1990s and early 2000s has moved distinctly towards turning the past into histotainment. Some presenters have the passion for history that allows them to present the past as a natural extension of their popular characters that has endeared them to TV-users in other non-history formats. Whether it is acting as Isambard Kingdom Brunel's advocate in *Great Britons*, or as writer and presenter of *The Victoria Cross: For Valour* (BBC2, 2003), Jeremy Clarkson, a motoring pundit, along with Fred Dibnah, steeplejack, demonstrate that their passion for the past is not an exclusive attribute of the professional historian.

Whether academic historians functioned as on-screen presenters and contributors, or non-historians served as presenters and narrators, the 1980s heralded a significant advance in factual history programming in both its type of presenters and style.

Yet the increase of history on our screen from the early 1990s cannot solely be laid at the doors of Starkey or Schama, influential as they are, because history programming has gradually adapted, developed and experimented in order for it to find its feet in terms of formats that attract TV-users.

With CGI firmly established as an integral addition to the programme maker's toolbox, how factual history programmes will develop around a presenter-led format is a moot point. For the BBC's specialist factual commissioner, Martin Davidson, there still seems to be faith in the presenter driven format:

> Davidson is keen to avoid the traditional 'voice of God' off-screen narrators – he wants more presenter-led histories. 'I am looking to bring on the next generation of presenters,' he says. 'History is one of those areas where I feel audiences

recognise knowledge, authority, passion.' Davidson is currently wooing Bettany Hughes, whose television work has included The Spartans and When the Moors Ruled in Europe on Channel 4. 'We can't just have men,' he says.[32]

Presumably, this 'next generation' includes Jeremy Paxman, a long-standing BBC journalist, presenter of *Newsnight*, host of *University Challenge* (BBC2, 1994–) and now a television historian with what the BBC Press Office claim yet again to be a 'landmark' series – in the four-part *The Victorians* (BBC1, 2009).

Retracing already well-trodden academic footprints, the programme-makers have come to the not so startling discovery that the Victorian artwork around which the series is based, 'was the cinema of its day. Viewed in the context of today, Victorian paintings offer a uniquely vivid, almost documentary account of the dramatic upheavals of the age'.[33] Paxman, no doubt to satisfy commissioning demands for action as a sop for the non-moving paintings, embraces Victorian experiences by relying on preserved mills or Victorian town halls that can be utilised as dynamic television illustrations.

The opening part, 'Painting the Town', set the historical tone and level of inquiry for Paxman's series. Directed by John Hay, written and presented by Paxman, here again was the crossover of a brand persona from the gladiatorial, combative *Newsnight* interviewer/interrogator into social historian.

Opening the programme with a summarisation on Victorian Britain from Dickens' *Tale of Two Cities* (1859), 'It was the best of times, it was the worst of times,' Paxman spent the next fifty-nine minutes creating a simplified comparative history of two extremes. Victorian paintings, Paxman promised, 'tell amazing stories', though the programme never covered any of the complex middle-ground between Paxman's polar extremes of Victorian society consisting of innovation and creativity versus poverty and degradation.

There is no doubt that Paxman is a seasoned and consummate professional in front of the camera with an interest for his subject as he indirectly explains how Victorian paintings functioned as social propaganda. Despite the *Radio Times* warning TV-users: 'You may groan at the thought of another suit-wearing senior broadcaster with a sweeping history about Britain,' the series and Paxman were praised for undercutting the 'heritage-TV look'.[34] But this has been overlaid by Paxman slamming dividing doors in a preserved workhouse as he describes how families were cruelly separated and categorised, before sampling gruel and smashing rocks with a sledgehammer presumably because no paintings of these Victorian scenes could be located.

Life in northern mills, driven by the Industrial Revolution – reinforcing the 'grim up north' myth – was, according to Paxman, hard, dangerous and dirty by comparison with their symbolic representation in Frederic James Shields' *Factory Girls at the Old Clothes Fair* (1875), or Eyre Crowe's *The Dinner Hour, Wigan* (1874). For artists there is a long tradition of producing 'beautiful' social propaganda as a commercial venture. The contracts between painters and their clients during the Renaissance aptly demonstrate this,[35] though Paxman made it appear a Victorian phenomenon. History then became a series of dramatic generalisations – 'rumours had reached the most remote villages and hamlets',[36] for instance – as Paxman, steering a canal barge, described the intensity of cultural change powered by the Industrial Revolution.

Paxman may have displayed passion of a sorts in his interpretation of the past, however his *Newsnight* persona trait of cynicism never seemed far from his inquisitorial style as a social historian. Despite the opening programme being praised as 'sharp, stimulating TV',[37] Paxman's generalisations as he glossed over ambiguities, simplifying Victorian society, meant that at times he appeared as: 'no great expert on his topic. He said that Victorian art "doesn't generally change hands for millions of pounds in auction rooms" while standing by one of Dante Gabriele Rossetti's portraits – which most certainly would do precisely that.'[38] Where some of the visual impact was at its strongest was not in paintings but in the cutaways.

In part two, 'Home Sweet Home', the cutaways following an observation by Paxman on the virtues or vices of Victorian home life are jarring, discordant, made up of random contemporary street scenes of mothers pushing prams, parents walking with children.

The cutaways in *The Victorians* only heighten the sense of history skimmed from the surface, rather than connecting past and present, as Paxman attempts to do in his pieces to camera and voice-overs. These snapshots of modern Britain force the past into a corner, making it more remote, a completely different 'Other' that has no bearing on the sophisticated, self-assured present that Paxman seemed more comfortable with than the past. Moving from one form of factual television does not necessarily ensure expertise in presenting factual history-based programming.

Not the first BBC series to uncover the story behind paintings, the twelve-part *Outlook: Painting in England 1700–1850* (BBC2, 1967) had also touched on Victorian life. Regional identity emerged from inside gilded frames with HTV West's *History on Canvas* (ITV, 1994), examining Bristol through the eyes of different artists. For Channel 4, Christopher Wood, an art historian, provided an informed insight into the social and cultural life of the Victorians in the six-part *Painters to the People* (C4, 1990), repeated by Discovery in 1993.

For Paxman and other professional historians involved in this new phase of factual programming, their success as 'active', on-screen practitioners will inevitably produce some new faces as 'television historians', though how many will actually become telly-dons, continuing a cult initiated in 1946 with Roger Manvell's *Early History of the Film*, and firmly established with A. J. P. Taylor remains to be seen.

The cult of the telly-don

Academia, according to Simon Schama, fails to believe or see how television history can be taken seriously, as it is not primarily a print medium, relies on images and must be practised by full-time 'trained' historians.[39] Coming out in defence of television history, Schama asserts that the Western tradition has been founded on, and developed from, non-print formats such as the oral and 'performative' tradition, with A. J. P. Taylor cited as the pioneer of television history.[40] Placing A. J. P. Taylor as the first historian to embrace television as a means of presenting the past to a non-academic audience, Jeremy Isaacs reasons that the historian alone, unaided by notes, graphics, images or special effects, is not an anathema to television history production because 'an intelligent talking-head is always visually compelling. A.J.P. Taylor's certainly was'.[41]

There is a no-nonsense, frank approach about Taylor's television lectures. In part one of his 1977 series for the BBC, *How Wars Begin* – 'The First Modern War: From French Revolution to French Empire', Taylor simply delivers the past informatively, without pomp or ceremony. The post-production script for this episode runs to seven pages and at no point is any extraneous material in the form of visual accessories allowed to disrupt Taylor's flow.[42] After the opening titles, accompanied by the *Lacrymosa* from Benjamin Britten's *Sinfonia da Requiem*, op. 20,[43] Taylor engages TV-users with the past without unnecessary preamble: 'Ladies and Gentlemen, well how *do* wars begin?'[44]

Although Taylor Downing claims that a return to the presenter-led format 'attracted millions of viewers to history who have never picked up an academic history book',[45] the presenter had never been absent, either as a non-historian or as historian. What is constantly, and sometimes conveniently, overlooked is that Michael Wood, David Starkey, Richard Holmes and Simon Schama were developing a personal style of presentation that had been honed to some considerable degree by previous presenters:

- Barry Cunliffe
  Outlook: Roman Britain (BBC2, 1966)
  Cradle of England (BBC1, 1972)
  The Making of the English (BBC1, 1973)

- Alec Clifton-Taylor
  Six English Towns (BBC2, 1978)
  Six More English Towns (BBC2, 1981)
  Another Six English Towns (BBC2, 1984)

- Anthony Burton
  The Past at Work (BBC2, 1980)
  The Past Afloat (BBC2, 1982)
  The Rise and Fall of King Cotton (BBC2, 1984)

Their contribution in a range of series provided a solid interpretation of the past that may not have had the range of John Roberts' *The Triumph of the West*, but each of them essentially championed the role of the informative historian as a presenter.

Michael Wood, perhaps the original role model for Stearn's mythical band of 'telegenic dishy dons',[46] has a natural screen presence that is 'liked in particular by women';[47] according to a 2001 BBC TV-user's research survey. Wood's secret of being able to tempt TV-users to sample historical journeys they may not have taken by themselves – looks would not be a good enough reason alone – is to construct programmes that Wood believes are: 'visually entertaining, exciting, accurate in their facts, provide a good arc of narrative and ensure an emotional grip on their audience'.[48] Jeremy Clarkson, not averse to wearing blue jeans and a Second World War leather flying jacket on occasion, can also turn the past into an entertaining adventure, especially when dealing with heroism, yet he lacks Wood's consummate knowledge.

This in-depth approach underwrites Wood's ability to create a contract with TV-users based on mutual trust that his experience and research will provide them with a rewarding programme. Praise for Wood's 1980 *In Search of…* series for the BBC was fulsome, described as 'compulsively watchable'.[49] Wood acknowledges that managing and presenting history within an allotted programme time frame of thirty-minutes or an hour inevitably constrains the presentation of the past.[50] For him, programmes have to be 'aesthetically satisfying, visually entertaining and accurate',[51] but above all, they must create what he terms as an 'emotional curve' in order to engage with TV-users.[52] What Wood regards as a threat to good television history, allowing it to be become

A. J. P. Taylor, an 'intelligent talking-head'   **3**

'vacuous and silly',[53] can only be guarded against by presenters who have a natural authority to inspire a genuine interest in the past, and David Starkey, like Wood, has demonstrated this ability throughout his television career.

David Starkey's rise to the status of telly-don, confirmed by his inclusion as a character in the comedy impressions show *Dead Ringers* (BBC2, 2003), played by Kevin Connelly, was no overnight ascendancy. His screen work included presenting episodes in *This Land of England* (C4, 1985), *The Making of Britain* (C4, 1985/1986), *Late Great Britons*, and *Henry VIII* (C4, 1988), before *Elizabeth* and *Monarchy* demonstrated that a relatively large TV-user share could be raised with an intelligent approach to the past. Generating over three million TV-users, Starkey puts the success of *Elizabeth* down to TV-user preferences:

> Programmes are like books, sometimes a success is planned, it's foreseen, is organised. Sometimes it is simply that a large number of people see something

that they like, and that was it, and of course from that point onwards you have this immense rush of imitative programming.[54]

Of course, the key to successfully presenting the past as contextualised phases of history is the vital interplay between narrative and a presenter's ability to handle narrative and convey a real sense of authority.[55] As Laurence Rees admits, 'as a general rule television is a profoundly narrative driven media', which for David Starkey highlights the strength of television in encapsulating stories within a dramatic framework of motivating forces.

> What television does extremely well is character and narrative, and it is brilliant for both of those, which is why in a medium or why in a form that combines the two of them, the soap opera works so brilliantly on television.[56]

Clearly then the narrative serves some purpose other than ensuring that the programme begins at point A, passes through point B and arrives at point C. Producing a discourse structure that TV-users can engage with requires characters and an environment from which their 'story' can be told. This systematic production of enunciation is not restricted to characters. Much in the same way that a literary text constructs spectator positions through what Shlomith Rimmon-Kenan identifies as 'focalization',[57] many factual history programmes rely on the presenter as a 'focalizer', functioning as a valued guide and interpreter.

Demonstrating this dominant bardic role, Kenneth Clark in part one of *Civilisation*, 'The Skin of our Teeth', transmitted on 23 February 1969, dryly observes, 'It took Gibbon nine volumes to describe the rise and fall of the Roman Empire and I'm not going to attempt that.' What he does do in this second segment, 'The Quest for Civilisation', is to use his personality, knowledge, experience and authority as a screen persona. This acts as a prism through which location and narrative are drawn and organised as supplementary commentary to Clark's masterful pieces to camera or bridging voice-overs.

The Quest for Civilisation

- Clark, standing on the Pont des Arts in Paris as he gives his piece to camera, mid-shot, wearing a brown suit, shirt and tie, asks: 'Is civilisation worth preserving?'
- Clark outlines the central theme: the period when Rome collapsed is a framework for the essential question, 'What is civilisation?' Clark concedes, 'I don't know–', adding, 'I can't define it in abstract terms.'
- As the camera pans along the Seine, Clark proposes that buildings – the very architecture – are civilisation.

- Clark voice-over states that barbarians created art, but it cannot be classed as civilisation.
- Clark proposes that Hellenistic imagination is superior to Viking or Northern imagination, and this is supported by shots of the Apollo of the Belvedere. Clark goes on to affirm that classical Greek and Roman art expresses and articulates a culture's desires. 'The children of his imagination are also the expressions of an ideal.'
- Voice-over as architecture from the Greco-Roman period appears on screen, including the Pont du Gard aqueduct at Nîmes.
- Back on Clark below the aqueduct: 'What happened? It took Gibbon nine volumes to describe the rise and fall of the Roman Empire and I'm not going to attempt that.'
- Tight mid-shot of Clark framed under the aqueduct. 'Civilisation requires confidence.' Clark then makes his proposition – 'Rome collapsed because it was exhausted.'
- Cut-to a frieze depicting a battle that is meant to represent the invasion and attacks of the Barbarians as Clark describes how the Northern tribes demonstrated a destructive tendency towards anything they couldn't understand. Here Clark's acerbic wit reflects a slight hint of class prejudice as he notes how the Barbarians 'preferred to live in pre-fabs and let the old places fall down'.

Clark's skill is being able to effortlessly weave together a complex insight into European development that neither simplifies nor talks down to TV-users. Here then, Clark becomes the historian/presenter as a bardic figure, a Shakespearian narrator, making the introduction, ushering in new scenes, closing old ones – what Daniel Dayan and Elihu Katz refer to as the 'highlighting process' that naturalises the television message. Accordingly, 'Television converts pronouncements of authority into exercises in seduction.'[58]

Being adept at seducing TV-users in Clark's style is a feature associated with Schama's delivery in *History of Britain*. In fact, *History of Britain* broke little new ground as far as formats go. As Jeremy Smither suggests, conventions that seem relatively fresh in *History of Britain* – reconstructions, no reliance on talking-heads because of Schama's on-screen performance – are nothing new and can be traced to *You Are There*, *Culloden* and *War Walks*, all employing one or all of the elements used by Schama.[59] If the series, according to Smither, reduced a need to have archive footage,[60] though this would not have been possible for much of the series in any case, using instead re-enactment groups, this is merely a format update on Clark's cutaways to paintings and sculpture to depict battles and events.

What all on-screen presenters achieve, whether they are aware of it or not, is being able to function as an 'official voice', representing what Jung identified as the archetypal figure of the 'wise old man'.[61] History, through its oral tradition, has always accommodated collective memory as an agent of storytelling framed by an archetypal position of narration. The narrator, a culturally located, knowledgeable bard – privileged by the fact that he or she has been 'chosen' to appear on television – produces narratives tightly controlled by binary opposition. These stories when 'told' as the framework for television history display causal effects and reactions that reinforce the morality of how and why citizenship, nation and nationality have evolved.

Though Schama does have his critics and has had to robustly defend *History of Britain*, it is usually by having to repudiate the claim by academics and critics that the series 'has been all kings and queens'.[62] Schama is also quick to dismiss the criticism that what in print would be read by academics as a scholarly piece of research into royal marriage and divorce is quickly accused of being nothing more than a 'soap opera' when included in a television history programme.[63] Here again is the paradox that academic work confined to print and designed primarily not to reach a large and popular audience is judged and assessed against the conventions of academic research; whereas television history, on the other hand, is automatically judged against other factual and fictional forms within its genres and compared to other popular forms such as drama and soap operas. A rather different accusation levelled against Schama and the producers of *History of Britain* comes in Martin Smith's polemical attack in *History Today*. Smith, a 'maker of documentaries and history films for television for over thirty years', attacks the production team, and Schama, by accusing them of cheating, and 'hoodwinking' the public over their use of archive film and reconstructions, though ruefully admits that he has also employed similar deceptions.[64]

In an industry where the conventions of programme-making are paramount, the manipulation of footage for instance, using specially shot footage of one location to represent another, seems for some programme-makers an acceptable price to pay in achieving good television. Gerda Jansen Hendriks, a trained historian and documentary film-maker, offers some startlingly naïve claims on the manipulation of reality, arguing that this has no bearing on historical accuracy.

By insisting that passing off archive footage from a different event as representing a totally unrelated story poses no threat to factual history programming, Hendriks is doing both television and history an injustice. This is particularly so when she claims that the appropriated footage was faked, distorted and therefore only symbolic.

> I deliberately made it that way [...] I must admit that I have learned on several occasions that most viewers do not take notice: they simply believe what they see. But I think that historians should not believe what they see, and should be very aware of all the tricks that filmmakers use to tell their stories.[65]

Just why anyone should be aware of deliberate covert deception, Hendriks does not say. Programme-makers such as Hendriks have an obligation to produce accurate formats without faking or cheating with visual elements simply because they believe this makes for good television, creating nothing less than an elliptical illusion.

Regardless of whether it is an academic historian or a personality/celebrity as presenter, one of the main problems in television history is that of control. The conflict between television professionals and professional historians often leads to a series of choices being made that, more often than not, have nothing whatsoever to do with the history element, but more with programme conventions designed to provide a tight, visually adhesive entertaining experience.

Accordingly, this pressure from television on the format and style of programmes is a factor in bringing history to a wider audience, argues Schama.[66] Budgets, scheduling and out-manoeuvring rival producers all impact on what becomes television history. The actual making of programmes has, for Schama, limitations through the conventions demanded by television. Constructing a programme requires an astute balancing act because Schama and his producers are 'attempting, in effect, to create a drama; to deliver the immediacy of a past world, but do it on a documentary budget'.[67] However, this professional responsibility to protect the past is always going to be in conflict with the demand to produce good television. Documentaries and factual series are no different from other television production commodities, capable of being bought, sold and co-produced in an international marketplace. Major factual history programmes are subject to the same market forces, particularly in terms of their appeal across large TV-user groups internationally.

This inevitably leads to formula-led programmes where the common denominator equates with appeal, profit and future sales. Co-production may stimulate new factual history projects, though they also bring an increasing danger that programmes produced in this way for international TV-users do fall into the trap of trying to be something for everyone.[68]

Time and money are the dual motivators of television production. Factual history programmes are no exception merely because they are dealing with such a sprawling chain of complex events. Factual series have to be tamed and managed within the confines of programme timings, scheduling and production budgets, which means that much ellipsis takes place as a necessity of production values. This also includes professional and personal values and beliefs.

History is always going to be crucial as a subject, and as much as some historians may prefer to deny it, as a prime commodity for popular history production, including television. When 'two-thirds of Britons have no idea why Guy Fawkes Night is celebrated',[69] or '36 per cent of 18 to 24-year-olds said Dame Ellen MacArthur was the first British person to sail around the world',[70] there is a real danger that history is in parlous state and will be deemed unimportant by future generations of TV-users.

Television history, however, should neither be dismissed as somehow being an inferior method of education nor overlooked that it can also entertain as it delivers its message on the past. National and regional histories are the dual nuclei of national self-image, constantly being redefined and remodelled.

For history to remain a successful genre, historians and critics are going to have to come to accept that formats that may not be to their personal liking offer the only opportunity to speak to certain groups of TV-users. Whether historians choose to take more of an active role or sit back as the past is entirely subsumed into histotainment, is going to require some difficult decisions.

Notes

1 A. L. Poole, *From Domesday Book to Magna Carta, 1087–1216* (Oxford: Clarendon Press, 2nd edn, 1955), p. 264.
2 Derek Pearsall, 'The visual world of the Middle Ages', in Boris Ford (ed.), *The New Pelican Guide to English Literature, Vol. 1, Medieval Literature, Part One: Chaucer and the Alliterative Tradition* (Harmondsworth: Penguin, rev. edn, 1982), p. 315.
3 Pearsall, 'Visual world of the Middle Ages', p. 315.
4 Starkey, interview with the author.
5 Sven Windahl, Benno H. Signitzer and Jean T. Olson, *Using Communication Theory* (London: Sage Publications, 1992), p. 137.
6 Davies, *Empiricism and History*, p. 127.
7 Keith Jenkins, *Re-thinking History* (London: Routledge, 1991), p. 12.
8 Macaulay, *History of England Vol. 1*, p. 3.
9 Isaacs, 'All Our Yesterdays', in Cannadine (ed.), *History and the Media*, p. 37.
10 Stearn, 'What's wrong with television history?', 26.
11 Stearn, 'What's wrong with television history?', p. 27.

12 Stearn, 'What's wrong with television history?', p. 27.

13 Ashley Davies, 'BBC2 Presenters Branded "Stiff and Stuffy"', www.guardian.co.uk/media/2001/may/04/bbc.broadcasting3.

14 Rees, interview with the author.

15 Michael Nelson, 'It may be history, but is it true?: The Imperial War Museum Conference', *Historical Journal of Film, Radio and Television*, 25:1 (2005), 141.

16 Data from TV-user survey, All Groups.

17 Data from TV-user survey, All Groups.

18 Foulkes, *Literature and Propaganda*, p. 11.

19 *Contrasts* – 'Marble Arch to Edgware Road', BBC Programme Catalogue

20 WAC, R9/37/14, BBC TV Viewing Barometer, *James Burke's Connections*, undated.

21 Anthony Masters 'Worthy Pursuit of the Miraculous', *The Times* (15 March 1984), p. 13.

22 Greg Myers, *Ad Worlds: Brands, Media, Audiences* (London: Arnold, 1999), pp. 6–7.

23 Andre Pettie, 'Tony Robinson's Crime and Punishment', www.telegraph.co.uk/culture/tvandradio/3673824/Tony-Robinsons-Crime-and-Punishment.html.

24 Sam Wollaston, 'Last Night's TV', www.guardian.co.uk/media/2008/jun/02/television.tvandradioarts.

25 Rory McGrath, 'Review TV; Why I Think History Is Bloody Marvellous', *Sunday Express* (4 April 2004), p. 65.

26 Nick Knowles, the author's transcript of a Teletext Report on Knowles' new history show – *Historyonics*, 9.32 a.m. (30 March 2004), Teletext page 135, this transcript taken from page 135's rolling pages 4,5 and 6.

27 Stephen Pile, 'Sometimes It Pays to Keep Up', *Daily Telegraph* (17 April 2004), p. 19.

28 Charlie Courtauld, 'Television: Get in Touch With Your Inner Thug', *Independent on Sunday* (11 April 2004), p. 11.

29 Simon Edge, 'Simon Edge … On Last Night's Telly', *Daily Star* (5 April 2004), p. 35.

30 James Walton, 'The Weekend on Television: Funny About That', *Daily Telegraph* (5 April 2004), p. 22.

31 James Rampton, 'Satellite, Cable and Digital Pick of the Day', *Independent* (5 April 2004), p. 20.

32 Brown, 'The End of an Era', guardian.co.uk

33 *The Victorians*, BBC Press Office www.bbc.co.uk/pressoffice/proginfo/tv/2009/wk7/unplaced.shtml#unplaced_victorians.

34 David Butcher, 'The Victorians', *RT* (21–27 February 2009), p. 56.

35 Michael Baxandall, *Painting and Experience in Fifteenth-Century Italy* (Oxford: Oxford University Press, 1972), p. 1.

36 Jeremy Paxman, *The Victorians* (transmitted BBC1, 15 February 2009)

37 Butcher, 'The Victorians', *RT*, p. 56.

38 Serena Davies, 'Paxman's Victorian Portrait Paints Only Half the Picture', *Daily Telegraph* (16 February 2009), p. 28.

39 Schama, 'Television and the trouble with history', in Cannadine (ed.), *History and the Media*, pp. 23–4.

40 Schama, 'Television and the trouble with history', p. 24.

41 Isaacs, 'All Our Yesterdays', p. 37.

42 WAC, copy of the post-production script *How Wars Begin*, Part 1. The First Modern War – From French Revolution to French Empire, 6447/1815 (transmitted BBC1, 11 July 1977).

43 *How Wars Begin.*

44 *How Wars Begin.*

45 Downing, 'Bringing the past to the small screen', in Cannadine (ed.), *History and the Media*, p. 15.

46 Stearn, 'What's wrong with television history?', p. 26.

47 Davies, 'BBC2 Presenters Branded "Stiff and Stuffy"', guardian.co.uk

48 Wood, telephone interview.

49 'Personal Choice', *The Times* (12 March 1980), p. 27.

50 Wood, telephone interview.

51 Wood, telephone interview.

52 Wood, telephone interview.

53 Wood, telephone interview.

54 Starkey, interview with the author.

55 Rees, interview with the author.

56 Starkey, interview with the author.

57 Rimmon-Kenan, *Narrative Fiction*, pp. 71–2.

58 Daniel Dayan and Elihu Katz, 'Media events', in Howard Tumber (ed.), *News: A Reader* (Oxford: Oxford University Press, 1999), p. 57.

59 Smither, 'Why is so much television history about war?', in Cannadine (ed.), *History and the Media*, p. 56.

60 Smither, 'Why is so much television history about war?', p. 56.

61 Jung, *Archetypes and the Collective Unconscious*, p. 183.

62 Schama, 'Television and the trouble with history', pp. 26–7.

63 Schama, 'Television and the trouble with history', p. 27.

64 Martin Smith, 'History and the media: Are you being hoodwinked?' *History Today*, 53:3 (2003), 28–30.

65 Gerda Jansen Hendriks, 'How to present riots that have not been filmed', in Roberts and Taylor (eds), *The Historian, Television and Television History*, p. 60.

66 Schama, 'Television and the trouble with history', pp. 21–2.

67 Schama, 'Television and the trouble with history', p. 29.

68 Kilborn and Izod, *Television Documentary*, pp. 187–8.

69 'Most Britons Fail Guy Fawkes Test', *Daily Telegraph* (2 November 2005), p. 6.

70 'Reality TV Winners Are Better Known Than Drake or Scott: British Heroes Lose Out to Big Brother', *Daily Mail* (22 February 2005), p. 19.

9

Nation, nationality and television history

Since resuming transmission in 1946, factual television history in Britain has travelled a long-way forward in its development and a greater distance back in time for its themes. A wealth of series and one-off programmes has, at consistent intervals, inexorably embedded the past into the present. This fusion of then and now has offered reviews of how a nation values, presents, re-presents and sees itself at crucial points of social and cultural development.

But what exactly is the concept of nation, nationality and national spirit? Is it a tangible quantifiable entity contained in institutions, the landscape, language custom and tradition, or is it amorphous and ephemeral, progressing and transforming itself with each new generation, forming a new spirit of the age? I believe that it is all of these things, and that nation, nationality and citizenship are a sense of shared experience and spirit made of memories real and artificial. Of course memories cannot be locked down or anchored without what Eric Hobsbawm defines as 'invented tradition', which involves 'a set of practices, normally governed by overtly or tacitly accepted rules and a ritual of symbolic nature ... [which] normally attempt to establish continuity with a suitable historic past'.[1]

Television, and the history it produces, is at the centre of such a system through a culturally and socially defined language system as its bardic voice. It also uses language as a visual logic to illustrate social and cultural change, delineating an established timeline of inherited traditions inscribed with national and regional customs.

Language as a cornerstone of nationality is a powerful modifier in terms of socialisation and conformity, a compressor of meaning that forms 'its own "grid" on our experiences ... by which we reduce our universe to order'.[2] Television, and the history it reproduces and re-represents as culturally important, is a central factor in this reductive process. Conversely, as television reduces the past to fit in with a one-off scheduling slot, or as parts in a series, it amplifies the events so that they assume importance in the fabric of national identity and national self-perception.

In the previous chapters, discussion has centred around the landscape as a binding ingredient in national spirit, on race, archetypes and stereotypes as national role models. Underpinning these raw materials of Britain past and Britain present is the influence that capitalism has brought to bear on how we value the past and present.

The rise of capitalism, together with print-based languages ensured that nationalism would become a central factor in a common, unified understanding of what the nation should represent. Television now serves the same purpose as the print-based media did in cohesively holding the nation-state fabric together around a central core of capitalist endeavour.

Capitalism is disguised within the holistic motivating concept of nationalism and is often understated when the past is brought to the small screen. As Benedict Anderson points out, asking people to die for their country, for an ideal mythical vision of what that country represents, is far more inspiring than asking people to give their lives to protect market forces and consumerism.[3] The past in one ideological form or another always has a value placed on it, not merely on financial terms as in Niall Ferguson's series *The Ascent of Money*, but as the value and worth of individual contributions to nation-state perspectives.

This can take the form of personal sacrifice and bravery, as in the six-part series *For Valour* (BBC2, 1979), neatly emulated by ITV with *For Valour* (ITV, 1985) or the 2008 version *Special Forces Heroes* (Five, 2008), reconstructing some of the SAS' most audacious exploits. National identity comprised of the collective mythical 'spirit' of Britain becomes more elusive and denser in its meaning as each generation adds its own contribution. It is hardly surprising that a scientific study has concluded that the reading of Victorian novels today still means that they 'act like "social glue", reinforcing beliefs that maintain the community and warning against destructive influences and character traits'.[4]

National characteristics were formed – so J. B. Priestley believed, writing in 1934 – as a central part of patriotism which was an inheritance gained through more than custom and tradition. It was the cumulative effect of class exploitation overwritten by individual and united endeavour.

> As I thought of what the nineteenth century has left us in every industrial area, I felt at once angry and ashamed. What right had we to go strutting about,

talking of our greatness, when all the time we were living on the proceeds of these muck-heaps? … But we have ravished for unjustly distributed profit the most enchanting countryside in the world […] Ours is a country that has given the world something more than millions of yards of calico and thousands of steam engines.[5]

George Orwell, never reluctant to examine cultural and social values, defines nationalism as an engine of power and patriotism as something quite separate, as a 'devotion to a particular place and a particular way of life'.[6] National-ism and nationalist tendencies are, for Orwell, divisive and defensive, formed from a simple 'us and them' mentality, with history created along these fracture lines.[7] It is more difficult, Orwell suggests, to actually ascribe a value as to what made his – now vastly changed – England different from other countries.

Are there really such things as nations? Are we not 46 million individuals, all different? And the diversity of it, the chaos! The clatter of clogs in the Lancashire mill towns, the to-and-fro of the lorries on the Great North Road, the queues outside the labour Exchanges, the rattle of pin-tables in the Soho pubs, the old maids biking to Holy Communion through the mists of the autumn mornings – all these are not only fragments, but characteristic, of the English scene. How can one make a pattern out of this muddle?[8]

The connectivity that Orwell has hit on is regional diversity, the fragmenta-tion of a country into constituent parts, that produces meaning for different people at their own level, but that, when joined, creates a collective impri-matur. More sights and smells are then added to Orwell's composite England – 'solid breakfasts and gloomy Sundays, smoky towns and winding roads, green fields and red pillar-boxes. It has a flavour of its own'.[9] Try as he can, Orwell still cannot put his finger on the nature of national identity. 'Moreover it is continuous, it stretches into the future and the past, there is something in it that persists, as in a living creature.'[10] J. B. Priestley, during his own *English Journey* undertaken in 1933, attempts to capture the regional variations that constitute a sense of nationality, criss-crossing the country as he unpicks the regional weave of a national fabric.

This quest to discover or rediscover what makes Britain different has been a continuous theme for factual history programming, including the novelist Beryl Bainbridge's *English Journey* (BBC2, 1984), celebrating Priestley's original. Perhaps proving how difficult and contentious a task it is, the brief genealogy overleaf demonstrates the different approaches taken.

The quest for national identity

This is Britain (BBC, 1947)

Our British Heritage (ITV, 1955)

Keeping in Step (ITV, 1958)

Farson's Guide to the British (ITV, 1959)

Insurrection: Easter Week, 1916 (BBC2, 1966)

Who Were the British? (ITV, 1966)

Who Are the Scots? (BBC1, 1971)

Milestones in Working Class History (BBC1, 1975)

The Troubles (ITV, 1981)

People to People (C4, 1983)

Built in Britain (C4, 1983)

Wales! Wales! (BBC2, 1984)

English Journey (BBC2, 1984)

Scotland's Story (C4, 1984)

The Dragon Has Two Tongues: A History of the Welsh (C4, 1985)

This Land of England (C4, 1985)

The Making of Britain (C4, 1985/1986)

The Story of English (BBC2, 1986)

The Spirit of England (BBC2, 1995)

England, My England (C4, 1998)

Britain and the Slave Trade (C4, 1999)

The Middle Classes: Their Rise and Sprawl (BBC2, 2001)

The British Empire in Colour (ITV1, 2002)

The Making of England (ITV1, 2003)

Class in Britain (C4, 2005)

How TV Changed Britain (C4, 2008)

Prescott: The Class System and Me (BBC2, 2008)

Citizen Smith (BBC4, 2009)

As much as the Labour Government attempts to redefine class on the basis of improvements in the General Certificate of Secondary Education (GCSE) exam results,[11] concepts of class are more ingrained into the national consciousness than correlations of statistical data suggest. The rise in GCSE pass rates may indicate social mobility, but for the Labour politician and former Deputy Prime Minister John Prescott, who earned the sobriquet 'two Jags' for his penchant use of ministerial limousines, inequality had to be confronted in a two-part documentary.

Prescott: The Class System and Me (BBC2, 2008) gave the former ship's steward the freedom to display 'a fine set of chips on both his shoulders as he bangs on about his working-class credentials',[12] as he met different examples of class. In neither part of the documentary, however, did he come close to getting to grips with class as a historical construction or its modified modern phenomenon of celebrity. For publisher/writer Michael Smith, a search for national identity involved six thirty-minute journeys around England in *Citizen Smith* (BBC4, 2009). A modern equivalent of Daniel Farson, Smith mixes with eccentrics, compares religion to consumerism, questions the existence of privilege through private members' clubs, before eventually deciding that the English have lost touch with their inherited identity, unlike the Scots.

With the elusiveness of national identity and its refusal to be dissected by documentary presenters, the one genre of factual history programming that *is* the nearest to marshalling a sense of what it means to be British is that of archive compilation films, shot by professionals and amateurs.

The nation on film

Invited by programme-makers to share ordinary and not so ordinary lives, the everyday and the extraordinary, archive compilations positions TV-users as *flâneurs*, observing the different stages of how society has evolved. These filmic archives of forgotten moments and obscure, outdated habits are capable of not only stirring individual memories but also creating new collective memories for different generations because of their emotive power.

Collective memories were one of the principal devices that the format of one of ITV's popular productions, *All Our Yesterdays*, aimed to stir, accounting for 60 per cent of all ITV factual production between 1960 and 1969.[13] Reconstructing the past from Movietone newsreel clips formed the presentational codes and conventions of *All Our Yesterdays*.[14] It was initially presented by journalist James Cameron from its launch in December 1960 to November 1961 when Brian Inglis became the programme's avatar. Inglis, with his historian's calm authoritative insight to the newsreel stories, provided a marked contrast to Cameron's 'austere' approach.[15]

The programme's final presenter, the Canadian actor Bernard Braden, known mainly for his 'consumer' shows, introduced the nostalgia-orientated programme for its final run between 1987 and 1989. A weekly programme networked across all ITV regions, its format originated from a deal between Granada Television, based in Manchester, and Movietone News, stipulating that only Movietone footage of twenty-five years ago could feature in each programme,[16] which provided TV-users with a very monocular reconstructed view of the world.

This concept of utilising newsreel as a primary source around which a programme is constructed was a format developed by the BBC in 1955, with *This Was Yesterday* – 'A Celebration of Pathé Pictorial' (BBC, 1955), that ITV quickly imitated with its 1957 *Flashback* series. Following the absence of *All Our Yesterdays* between 1973 and 1987, compilation series were rare, with the BBC producing a one-off with *Festival 77* (BBC2, 1977), a retrospective look at television newsreel from 1952. Newsreel did eventually return, providing a conceptual framework for the BBC's *Vision of Change* (BBC1, 1983) and *The World of the Thirties* (BBC2, 1987), which offered an informative insight into the past.

These would be followed by another two newsreel-based series, *A Week To Remember* (BBC2, 1992–95), centred on Pathé newsreel of forty-years earlier, and *Today's The Day* (BBC2, 1993–99), a quiz based on history and news, presented first by Andrew Rawnsley and then by Martyn Lewis.

It was *All Our Yesterdays*, however, that defined the style of compilation formats. From its original early evening slot on Monday in the 1960s, *All Our Yesterdays* suffered from the vagaries of scheduling, shunted between late night and early morning slots to weekday and weekend afternoons in the 1970s, which would be enough to ensure that any programme's TV-user share would quickly fall and disappear.

Re-presenting past events in *All Our Yesterdays* is designed to engage with TV-users through a contract based on the television equivalent of a weekly periodical. History becomes more manageable, with each programme narrative not continuous but broken into guided segments. In this way, TV-users never become totally detached from the action but engage with history as an already known or newly known experience. Experienced and inexperienced TV-users are conducted on a guided tour into the past controlled by an on-screen 'guide', whether that be Cameron, Inglis or Braden.

In the *All Our Yesterdays* titled 'Abdication', transmitted on 11 December 1961, it is possible to reveal these different aspects of serialised re-presentation. According to Jeremy Isaacs, the producer for the series during 1961, the Abdication episode was, 'bulked out' in order for the programme to run the story over two successive weeks.[17] Part one of the Abdication programmes evolves through five clearly defined segments: 'Introduction', 'Setting the Scene', 'Edward's Life and Times', 'Portrait of a Prince and King' and 'The Impending Crisis'.

The opening rostrum camera shot marking the introduction contextualises the period through archive material, the 'Instrument of Abdication', filling the screen under the title – *All Our Yesterdays*. Put together on a small budget, *All Our Yesterdays* was 'intended to entertain, as well as inform',[18] with the rostrum camera bringing still photographs to life, what Isaacs refers to as creating 'action-stills'.[19]

In contrast to factual history programme presenters who move through shots or play an active on-screen narratorial role, Brian Inglis sits facing the camera in a leather swivel chair. To his right is a small coffee table dressed with a table lamp, decanter and glass of water, book and script. Inglis is composed, providing the impression of being relaxed, with one leg crossed over the other. Wearing a two-piece suit, white shirt and dark tie, this full-length shot positions Inglis slightly to the right of the frame in a classic documentary convention. Immediate contact is formed with TV-users, subject to Inglis' on-screen control and authority as guide and narrator.

Acceptance of Inglis' role as gatekeeper to the past is naturalised through television's convention that allows TV-users to feel special, as a chosen companion for the presenter. The TV-user is then drawn into the text and positioned in such a way that ideological channels of communication form a receptive space – not a blank space, but one created to appear natural.

Far from being a shared space, this space is dominated by a direct one-way flow of information governed by the expectations and assumptions of power and knowledge held by the production team. In this one-sided relationship, Inglis is clearly the provider, the TV-user the receiver of this lens-based journey into the past.

Eye contact from Inglis forms a direct relationship with TV-users, inviting them into his tour of the abdication crisis built on a carefully crafted narrative. This invisible construction of authority and insight behind Inglis' point of view allows him to question contradictions present in newsreel footage, stills, diaries or other evidence that may emerge.

This factor becomes evident in the second segment, 'Setting the Scene', where the abdication is contextualised by a selective review of social and cultural framing devices, bridging past and present. In this case, it is the Madrid air raids of October 1936, which killed sixteen and wounded sixty, with reference also made to the German–Japanese Treaty of November 1936. Inglis points out that at the time it may have been thought that there may have been nothing much exciting happening abroad; however, he concedes there would be ample reason in the coming years to view this period as one of increasing

4   Brian Inglis, the calm, authoritative guide to *All Our Yesterdays* (ITV, 1960–73)

destabilisation, where mechanisms of order and control began to fracture.

Home events are framed by newsreel coverage of the Eton Wall Game, a move to have card games introduced into schools, and the editor of the *Times*, Geoffrey Dawson, complaining of a news famine, followed by the Bishop of Bradford's appeal for the 'King's need for divine grace'. This Inglis impishly quotes as a bridge into the next segment, 'Edward's Life and Times'.

To construct a picture of Edward as Prince of Wales, archive newsreel footage runs over Inglis' commentary – a compilation of shots of the future king hunting, playing polo and piloting an aircraft. Between archive newsreels, Inglis, in mid-shot, links each segment of footage with details and opinion on Edward's life as the impending crisis looms. One reason why retrospective compilation programmes such *All Our Yesterdays* enjoy popular appeal is because the past has been tamed, is contained and poses no threat. They consist of the known, as opposed to the unpredictable unknown of the present and future. In the segment 'Portrait of a Prince and King', Edward's contribution to the Great War is sympathetically handled by Inglis, who points out the dangers, the fact Edward ventured close to the front line and that his driver was killed.

The footage then skims over Edward's 1924 visit to America, his relationship with his father, overseas travel, state occasions, garden parties and guards of honour. During this biographical element, Inglis constructs a portrait of Edward as a man not much valued by his own father and as a royal attempting to find a means of justifying what his duties demand of him. Inglis' compassion is evident over footage of Edward during a state visit: as Inglis dryly observes, it consisted of 'speeches, speeches, speeches', summing up the schedule of a visiting royal.

If Edward faced pressure overseas, at home the routine of the court brought no respite. In a sequence dealing with the presentation of debutantes at a garden party, Inglis describes Edward's lack of patience with what is expected of him: 'The prince, as you could see, was rarely at ease.' Here Inglis' exhortation is for TV-users to actively share his interpretation through the conspiratorial 'as you could see', highlighting the constructed role of the TV-user as a valued fellow traveller into the past.

As the newsreel excerpts cover the death of King George, his lying in state, Inglis comments on Edward's decision to perform an all-night vigil as a symbol of his respect for the monarchy, 'Surely the new King could live up to their expectations.' This enables Inglis to guide TV-users into a position from where they can make value judgements on the binary constructed roles of the monarchy and the British public and the monarchy's role as a core unit of nationality.

On Mrs Simpson, Inglis wryly describes how the relationship was kept out of the papers and why any newsreel footage rarely revealed her or the King together: 'Mrs Simpson was either out of focus or out of shot.' In the final programme segment, 'The Impending Crisis', Inglis uses biographies, news stories and newspaper front page headlines as stills to detail the build-up to the abdication. Quoting directly from Edward on meeting Mrs Simpson, Inglis observes how the King had a 'disliking for humbug', a characteristic that one assumes may have been shared by Inglis. Finally, Inglis prepares for the next instalment of *All Our Yesterdays* by laying out the opposition of Baldwin to the King's marriage to Mrs Simpson and Edward remaining as monarch.

All Our Yesterdays' success at informing and entertaining was largely due to Brian Inglis' mode of presentation. Inglis comes across as an avuncular figure, hard but fair, not given to taking fools lightly, slightly sceptical, and prepared to put forward his own values and beliefs. The programme is certainly basic and static compared with today's factual history programming, with abrupt silent pauses accompanying the end of archive footage. Perhaps the most telling indication of Inglis' style comes through his narration, with one scene perhaps more than any other evoking Inglis' sympathy as a historian for Edward. The Movietone footage captures Edward launching a ship, the *Empress of India*, and the microphone picks up Edward's asides, relating how he was asked why he was launching a ship, to which he jokingly replies that he did not know – it was a woman's job.

This choice of clip, the way it is deftly crafted into the narrative, demonstrates why factual television history is popular; it is because of its ability to reveal an intimate insight into its subjects. Here, Edward, reconstructed by Inglis, became human, an individual rather than a stereotypical caricature. *All Our Yesterdays* may have been produced on a small budget, yet its appeal is entirely down to this contract between the TV-users and Inglis, someone able to provide an authoritative insight into past events.

The success of *All Our Yesterdays* would lead to another series constructed from newsreels, ITV's *Time to Remember*, repeated by Channel 4 (1987–88), which utilised sequences from the extensive Pathé News Library on a wide spread of events, produced by ABC Television and Pathé News, and broadcast by Thames Television.[20]

One of the BBC's strengths in factual history programming has been in devising formats that are simple, well written and effectively constructed to create incisive ways forward that text-based historiography cannot always match. This has been achieved through the BBC's experience and skill in working with moving, visual history, forming entertaining series around archive film such as *Propaganda With Facts* (BBC2, 1978), a six-part series dealing with Second World War propaganda films. Equally illuminating is the untapped footage of amateur filmmaking in the nine-part *Everybody's Doin' It* (BBC2, 1980), narrated by John Julius Norwich.

It is this concept of the 'unseen' past that the BBC and other broadcasters maximise. An innovative format, it projects different eras into the present, their simplicity allowing the footage itself to emphasise difference, an opportunity closed to text based historians. One example of the 'unseen past', *The Lost World of Mitchell and Kenyon* (BBC2, 2005), a three-part journey into different aspects of the past using restored footage, does give the past a very strong presence, though the pedestrian, mundane narration of Dan Cruickshank stifled the film's own powerful voice.

Archive compilations were an important theme for Channel 4 during the 1980s, with six series highlighting the coverage of events provided by the American cinemagazine, *The March of Time*.

- *On the March* (C4, 1985)
- *The American Century* (C4, 1986)
- *In Time of War 1939–1945* (C4, 1986)
- *Dust and Dreams: America 1935–51* (C4, 1987)

- *Reporting the Dictators* (C4, 1988)
- *The White Man's Burden* (C4, 1989)

It is the amateur footage strung together by voice-over or cutaway commentary by talking heads, that comes closest to achieving a sense of time and place, of how the mundane and seemingly isolated characteristics amalgamate into national spirit and outlook. Not that Orwell found identifying what makes a nation from its past and present parts an easy task. 'National characteristics are not easy to pin down, and when pinned down they often turn out to be trivialities or seem to have no connexion with one another.'[21]

The archive compilation format is garnered from such trivialities. An early example of this format is the BBC's thirteen-part *Caught in Time* (BBC2, 1978), presented by James Cameron. Scheduled for a late Sunday slot – 10.20–11.45 p.m. – the amateur footage from the 1920s and 1930s, also included a documentary, the *Turn of the Tide*.

Everybody's Doin' It, with its pre-war amateur footage showing the nation at work and play, was followed by rediscovered home movie film in *Attic Archives* (BBC2, 1988). During the 1990s, the BBC retained its enthusiasm for this personal and once private realm of the past with *Cine Memo* (BBC2, 1991), showing life in Britain, France and Germany through the lens of enthusiasts, and Channel 4 used amateur cine film for *Home Movies* (C4, 1995).

It was not only the everyday events that were captured and documented by amateurs. *The Late Show* – 'The Zapruder Footage' (BBC2, 1993) examined the twenty-two seconds of footage recording the assassination of President Kennedy, and *Pearl Harbor: Death of the Arizona* (Discovery, 2002) covered the Japanese attack on Pearl Harbor.

Archive footage that could be repackaged and rebranded as integral cultural signifiers also became a prized commodity, with the BBC's aptly titled *Nation on Film*, beginning its BBC2 run in 2003 with 'Off the Rails', questioning, with eyewitness accounts, if Britain's railways did have a golden period in the 1930s. Regional nostalgia for a past long modernised featured in *The Way We Were …* (ITV, 2004), with regional providers such as Anglia, Granada, Meridian and Yorkshire tailoring archive footage for their own TV-users. The eight-part series in 2008 on ITV1, *The Way We Were on Holiday*, used archive footage to reveal how the British idea of a holiday has significantly altered through social and cultural shifts in personal leisure and travel.

The past in terms of the nation composed of a united spirit, a defining identifiable essence, simply does not exist, as the Prime Minister Gordon Brown has discovered with his vision for a museum of Britishness widely derided.[22]

Nation, nationality and citizenship are individually held beliefs that may take all of the collective influences and myths into play, or a small number of them. The important point is that the concept of Englishness or Britishness is individual, conditioned by individual circumstances, individual experience, individual beliefs, education, occupation, knowledge and location. When these become collective at a regional level and national level they form a 'brand' of the nation constructed through myth, heritage and tradition bound by real and artificial memories. The consumption of this brand of nation and nationality is modified and adapted, then re-consumed, and the cycle begins once more.

Decade by decade, this collectively imagined brand is reworked, with layers of meaning added through time, creating what Henrietta Lidchi deems 'palimpsests of meaning',[23] in order to represent historically mediated values. Without this type of popular, easily to engage with archive format of forgotten professional and amateur film – and of course, living history series such as *Coal House* – the shared bond between generations may be in danger of being broken so that contact with a collective national identity is ruptured. As one TV-user to *The Way We Were* put it:

> Did anyone see it? Does anyone know where I can get a copy of this episode for my Nan? Our street was featuring it [*sic*] and the press article on this particular episode said the episode was going to be 24th Sep 2008 so sadly everyone on our street has missed it.[24]

For some TV-users, the reality of the past in *Coal House* was also a means of joining generations together to form a mutual understanding on how the present has formed:

> We watched the first *Coal House* series last year and this new series, *Coal House at War*, is just as absorbing. My 15 year old daughter loves watching it and won't miss an episode, it really is living history and a great way for us all to learn about the past.[25]

Television history in all its formats is essential if history is to be passed on to the next generation. In future it will not be clear, as Orwell maintained, that the peculiar arrangement of individual views loosely organised around class will motivate Britain and 'all its inhabitants to feel alike and act together in moments of supreme crisis',[26] as it is assumed they did during the Second World War.

Factual television history has become a valuable commodity, and in many ways television history is a history of Britain as a nation-state. Clearly, despite some very deeply ingrained mistrust towards factual television history on the part of some historians, there are some similarities between the production of academic history and popular history produced for television. These shared points of interaction arise from the reliance of the past being re-presented through the careful managing of narratives that are produced, shaped and constrained by professional practices governing academic historians, as well as those practices accepted as institutional frameworks by television producers. This is particularly true with the reliability of sources when oral history or actuality footage is involved. Laurence Rees recognises that there was wide-spread and bitter resentment towards television's handling of the past by some academics ten years ago, though this he believes has decreased significantly.[27]

History produced for public consumption, inevitably becomes defined as 'popular', always drawing criticism from a variety of quarters. In some cases, Nick Knowles and his *Historyonics* deserved all the criticism they received. Television history and academic history may well be divided by methodology and their respective consumers, yet they both share the same intention of creating understanding from interpreting past events.

If television is the first port of call for individuals who have been failed by a national curriculum that is rudderless, then factual history programming should be regarded as an irreplaceable vehicle for generating interest in Britain and its relationship with the world. As the anonymous diarist who experienced the Great War declares, 'We are all strangers when we look back on our pasts',[28] and television has the means to function as a vehicle for making this journey as familiar as possible. Here then, is the opportunity for professional historians to recognise that television history and professional academic history can exist side by side, not necessarily as mutually exclusive forms but as a means of opening up debate and interest in the past.

For many people history is an affirmation of tradition, hard won rights, the projection of an international reputation and cultural heritage. It is not, however, an autonomous agent that works and exists outside society. What makes history so important is the selection, recording and interpretation of events, people and places that define and shape cultural expectations and a society's perception of nation, national interest and national identity.

Television does simplify; it reduces. But that is what makes it attractive, informative, entertaining and popular. Its ellipsis is constructed from meeting the challenges of constraints imposed by scheduling regimes and genre conventions. It is also history edited to meet the expectations of TV-users, whose perceptions vary according to their own social demographics.

Perception is an important factor in how people see the past, with claims that television history is obsessed with the Second World War. My own modest survey of TV-users found that from responses covering all three groups, 34 per cent believed that there was not too much focus devoted to war, 29 per cent disagreed and 16 per cent did not know.[29] This is supported by the BBC's own statistical breakdown of its factual history production carried out in 2004.

> In the academic community, there's often the sense that we over concentrate on certain periods, which I don't think is valid. We did a survey last year [2004] of BBC output in History, and 89 per cent of what was made last year was nothing to do with the Second World War.[30]

History, at its basic level, emerges from selected past events because historians and programme-makers have the professional opportunity and frameworks to access the past according to their own interests. One of the advantages of television is that this privileged position is not restricted to professional historians.

> Phillip Donnellan, the man who collected all the songs, the letters, the diaries, the orders and the reports, and all the pictures and film for *Gone for a Soldier* on BBC2 last night is not a historian, a political commentator or a propagandist. He is instead a poet.[31]

When history becomes a commodity in this way, it demonstrates the ease with which television affords other views and voices to be heard. History has long been a commodity between the covers of academic books and monographs and as material for conferences. The moment that its value is recognised as a means of generating sales of non-academic books on the subject, or of attracting large numbers of TV-users to factual television history, its status as a commodity established by academics is overlooked. History is not solely about the events from which its narrative threads are drawn, the weight of its characters, the impact of its events; history is about interpretation, and individuals and groups will differ on how the past should be re-presented. From those TV-users who admitted to having no interest in history in my survey, the reasons given are quite revealing.

Out of all the groups representing a broad age range, 20 per cent of TV-users classed television history as not being interesting enough. A further 20 per cent said that it did not interest them, and 13 per cent could not find their own interests in history amongst the themes covered by terrestrial, cable and satellite channels.[32] Television cannot please all TV-users all the time. Just as all individuals cannot be forced to enjoy history during their education, or have a desire to read history for themselves, factual history programming can only offer a contract to engage with the past to TV-users who have a commitment to do so.

When factual history has to survive with other popular forms and genres within television's competitive schedules, history does not seem to equate with entertainment. When 'top' or 'favourite' programme lists spanning each decade from the 1950s onwards are compiled on the basis of viewing figures such as those put together by the BFI for Channel 4's *Britain's Most Watched TV* (C4, 2005),[33] or selected by industry insiders who voted for their preferences in the BFI's 'TV 100',[34] the inclusion of factual history programming varies enormously.

Factual history was unrepresented by any history programmes generating high enough TV-user figures to qualify in any of the top twenty positions spanning the 1950s to the 2000s for *Britain's Most Watched TV*. It fared only slightly better when programme-makers had their say in the BFI's 'TV 100'.[35]

The television industry's favourites: factual history in the top 100

Position	Programme
19	*The World at War*
48	Ken Russell's 'Elgar' for *Monitor*
64	*Culloden*
65	*The Ascent of Man*
67	*Civilisation*
93	*Nazis: A Warning from History*
95	*Arena*

Only in the 'Top 20 Factual Category' did history programmes gain any merit in the ranking they received from the votes cast.[36]

The television industry's favourites: factual history in the top 20

Position	Programme
1	*The World at War*
4	Ken Russell's 'Elgar' for *Monitor*
7	*The Ascent of Man*
8	*Civilisation*
12	*Nazis: A Warning from History*
13	*Arena*
14	*The Great War*
16	*Horizon*
17	*The Rock 'n' Roll Years*

Factual television history is an important part of understanding the complex systems forming national identity, due in no small part because television is an integral factor in producing narratives as a visual reinforcement of citizenship. This, along with language, landscape, institutions, individual values and regional diversity, forms what Orwell classes as 'an invisible chain' that binds the nation together.[37] Television has had a dominant role in constructing society and culture, as George Gerbner *et al*, suggest: 'Television is the source of the most broadly shared images and messages in history',[38] though the encroachment of the personal computer could make that a thing of the past.

The past, television and the future

Immersed as it is in a technological media revolution, factual television history programming will be under intense pressure to radically adapt in the years ahead as digitally driven media convergence accelerates. Michael Grade, the Executive Chairman of ITV, concerned about the network being punished through archaic 'regulatory burdens', has warned that 'we're heading towards a situation where commercial investment in original programming in the UK becomes unsustainable'.[39]

Efforts to save Channel 4 from its dire financial situation have led to speculation that it may be merged with Five, or with the BBC's successful commercial arm, BBC Worldwide,[40] though Channel 4 appears wilfully oblivious to the fact that its commissioning strategy is still skewed towards young TV-users who do not count television as their prime source of education, knowledge or entertainment.

With the internet already radically changing the way in which individuals engage with visual culture, choosing their own terms along with their own selections, factual history has already had to adopt a multiplatform approach. Innovative programming with multiplatform support comes at a price, however, and with greater competition, creativity is usually an expensive option when compared to easy-to-use genre formulas.

Intense competition for ratings and prestigious channel-branding programmes and series capable of winning awards may spur some broadcasters on, but the control of programme supply through the move to digital television as analogue is phased out is likely to prove a bigger incentive to maximise production costs by selling-on formats and series rather than by taking risks with original commissioning ventures that may not prove as financially lucrative or rewarding. The very use of television as a family custom, a ritual sharing of an evening's entertainment, has disappeared. Television, for younger TV-users, has moved from the living room to the bedroom. Mass-appeal, generating millions of TV-users for a single programme or series, is decreasing, as narrowcast, niche markets become the norm.

Production values, when capped by licence fee increases or a decline in advertising revenue, will have to satisfy the demand and expectation of a diversified marketplace. In many cases this is a media-rich home landscape peopled by individuals who, after the freedom afforded by the VCR in the 1980s, have become sophisticated and demanding TV-users. Any downturn or stagnation in market share tends to create a stimulus for pledges of greater investment in programmes or a change in the way that TV-users receive and engage with programmes. The introduction of cable and satellite television added to the levels of appeal the industry has maintained through technological innovation. Colour sets, the remote control device, the VCR, digital and high-definition television have created a viable means of generating continued interest from TV-users.

Television, cable and satellite providers have altered the patterns of sharing entertainment and information. Each new technological phase permits TV-users to experience the past on demand and on their own terms within their own preferred individual schedules. This can only be beneficial for television history, though quality programming may be an ideal that is ultimately offered for sacrifice, as the latest technology becomes a lynchpin in attracting new TV-users. Sky is offering the viewing experience as a form of personal freedom and a lifestyle statement: 'Watch different Sky TV channels in different rooms at the same time … Fit your TV around your life – with a Sky⁺ box'.[41] Technical freedom, no matter how innovative or lifestyle-reforming it may be, requires more schedules to be filled, often with repeats or series culled from terrestrial providers.

This reinvention of the VCR in the form of 'catch up' television offered by Virgin Media, which engineered a takeover of Telewest in 2006, as well as by its main rival Sky, enhances the ability to time shift. Adding to this, the ease and availability of programmes offered as downloads by the BBC and commercial stations means that the 'revolution in television viewing and the beginning of the end of "prime-time television"',[42] is already a factor. With the loss of prime-time slots attracting the best rates of commercial advertising and the long overdue demise of rating figures, new methods of financing television will need to be established by the BBC and commercial broadcasters.

If TV-users become increasingly fragmented, dissolving into electronic communes, an imagined space with no defined boundaries, then the whole style of factual history programming is likely to change to ensure that not only are relatively small-core TV-users retained but new TV-users are recruited to maintain profitability.

TV-users of factual history programming may have the 'time' and opportunity to create their own viewing regime, yet there is a very real danger that TV-users are going to be caught in a no-man's land of the production chain. Under incessant pressure from trailers, press and pre-publicity campaigns, direct mail shots and TV listings, they will have to make more complex choices of where and how they want their factual history programming.

There is a growing tendency from programme providers to maximise their return on new digital technology by encouraging increased usage, or by persuading TV-users to sample programmes they may not be inclined to normally watch.[43] With greater choice, high-definition television, and digital convergence, factual history programming will have to fight hard to attract younger TV-users in what is set to become a ruthless, cut-throat marketplace.

Television history in a popular vacuum

History does not appear out of thin air. For the academic pursuit of history, as for popular television history, the past is revisited out of the interests of its producers. Historians manufacture a specific view of the past that fits their own social, political, cultural and professional needs,[44] as do programme-makers.

There can be little doubt that the moving images of cinema and television are able to capture the imagination far more than other, non-moving, media. Through that greater interaction comes insights into the past that are more convincing because they are packaged in drama and spectacle and bring with them the promise of entertainment. Denis McQuail suggests that all media production, television history not excepted, does have to conform to what he describes as 'economic logic, a technological logic and a media cultural logic, each of which leaves a distinctive mark on the cultural product through its influence on production decisions'.[45] This, taken with professional considerations of the production team and the historian or presenter, will ultimately shape and define how the programme or series looks. Accordingly, it can be argued that any visual bridge into the past is constructed to a finite budget. Needless to say, this limits not merely its span, its type of construction, but also its weight, its ability on how much is carried back from the past.

In this way, television sets up relationships of engagement through a standardisation process that is embedded in its codes and conventions operating as a taken-for-granted system of communication. When television is taken for granted, its central role of using storytelling as models for citizenship and socialisation often goes unquestioned. However, broadcasting cannot be divorced from history, as much as some historians and critics would prefer it to be. The evolution of channels, programmes, presenters, genres and TV-users reflects a cultural and social dimension that is in itself history,[46] a stylised, manufactured aspect of history none the less.

Collecting and transmitting memories

If memory and history share one common feature, it is that they can be framed and referenced by archetypal visual tropes, aligned to powerful traces linked to the immediacy of events. Visual traces of history never operate as passive elements once they have been integrated into different forms of communication designed to interpret or commodify the past. As soon as they begin to become circulated and consumed, they become culturally embellished as they progress from individual to individual and from group to group. This amassing of first-hand and artificially mediated experience that make up memory influences individual memory, primed and prompted by social and public groups, and media such as television. If the oral tradition served factual history programming well from the 1950s, there appears to be no reason why it should not continue as a staple convention.

One of the major problems with the immediacy of television is its dependency on visual storytelling techniques. Here, the surface detail, the visual attraction, generates a false impression that the past is highly accessible without any real effort. This suggests that the past can be visualised in much the same way as a drama, a news report or a reality show, when in fact, travelling back into the past is fraught with problems.

Memory is fickle. Where some events can be recalled instantly, others remain stubbornly detached from the power of memory, which refuses all attempts to draw fragments of the past into the present cohesively or accurately. Connecting past and present together through collective memory is a sphere of remembering where television has a powerful and long-term effect through its visual articulation of events and characters.

In attempting to define the relationship between individual memory and collective memory it is important to assess, rather than dismiss out of hand, how – or indeed if – memory can be relied upon as a basis for an accurate representation of the past. Memory is not some encapsulated archival reference system, the sole preserve of eyewitnesses, survivors or veterans. It is an integral component in everyday professional and social activities, which includes historians, researchers, writers and programme-makers.

Factual history programming where 'memory work' is made visible on-screen, particularly in dealing with war and conflict, is no less important than the unseen memory work involved in shaping the past to fit the screen. In this sense, television operates as a visual theatre where much inherited, mediated memory reinforces a shared, collective past. However, this collective or popular memory is open to the effects of distortion, as is individual memory.

In many factual programmes, history and memory run in parallel when eyewitness accounts are featured. Some events are sharply delineated, others skimmed over, whilst some are ignored or deliberately forgotten across a range of group and individual recollections. For Jacques Le Goff, the formation of collective or popular memory is a process of struggle and negotiation between groups and individuals, where 'collective memory has been an important issue in the struggle for power among social forces'. [47] Even if one shared event may become strikingly memorable for diverse groups of people, their own individual memories will be unique, personal narratives.

If these narratives are made public or passed on to another generation, the original memory traces may be completely overwritten, modified beyond recognition or distorted. In any case, the inherited memories will have no resemblance to their originals and will have become, through transference, strands of cultural, family, social or national myths.

Memory cannot be classed as simply being an individual product that operates outside society, but as Henry Rousso suggests, memory is part of a nation's fabric,[48] part of its national identity created to maintain social values and cultural mores. In this case, memory is carried forward by different groups for different reasons. Personal memory, popular collective memory and official memory operate on diachronic and synchronic axes.

The process of memory formation operates along the synchronic axis, activated by events, images, sounds, smells or any other form of memory trigger. Transforming memory into sense-making narratives has equivalence to what T. S. Eliot termed 'objective correlatives',[49] opening links down the diachronic axis in order to find matches that substantiate meaning and offer answers, explanations and clarity. Deposited along the diachronic axis are sites of reference, cultural and social archetypes, together with myths formed by official and collective memories.

When collective memories attempt to handle and define what being British means – an amorphous cultural and historic construct in itself – collective memory is constantly shifting,[50] unable to be neatly tied down to provide a definitive answer. National identity and units of the nation-state are founded on nothing more binding than language, providing an opportunity to be 'invited' into 'the imagined community'.[51]

This is a feature that television history programmes display each and every time they are transmitted. Organised around the binding relationship between televisual discourses, TV-users and socio-cultural boundaries, television and factual history programming have an important role to play in the regeneration of society. To deny them a part to play because some programmes treat history as entertainment is to deny society a powerful means of recognising what shared and individual pasts stands for. This refusal to accept television history as a valid and important guardian of the past is a rejection of how collective and personal histories are re-presented as citizenship within the ever-changing concept of nation and nationality.

Notes

1 Eric Hobsbawm, 'Introduction: Inventing traditions', in Eric Hobsbawm and Terence Ranger (eds), *The Invention of Tradition* (Cambridge: Cambridge University Press, 1983), p. 1.

2 Geoffrey Leech, *Semantics* (Harmondsworth: Penguin Books, 2nd edn, 1981), p. 26.

3 Anderson, *Imagined Communities*, p. 144

4 Richard Alleyne, 'Guide Books: Classic Novels Teach Us Good Behaviour, Say Scientists', *Daily Telegraph* (15 January 2009), p. 8.

5 J. B. Priestley, *English Journey* (London: Book Club Associates, 1984), pp. 310–11.

6 George Orwell, *Decline of the English Murder and Other Essays* (Harmondsworth: Penguin Books, 1965), p. 156.

7 Orwell, *Decline of the English Murder*, p. 165.

8 George Orwell, *Inside the Whale and Other Essays* (Harmondsworth: Penguin, 1962), p. 64.

9 Orwell, *Inside the Whale*, p. 64.

10 Orwell, *Inside the Whale*, p. 64.

11 Martin Beckford, 'Britain's Class Divide "Is In Decline"', *Daily Telegraph* (4 November 2008), p. 14.

12 Alison Graham, 'Prescott: The Class System and Me', *RT* (25–31 October 2008), p. 68.

13 Data from the *RT et al.*

14 Isaacs, 'All Our Yesterdays', in Cannadine (ed.), *History and the Media*, p. 35.

15 Isaacs, 'All Our Yesterdays', p. 35.

16 Isaacs, 'All Our Yesterdays', p. 35.

17 Isaacs, 'All Our Yesterdays', pp. 35–6.

18 Isaacs, 'All Our Yesterdays', p. 35.

19 Isaacs, 'All Our Yesterdays', p. 35.

20 *Time to Remember*, BFI Film and Television Database. http://ftvdb.bfi.org.uk/sift/series/14461.

21 Orwell, *Inside the Whale*, p. 65.

22 Simon Tait, 'PM's Plan for "Britishness" Museum Consigned to History', *Independent* (30 January 2009), p. 13. See also James Kirkup, 'The Story of Britain "Can Be Told With a Collection of Websites"', *Daily Telegraph* (30 January 2009), p. 13.

23 Henrietta Lidchi, 'The Poetics and the politics of exhibiting other cultures', in Hall (ed.), *Representation, Cultural Representations and Signifying Practices*, p. 167.

24 *The Way We Were*. http://forums.itv.com/thread/742786.aspx.

25 www.bbc.co.uk/wales/coalhouse2/sites/programmes/?page=7#comments-pager.

26 Orwell, *Inside the Whale*, p. 77.

27 Rees, interview with the author.

28 Anonymous, *A Soldier's Diary of the Great War*, introduction by Henry Williamson (London: Faber and Gwyer, 1929), p. xi.

29 Data from TV-user survey, All Groups.

30 Rees, interview with the author.

31 Stanley Reynolds, 'Gone for a Soldier', *The Times* (10 March 1980), p. 11.

32 Data from TV-user survey, All Groups

33 *Britain's Most Watched*, BFI. www.bfi.org.uk/features/mostwatched/research.html.

34 BFI 'Top 100'. www.bfi.org.uk/features/tv/100/biglist/.

35 BFI 'Top 100'. www.bfi.org.uk/features/tv/100/list/list.php.

36 BFI 'Top 100'. www.bfi.org.uk/features/tv/100/list/genre.php?gid=4 .

37 Orwell, *Inside the Whale*, p. 77.

38 George Gerbner, Larry Gross, Michael Morgan and Nancy Signorielli, 'Growing up with television: The cultivation perspective', in Jennings Bryant and Dolf Zillmann (eds), *Media Effects: Advances in Theory and Research* (Hillsdale: Lawrence Erlbaum Associates, 1994), p. 17.

39 Michael Grade, 'I have Bad News for British Viewers', *Daily Telegraph* (13 January 2009), p. 21.

40 Nick Clark, 'TV Regulator Says C4 Should Merge in Order to Survive', *Independent* (22 January 2009), p. 38. See also Neil Midgley 'Channel 4 May Be Saved by Link With BBC Worldwide', *Daily Telegraph* (23 January 2009), p. 8.

41 BSkyB promotional flyer, B2B1 8620 (02/07).

42 Stephanie Condron, 'Channel 4 to Let Viewers Download its Programmes', *Daily Telegraph* (7 December 2006), p. 15.

43 David Derbyshire, 'Free Downloads of Top BBC Shows', *Daily Telegraph* (1 February 2007), p. 9.

44 Richards, 'Popular memory and the construction of English history', pp. 1–2.

45 McQuail, *Mass Communication Theory*, p. 229.

46 Jean Seaton, 'Writing the history of broadcasting', in Cannadine (ed.), *History and the Media*, p. 143.

47 Le Goff, *History and Memory*, p. 54.

48 Rousso, *Vichy Syndrome*, p. 219.

49 T. S. Eliot, 'Hamlet', in Frank Kermode (ed.), *Selected Prose of T.S. Eliot* (London: Faber and Faber, 1987), p. 48.

50 Samuel, *Island Stories*, p. 22.

51 Anderson, *Imagined Communities*, p. 145.

Bibliography

BBC Written Archive

Scripts

First Hand – Part 10, 'Edward VII' (camera script), produced by Paul Johnstone, presented by Peter West (transmitted 20 December 1957).

Great Britons – Part 4, 'Florence Nightingale' (post-production script) written and presented by Philippa Stewart (transmitted 8 August 1978).

How Wars Begin – Part 1, 'The First Modern War – From French Revolution to French Empire' (post-production script), written and presented by A. J. P. Taylor (transmitted 11 July 1977).

Living Legends – Part 3, 'Robin Hood' (post-production script), produced by Jane Coles, presented by Magnus Magnusson (transmitted 10 May 1979).

The Trial of Madeleine Smith, written by John Gough, produced by Royston Morley (transmitted 9 January 1949).

Letters, memos, audience research and programme notes

Buried Treasure, WAC T32/96/3, T32/96/2, T32/96/1, T32/96/17, 1954–58.

Early History of the Film, WAC T32/190, 1946–50.

Historic Houses, letter from John Read, 29 January 1952, WAC T32/189.

Historic Houses, memo from John Read, WAC T32/189, undated.

Historic Houses, report from John Read, WAC T32/189, undated.

Historic Houses, WAC T32/189, 1950–52, undated.

Historic Houses, Viewer Research Report on programme 2, West Wycombe (week 31) VR/50/315, WAC T32/189, undated.

James Burke's Connections, BBC TV Viewing Barometer, WAC R9/37/14, undated.

London Town, WAC T4/29/2, 1945–55.

Music Through the Centuries, memo from Cecil McGivern, WAC T13/78), undated.

Secret Mission, WAC T32/310 (transmitted 11 October 1948).

Victory at Sea, letter from Jock Colville to B.E. Nicolls, 27 October 1952, WAC T6/290.

Victory at Sea, letter from B.E. Nicolls to Jock Colville, 28 October 1952, WAC T6/290.

Victory at Sea, letter from Winston Churchill to Sir Alexander Cadogan, Chairman of the BBC Board of Governors, 29 October 1952, WAC T6/290.

Victory at Sea, letter from Sir Alexander Cadogan to Winston Churchill, 31 October 1952, WAC T6/290.

Victory at Sea, memo from George Barnes, Director of BBC Television, to Cecil McGivern, Controller of Television Programmes, 28 October 1952, WAC T6/290.

Victory at Sea, National Broadcasting Corporation (NBC) Fact Sheet, WAC T6/290, undated.

Victory at Sea, Phillip Dorté, Head of BBC Television Films, advance publicity copy for an article for the *Radio Times*, 13 October 1952, WAC T6/290.

Newspapers and programme features/listings

Alleyne, Richard, 'Guide Books: Classic Novels Teach Us Good Behaviour, Say Scientists', *Daily Telegraph* (15 January 2009).

Armstrong, Stephen, 'Ode to a Nightingale', *Radio Times,* North West/Yorks/N East edition (31 May–6 June 2008).

'Asians' Strike Threat Over Skinheads', *The Times* (27 May 1970).

'A.T.V. to Pay £89,300 for U.S. Films', *The Times* (29 August 1957).

'BBC's "Critical Phase" After Lavish Rivals Offers to Staff', *The Times* (29 July 1955).

'BBC Dispute Likely to Be Extended', *The Times* (13 January 1978).

'B.B.C. Talks on Filling Television Gap', *The Times* (11 January 1957).

Beckford, Martin, 'Decline of Christian Values "Is Destroying Britishness"', *Daily Telegraph* (29 May 2008).

Beckford, Martin, 'Britain's Class Divide "Is In Decline"', *Daily Telegraph* (4 November 2008).

Beckford, Martin, 'BBC Favours £18m Ross Over Songs of Praise, Say Bishops', *Daily Telegraph* (9 December 2008).

Bignell, Paul, 'BBC Hit by Row Over "History of Scotland"', *Independent on Sunday* (9 November 2008).

Bird's-Eye View, Radio Times, South and West edition (5–11 April 1969).

Black & White Minstrel Show, Radio Times, South and West edition (11–17 April 1970).

Bloxham, Andy, 'Do the English Build Castle Ruins?', *Daily Telegraph* (11 August 2008).

Butcher, David, 'The Victorians', *Radio Times*, North West/Yorks/N East edition (21–27 February 2009).

Cassidy, Sarah, 'History Man Starkey in "Golden Handcuffs" Deal', *Independent* (15 February 2002).

'Channel 4 Switch-On Despite Dispute', *The Times* (1 November 1982).

Christianity: A History, Radio Times, North West/Yorks/N East edition (10–16 January 2009).

'Christmas TV Has 500 Hours of Repeats', *Independent* (19 December 2008).

Clark, Nick, 'TV Regulator says C4 Should Merge in Order to Survive', *Independent* (22 January 2009).

Cochrane, Alan, 'A Britishness Day Is Not the British Way', *Daily Telegraph* (4 June 2008).

Condron, Stephanie, 'Channel 4 to Let Viewers Download its Programmes', *Daily Telegraph* (7 December 2006).

Conlan, Tara, 'ITV's Big Switch-Off', *Daily Mail* (5 August 2004).

Conlan, Tara, 'BBC TV Ratings Melt Away to Hit a New Low', *Daily Mail* (5 January 2005).

Courtauld, Charlie, 'Television: Get in Touch With Your Inner Thug', *Independent on Sunday* (11 April 2004).

Davalle, Peter, 'Today's Television and Radio Programmes: Choice', *The Times* (20 February 1985).

Davies, Serena, 'Paxman's Victorian Portrait Paints Only Half the Picture', *Daily Telegraph* (16 February 2009).

Derbyshire, David, 'Free Downloads of Top BBC Shows', *Daily Telegraph* (1 February 2007).

Dunkley, Chris, 'MPs Criticize Running of Commercial TV and Call for Inquiry into Broadcasting', *The Times* (28 September 1972).

Eden, Richard and Wynne-Jones, Jonathan, 'Why I Am Scared to Talk About My Christianity On Air, by Jeremy Vine', *Daily Telegraph* (18 January 2009).

Edge, Simon, 'Simon Edge… On Last Night's Telly', *Daily Star* (5 April 2004).

Evans, Nick, 'Nazi Doctor and the Mystery of "Twins Town"', *Daily Telegraph* (22 January 2009).

'First Night of the I. T. A. Emphasis On the "Stars"', *The Times* (23 September 1955).

'Go-Ahead Given by Mr Chataway to 24-hour Radio and Television', *The Times* (20 January 1972).

Grade, Michael, 'I have Bad News for British Viewers', *Daily Telegraph* (13 January 2009).

Graham, Alison, 'Secret History: Britain's Boy Soldiers', *Radio Times*, North West/Yorks/N East edition (12–18 June 2004).

Graham, Alison, 'Florence Nightingale', *Radio Times*, North West/Yorks/N East edition (31 May–6 June 2008).

Graham, Alison, 'Britain from Above', *Radio Times*, North West/Yorks/N East edition (9–15 August 2008).

Graham, Alison, 'Prescott: The Class System and Me', *Radio Times*, North West/Yorks/N East edition (25–31 October 2008).

Greatest Comedy Catchphrases, Radio Times, North West/Yorks/N East edition (22–28 November 2008).

'Hitler a Real Person? Who Do You Think You're Kidding?' *Daily Mail* (5 April 2004).

Hope, Christopher, 'Bad Parents Have Caused Britain's Decline Since the 1950s, Says MP', *Daily Telegraph* (27 November 2008).

Industrial Grand Tour, Radio Times, South and West edition (22–28 July 1972).

Kennet, Lord, Letters to the Editor, 'Scott and Reality', *The Times* (18 February 1985).

Khan, Urmee, 'Selina Scott Wins Ageism Battle Over Job With Five', *Daily Telegraph* (6 December 2008).

Kirkup, James, 'The Story of Britain "Can Be Told with a Collection of Websites"', *Daily Telegraph* (30 January 2009).

Lennon, Peter, 'Lord Reith's Last Blast', *The Times* (1 November 1982).

Leonard, Tom, 'Truman Show Syndrome: When Reality TV Takes Over Your World', *Daily Telegraph* (26 November 2008).

McGrath, Rory, 'Review TV; Why I Think History Is Bloody Marvellous', *Sunday Express* (4 April 2004).

Man Alive, Radio Times, South and West edition (12–18 September 1970).

Martin, Nicole, '"Pretty" Newsreaders Will Be Found Out, Says ITV's Austin', *Daily Telegraph* (16 September 2008).

Martin, Nicole, 'Wales Documentary Was Biased Against Thatcher, Admits BBC', *Daily Telegraph* (14 November 2008).

Massie, Allan, 'The Final Highland Fling?', *Daily Telegraph* (14 April 2007).

Masters, Anthony, 'Worthy Pursuit of the Miraculous', *The Times* (15 March 1984).

Midgley, Neil, 'Channel 4 May Be Saved by Link With BBC Worldwide', *Daily Telegraph* (23 January 2009).

Monitor: Elgar, Radio Times, South and West edition (13–19 July 1968).

Moreton, Cole, 'What the Dickens?', *Independent* (26 October 2008).

'Most Britons Fail Guy Fawkes Test', *Daily Telegraph* (2 November 2005).

Night in the City, Radio Times, South and West edition (21–27 July 1962).

'No More Men to Be Called Up', *The Times* (19 November 1960).

Parker, Derek, 'This Week – 1844', *The Times* (22 January 1975).

Paterson, Peter, 'Angels Fail to Delight', *Daily Mail* (21 June 2004).

'Personal Choice', *The Times* (12 March 1980).

Pile, Stephen, 'Sometimes It Pays to Keep Up' *Daily Telegraph* (17 April 2004).

'Pilkington Report "Biased"', *The Times* (2 March 1964).

Porter, Andrew, 'BBC Must Help to Heal Broken Society, Says Tories', *Daily Telegraph* (29 September 2008).

'Programme Extension Sought by I. T. A. Move to End Evening "Closed Hour"', *The Times* (25 August 1956).

Rackham, Jane, 'Timewatch – Young Victoria', *Radio Times* (18–24 October 2008).

Rampton, James, 'Satellite, Cable and Digital Pick of the Day', *Independent* (5 April 2004).

'Reality TV Winners Are Better Known Than Drake or Scott: British Heroes Lose Out to Big Brother', *Daily Mail* (22 February 2005).

Reynolds, Stanley, 'Gone for a Soldier', *The Times* (10 March 1980).

'Rule on Television Hours. Announcement of Change Expected To-Day', *The Times* (12 December 1956).

Secret Mission, Radio Times, North West edition (10–16 October 1948).

Sights and Sounds of Britain, Radio Times, South and West edition (10–16 January 1970).

Singh, Anita, 'Ageism Row at BBC as Countryfile Gets a New Presenter', *Daily Telegraph* (10 December 2008).

'Social Effects of Television. Extended Time Criticized', *The Times* (24 January 1957).

'Suicides Dropped After Terrorist Attack Thanks to Blitz Spirit', *Daily Telegraph* (6 January 2009).

Tait, Simon, 'PM's Plan for "Britishness" Museum Consigned to History', *Independent* (30 January 2009).

'Television For Two Audiences. B.B.C.'s Aim in Extra Programmes', *The Times* (16 January 1957).

'1066 and All *What?*', *Daily Mail* (5 August 2004).

The Bristol Entertainment, Radio Times, South and West edition (27 November–3 December 1971).

'The End of the Monopoly', *The Times Radio and Television Supplement* (19 August 1955).

The Heart of an Empire, Radio Times, North West edition (10–16 November 1946).

The Noble Game, Radio Times, South and West edition (18–24 August 1962).
'The War Underwater', *Radio Times,* North West edition (17–23 November 1946).
The World About Us, *Radio Times*, South and West edition (18–24 March 1972).
'TV Workers Protest at Early Close-Down', *The Times* (1 February 1974).
Tweedie, Neil, 'Taking On a Nation in Crisis', *Daily Telegraph* (10 January 2009).
Walton, James, 'The Weekend on Television: Funny About That', *Daily Telegraph* (5 April 2004).
Walton, James, '19th-Century Nostalgia to Rival Lark Rise to Candleford', *Daily Telegraph* (9 January 2009).
Wansell, Geoffrey, 'A Profile of A. J. P. Taylor: "A Pyrotechnic Academic." How Vanity Led an Unquiet Don into New Fields', *The Times* (30 August 1971).
Wyver, John, 'Hero Caught in an Icy Blast', *The Times* (11 February 1985).
Yesterday's Witness, Radio Times, South and West edition (22–28 March 1969).

Emails

Jeff Walden, BBC Written Archives, Caversham, email reply to the author (13 January 2006).

Interviews

Adam Hart-Davis, written responses to the author's questionnaire (14 May 2004).
Bamber Gascoigne, written responses to the author's questionnaire (16 December 2004).
Bettany Hughes, written responses to the author's questionnaire (31 February 2005).
David Starkey, interview with the author, Department of History, Lancaster University (14 July 2004).
Laurence Rees, Creative Director BBC History, interview with the author, BBC Television, White City, London (26 October 2005).
Michael Wood, telephone interview with the author (27 April 2004).

Letters

Frank Rosier, Secretary, The Normandy Veterans Associations, Portsmouth Branch, in a letter to the author (30 November 2004).

Advertising material

BSkyB promotional flyer, B2B1 8620(02/07).

Teletext

Report on Nick Knowles and *Historyonics*, Teletext page 135, this transcript taken from page 135's rolling pages 4, 5 and 6 (30 March 2004).

Books

Abercrombie, M. L. J., *The Anatomy of Judgment* (London: Free Association Books, 1989).

Alberti, Leon Battista, *On Painting*, trans. John R. Spencer (New Haven: Yale University Press, rev. edn, 1966).

Allen, Robert C. (ed.), *Channels of Discourse Reassembled* (London: Routledge, 2nd edn, 1992).

Allen, Walter, *The English Novel: A Short Critical History* (Harmondsworth: Penguin Books, 1984).

Anderson, Benedict, *Imagined Communities* (rev. edn, London: Verso, 1991).

Anonymous, *A Soldier's Diary of the Great War*, introduction by Henry Williamson (London: Faber and Gwyer, 1929).

Aristotle/Horace/Longinus, *Classical Literary Criticism*, trans. T.S. Dorsch (Harmondsworth: Penguin Books Ltd, 1965).

Attridge, Derek, Geoff Bennington and Robert Young (eds), *Post-structuralism and the Question of History* (Cambridge: Cambridge University Press, 1987).

Bal, Mieke, *Narratology: Introduction to the Theory of Narrative* (Toronto: University of Toronto Press, 2nd edn, 1997).

Barthel, Diane, *Historic Preservation: Collective Memory and Historical Identity* (New Brunswick: Rutgers University Press, 1996).

Barthes, Roland, *Elements of Semiology*, trans. Annette Lavers and Colin Smith (New York: Hill and Wang, 1967).

Barthes, Roland *Image, Music, Text*, trans. Stephen Heath (London: Fontana Press, 1977).

Barthes, Roland, *Camera Lucida: Reflections on Photography*, trans. Richard Howard (London: Jonathan Cape, 1982).

Barthes, Roland, *Mythologies*, trans. Annette Lavers (London: Vintage, 1993).

Baxandall, Michael, *Painting and Experience in Fifteenth-Century Italy* (Oxford: Oxford University Press, 1972).

BBC Yearbook 1947 (London: British Broadcasting Corporation, 1947).

BBC Year Book 1950 (London: British Broadcasting Corporation, 1950).

BBC Handbook 1956 (London: British Broadcasting Corporation, 1956).

Bede, *The Ecclesiastical History of the English People,* ed. Judith McClure and Roger Collins (Oxford: Oxford University Press, 1998).

Berger, John, *Ways of Seeing* (London: BBC/Penguin, 1972).

Beowulf, trans. Michael Alexander (Harmondsworth: Penguin, 1973).

Briggs, Asa, *The History of Broadcasting in the United Kingdom, Volume V. Competition* (Oxford: Oxford University Press, 1995).

Bryant, Jennings and Dolf Zillmann (eds), *Media Effects: Advances in Theory and Research* (Hillsdale: Lawrence Erlbaum Associates, 1994).

Burckhardt, Jacob, *The Civilisation of the Renaissance in Italy*, trans. S. G. C. Middlemore (London: Penguin Books, 2004).

Bygrave, Stephen (ed.), *Romantic Writings* (London: Routledge/The Open University, 1996).

Calder, Angus, *The People's War 1939–1945* (London: Pimlico, 1992).

Callinicos, Alex, *Theories and Narratives, Reflections on the Philosophy of History* (Cambridge: Polity Press, 1995).

Carroll, Noel, *Philosophy of Art* (London: Routledge, 1999).

Cannadine, David, *What is History Now?* (Basingstoke: Palgrave Macmillan, 2002).

Cannadine, David (ed.), *History and the Media* (Basingstoke: Palgrave Macmillan, 2004) .

Carr, Edward Hallett, *What is History?* (Harmondsworth: Penguin, 1964).

Chapman, James, *The British at War: Cinema, State and Propaganda 1939–1945* (London: I.B. Taurus, 1998).

Cherry-Garrard, Apsley, *The Worst Journey in the World: Antarctica 1910–1913* (London: Pimlico, 2003).

Collingwood, R. G., *The Idea of History* (Oxford: Oxford University Press, 1961).

Connerton, Paul, *How Societies Remember* (Cambridge: Cambridge University Press, 1989).

Corner, John (ed.), Popular *Television in Britain* (London: BFI Publishing, 1991).

Corner, John, *Critical Ideas in Television Studies* (Oxford: Oxford University Press, 1999).

Curran, James and Michael Gurevitch (eds), *Mass Media and Society* (London: Hodder Arnold, 4th edn, 2005).

Davies, Stephen, *Empiricism and History* (Basingstoke: Palgrave Macmillan, 2003).

Deary, Terry, *Horrible Histories: The Cut-Throat Celts* (London: Hippo, 1997).

Debord, Guy, *The Society of the Spectacle*, trans. Donald Nicholson-Smith (New York: Zone Books, 1994).

Easthope, Antony, *Poetry as Discourse* (London: Methuen, 1983).

Edgerton, Gary R., and Peter C. Rollins (eds), *Television Histories, Shaping Collective Memory in the Media Age* (Lexington: The University Press of Kentucky, 2001).

Erens, Patricia (ed.), *Issues in Feminist Film Criticism* (Bloomington: Indiana University Press, 1990).

Evans, Martin, and Ken Lunn (eds), *War and Memory in the Twentieth Century* (Oxford: Berg, 1997).

Evans, Richard, *In Defence of History* (London: Granta Books, 2000).

Febvre, Lucien, *A New Kind of History*, ed. Peter Burke (London: Routledge and Kegan Paul, 1973).

Fiske, John, *Television Culture* (London: Routledge, 1987).

Fiske, John, and John Hartley, *Reading Television* (London: Routledge, 1989).

Ford, Boris (ed.), *The New Pelican Guide to English Literature, Vol. 1, Medieval Literature, Part One: Chaucer and the Alliterative Tradition* (Harmondsworth: Penguin, rev. edn, 1982).

Ford, Boris (ed.), *The New Pelican Guide to English Literature, Vol. 1, Medieval Literature, Part Two: The European Inheritance* (Harmondsworth: Penguin, rev. edn, 1982).

Ford, Boris (ed.), *The New Pelican Guide to English Literature, Vol. 6, From Dickens to Hardy* (Harmondsworth: Penguin, rev. edn, 1982).

Foucault, Michel, *Language, Counter-Memory, Practice. Selected Essays and Interviews with Michel Foucault,* ed. F. Bouchard (Ithaca: Cornell University Press, 1980).

Foucault, Michel, *Power/Knowledge, Selected Interviews and other Writings 1972–1977*, trans. Colin Gordon, Leo Marshall, John Mepham, Kate Soper, ed. Colin Gordon (Harlow: Longman, 1980).

Foucault, Michel, *Discipline and Punish: The Birth of the Prison*, trans. Alan Sheridan (London: Penguin, 1991).

Foulkes, A. P., *Literature and Propaganda* (London: Methuen, 1983).

Frye, Northrop, *Anatomy of Criticism* (Princeton, New Jersey: Princeton University Press, 1971).

Gardiner, Juliet (ed.), *What Is History Today?* (London: Palgrave Macmillan, 1988).

Gibbon, Edward, *The Decline and Fall of the Roman Empire*, A one-volume abridgement by D. M. Low (London: Book Club Associates, 1979).

Green, Anna, and Kathleen Troup (eds.), *The Houses of History: A Critical Reader in Twentieth-Century History and Theory* (Manchester: Manchester University Press, 1999).

Halbwachs, Maurice, *On Collective Memory*, ed. and trans. Lewis, A. Coser (Chicago: The University of Chicago Press, 1992).

Hall, Stuart (ed.), *Representation, Cultural Representations and Signifying Practices* (London: Sage/The Open University, 1997).

Hampson, Norman, *The Enlightenment* (London: Penguin Books, 1990).

Hastings, Max, and Simon Jenkins, *The Battle for the Falklands* (London: Pan Books, 1997).

Herodotus, *The Histories*, trans. Aubrey De Sélincourt (London: Penguin Books, rev. edn, 2003).

Hill, John, and Pamela Church Gibson (eds), *The Oxford Guide to Film Studies* (Oxford: Oxford University Press, 1998).

Hobsbawm, Eric, and Terence Ranger (eds), *The Invention of Tradition* (Cambridge: Cambridge University Press, 1983).

Hobsbawm, Eric, *The Age of Revolution: Europe 1789–1848* (London: Abacus, 1992).

Hooson, David (ed.), *Geography and National Identity* (Oxford: Blackwell Publishers, 1994).

Hutton, Patrick, *History as an Art of Memory* (Hanover: University Press of New England, 1993).

Jenkins, Keith, *Re-thinking History* (London: Routledge, 1991).

Jenks, Chris (ed.), *Visual Culture* (London: Routledge, 1995).

Jhally, Sut, *The Codes of Advertising* (New York: Routledge, 1990).

Johnson, Richard, Gregor McLennan, Bill Schwarz, and David Sutton (eds), *Making Histories: Studies in History Writing and Politics* (Minneapolis: University of Minnesota Press, 1982).

Jordanova, Ludmilla, *History in Practice* (London: Arnold, 2000).

Jung, Carl Gustav, *The Archetypes and the Collective Unconscious*, trans. R.F.C. Hull (London: Routledge, 2nd edn, 1968).

Kemal, Salim, and Ivan Gaskell (eds), *Landscape, Natural Beauty and the Arts* (Cambridge: Cambridge University Press, 1993).

Kermode, Frank (ed.), *Selected Prose of T.S. Eliot* (London: Faber and Faber, 1987).

Kilborn, Richard, and John Izod, *An Introduction to Television Documentary* (Manchester: Manchester University Press, 1997).

Leech, Geoffrey, *Semantics* (Harmondsworth: Penguin Books, 2nd edn, 1981).

Le Goff, Jacques, *History and Memory*, trans. Steven Rendall and Elizabeth Claman (New York: Columbia University Press, 1992).

Liddell Hart, Basil, *History of the First World War* (London: Book Club Associates, 1973).

Lodge, David (ed.), *20th Century Literary Criticism* (London: Longman, 1972).

Lorey, David E., and William H. Beezley (eds), *Genocide, Collective Violence, and Popular Memory* (Wilmington: Scholarly Resources, 2002).

Lummis, Trevor, *Listening to History: The Authenticity of Oral Evidence* (London: Hutchinson, 1987).

Lyotard, Jean-François, *The Postmodern Condition: A Report on Knowledge*, trans. Geoff Bennington and Brian Massumi (Manchester: Manchester University Press, 1986).

Macaulay, Thomas Babington, *History of England Vol. 1* (London: Heron Books, 1967).

Machiavelli, Niccolò, *The Prince,* trans. George Bull (London: Penguin Books, 2003).

Marwick, Arthur, *The Nature of History* (Basingstoke: Macmillan, 2nd edn, 1981).

Marwick, Arthur, *Culture in Britain Since 1945* (Oxford: Blackwell, 1991).

Marwick, Arthur, *The New Nature of History* (Basingstoke: Palgrave, 2001).

Marx, Karl, and Frederick Engels, *The German Ideology, Part One*, ed. C. J. Arthur (London: Lawrence and Wishart, 2nd edn, 1974).

Miller, David, *On Nationality* (Oxford: Clarendon Press, 1997).

McQuail, Denis, *Mass Communication Theory* (London: Sage Publications, 3rd edn, 1994).

Myers, Greg, *Ad Worlds: Brands, Media, Audiences* (London: Arnold, 1999).

Newcomb, Horace (ed.), *Television, The Critical View* (New York: Oxford University Press, 3rd edn, 1982).

Nichol, John, and Tony Rennel, *The Last Escape: The Untold Story of Allied Prisoners of War in Germany 1944–45* (London: Viking, 2002).

Orwell, George, *Inside the Whale and Other Essays* (Harmondsworth: Penguin, 1962).

Orwell, George, *Decline of the English Murder and Other Essays* (Harmondsworth: Penguin Books, 1965).

O'Sullivan, Tim, and Yvonne Jewkes (eds), *The Media Studies Reader* (London: Arnold, 1997).

Palmer, Svetlana, and Sarah Wallis, *A War in Words* (London: Simon & Schuster, 2003).

Pitt, Barrie (ed.), *The Military History of World War II* (London: Chancellor Press, 1994).

Plumb, J. H., *The Death of the Past* (Harmondsworth: Pelican, 1973).

Poole, A. L., *From Domesday Book to Magna Carta, 1087–1216* (Oxford: Clarendon Press, 2nd edn, 1955).

Price, Monroe E., *Television: The Public Sphere and National Identity* (Oxford: Oxford University Press, 1995).

Priestley, J. B., *English Journey* (London: Book Club Associates, 1984).

Richards, Denis, and J. W. Hunt, *An Illustrated History of Modern Britain 1783–1964* (London: Longman, 2nd edn, 1965).

Richards, Jeffrey, 'Popular memory and the construction of English history', *The Ninth Annual Bindoff Lecture, Queen Mary and Westfield College, University of London* (London: University of London, 1998).

Rimmon-Kenan, Shlomith, *Narrative Fiction: Contemporary Poetics* (London: Methuen, 1983).

Roberts, Andrew, *Hitler and Churchill: Secrets of Leadership* (London: Weidenfeld & Nicolson, 2003).

Roberts, Graham, and Phillip M. Taylor (eds), *The Historian, Television and Television History* (Luton: University of Luton Press, 2001).

Rousso, Henry, *The Vichy Syndrome, History and Memory in France since 1944*, trans. Arthur Goldhammer (Cambridge, Mass.: Harvard University Press, 1991).

Samuel, Raphael, *East End Underworld: Chapters in the Life of Arthur Harding* (London: Routledge and Kegan Paul, 1981).

Samuel, Raphael, *Island Stories, Unravelling Britain, Theatres of Memory, Volume II*, ed. Alison Light (London: Verso, 1998).

Scott, Joan Wallach (ed.), *Feminism and History* (Oxford: Oxford University Press, 1996).

Solomon, Susan, *The Coldest March: Scott's Fatal Antarctic Expedition* (New Haven: Yale University Press, 2001).

Sophocles, *The Theban Plays*, trans. E. F. Watling (Harmondsworth: Penguin Books, 1986).

Strinati, Dominic, *Popular Culture* (London: Routledge, 1995).

Taylor, Richard (ed.), *The Eisenstein Reader* (London: British Film Institute, 1998).

Thompson, Edward Palmer, *The Making of the English Working Class* (Harmondsworth: Pelican Book, 1963).

Thompson, Paul, *The Voice of the Past* (Oxford: Oxford University Press, 2nd edn, 1988).

Tosh, John, *The Pursuit of History* (London: Longman, revised 3rd edn, 2002).

Trevelyan, George Macaulay, *English Social History: A Survey of Six Centuries, Chaucer to Queen Victoria* (London: Book Club Associates, 1973).

Tumber, Howard (ed.), *News: A Reader* (Oxford: Oxford University Press, 1999).

Vico, Giambattista, *The New Science of Giambattista Vico*, trans. Thomas Goddard Bergin and Max Harold Fisch (Ithaca: Cornell University Press, 1984).

Vico, Giambattista, *On the Most Ancient Wisdom of the Italians*, trans. L. M. Palmer (Ithaca: Cornell University Press, 1988).

Wallach, Joan Scott (ed.), *Feminism and History* (Oxford: Oxford University Press, 1996).

Warren, John, *The Past and Its Presenters* (London: Hodder and Stoughton, 1998).

White, Hayden, *Metahistory* (Baltimore: The John Hopkins University Library, 1975).

Whiteclay Chambers II, John, and David Culbert, *World War II Film and History* (New York: Oxford University Press, 1996).

Williams, Raymond, *Culture and Society 1780–1950* (Harmondsworth: Penguin, reprinted with a postscript, 1963).

Windahl, Sven, Benno H. Signitzer and Jean T. Olson, *Using Communication Theory* (London: Sage Publications 1992).

Winston, Brian, *Media Technology and Society. A History: From the Telegraph to the Internet* (London: Routledge, 1998).

Winter, Jay, and Emmanuel Sivan (eds), *War and Remembrance in the Twentieth Century* (Cambridge: Cambridge University Press, 1999).

Wordsworth, William, *Selected Poems,* ed. Walford Davies (London: Dent, 1975).

Journals, online papers and e-journals

Baer, Alejandro, 'Consuming history and memory through mass media products', *European Journal of Cultural Studies*, 4:4 (2001) http://ecs.sagepub.com/cgi/content/abstract/4/4/491.

Bain, A. D., 'The growth of television ownership in the United Kingdom', *International Economic Review*, 3:2 (1962).

Bourdon, Jérôme, 'Some sense of time', *History and Memory*, 15:2 (2003).

Coase, Ronald H., 'The development of the British television service', *Land Economics*, 30 (1954).

Collins, Norman, 'The nature of "competitive" television', *Political Quarterly* (1953).

Confino, Alon, 'Collective memory and cultural history: Problems of method', *The American Historical Review*, 102:5 (1997).

Emmett, B. P., 'The television audience in the United Kingdom', *Royal Statistical Society Journal*, 119:3 (1956).

Gardiner, Juliet, 'The Edwardian country house', *History Today*, 52:7 (2002).

Henson, Don, 'Television archaeology: Education or entertainment?' Institute for Historical Research (2007) www.history.ac.uk/education/conference/henson.html.

Nelson, Michael, 'It may be history, but is it true?: The Imperial War Museum Conference', *Historical Journal of Film, Radio and Television*, 25:1 (2005).

Palmer, Catherine, 'Tourism and symbols of identity', *Tourism Management*, 20 (1999).

Porter, Bernard, 'My country. Right or wrong?', *History Today*, 56:7 (2006).

Ramsden, John. A., '*The Great War*: The making of the series', *Historical Journal of Film, Radio and Television*, 22:1 (2002).

Smith, Martin, 'History and the media: Are you being hoodwinked?' *History Today*, 53:3 (2003).

Stearn, Tom, 'What's wrong with television history?' *History Today*, 52:12 (2002).

Thomas, Peter ' Reappraisals: The structure of politics at the accession of George III', Institute of Historical Research (1997) www.history.ac.uk/reviews/reapp/lewis.html.

Internet sources

British Broadcasting Corporation (General)

Castle in the Country (2008) www.bbc.co.uk/programmes/b006mk00.

Coal House (2008) www.bbc.co.uk/wales/coalhouse/sites/families/. www.bbc.co.uk/wales/coalhouse/sites/behindthescenes/pages/chriswilliams.shtml.

Coal House at War (2008) www.bbc.co.uk/wales/coalhouse2/sites/programmes/?page=1#comments-pager. www.bbc.co.uk/wales/coalhouse2/sites/programmes/?page=4#comments-pager. www.bbc.co.uk/wales/coalhouse2/sites/programmes/?page=6#comments-pager. www.bbc.co.uk/wales/coalhouse2/sites/programmes/?page=7#comments-pager. www.bbc.co.uk/wales/coalhouse2/sites/cast.

Contrasts – 'Marble Arch to Edgware Road', BBC Programme Catalogue (2007).

Great Britons (2008) http://web.archive.org/web/20060514084331/www.bbc.co.uk/history/programmes/greatbritons.shtml.

I Love the 70s (2008) www.bbc.co.uk/cult/ilove/years/70sindex.shtml.

Royal Charter for the continuance of the British Broadcasting Corporation (2009) www.bbc.co.uk/bbctrust/framework/charter.html.

Television Is Here Again, BBC Programme Catalogue (2007).

The Victorians (2009) www.bbc.co.uk/pressoffice/proginfo/tv/2009/wk7/unplaced.shtml#unplaced_victorians.

Victorian Farm (2009) www.bbc.co.uk/programmes/b00gn2bl.

British Film Institute (General)

Britain's Most Watched, BFI (2005) www.bfi.org.uk/features/mostwatched/research. html.

BFI 'Top 100' (2005) www.bfi.org.uk/features/tv/100/.

www.bfi.org.uk/features/tv/100/biglist/.

www.bfi.org.uk/features/tv/100/list/list.php.

BFI 'Top 100' (2005) www.bfi.org.uk/features/tv/100/list/genre.php?gid=4.

British Film Institute (Film and Television Database)

Time to Remember (2007) http://ftvdb.bfi.org.uk/sift/series/14461.

Today's History (2007) http://ftvdb.bfi.org.uk/sift/series/14477.

Western Civilisation – Saints and Sinners (2007) http://ftvdb.bfi.org.uk/sift/title/ 179201.

Hansard

Fisher, Sir Nigel, and Douglas Jay, House of Commons Hansard debates for 3 April 1982. Vol. 21, Cols. 632–68 (2009) http://hansard.millbanksystems.com/commons/ 1982/apr/03/falkland-islands.

Hurd, Douglas, Home Secretary, House of Commons Hansard debates for 8 February 1989, Vol. 146, Cols. 1007–08 (2007) www.publications.parliament.uk/pa/ cm198889/cmhansrd/1989-02-08/Debate-4.html.

General websites

Appleyard, Bryan, 'Report: TV Needs a History Lesson' (2005) http://entertainment. timesonline.co.uk/tol/arts_and_entertainment/tv_and_radio/article586608.ece.

Barnes, Julian, 'The Worst Reported War Since the Crimean', guardian.co.uk (2002) www.guardian.co.uk/Archive/Article/0,4273,4362424,00.html.

Brown, Maggie, 'The End of an Era', guardian.co.uk (2008) www.guardian.co.uk/ media/2008/nov/10/bbc-history-programmes.

Channel 4, *100 Worst Britons We Love to Hate* (2007) www.channel4.com/ entertainment/tv/microsites/G/greatest/britons/results.html.

Channel 4 Commissioning, Factual Entertainment (2009) www.channel4.com/ corporate/4producers/commissioning/factualentertainment.html.

Davies, Ashley, 'BBC2 Presenters Branded "Stiff and Stuffy"', guardian.co.uk (2009) www.guardian.co.uk/media/2001/may/04/bbc.broadcasting3.

'Ernest Labrousse and the rise of Cliometrics', Cambridge Forecast Group (2009) http://cambridgeforecast.wordpress.com/2008/04/06/ernest-labrousse-and-the-rise-of-cliometrics/.

Extreme Archaeology (2009) www.channel4.com/history/microsites/E/ extremearchaeology/exa.html.

Fincham, Peter, '2008 MacTaggart Lecture at the Edinburgh International Television Festival' (2008) http://image.guardian.co.uk/sys-files/Media/documents/2008/08/22/ MacTaggartLecture2008.pdf

Gillard, Michael Sean, and Laurie Flynn, 'Channel 4 in New Documentary Fake Row', guardian.co.uk (2009) www.guardian.co.uk/uk/1999/mar/23/8.

History Channel, *Hidden House History* (2008) www.hiddenhousehistory.co.uk/press/view.php?Id=88.

Humphrys, John, '2004 MacTaggart Lecture to the Edinburgh International Television Festival' (2005) www.mgeitf.co.uk/home/news.aspx/John_Humphrys_Delivers_the_2004_MacTagga.

Lost Treasures (2009) www.media53.co.uk/clizone/treasures/series1/index.html.

Office of Communications (Ofcom), 'The television viewer proportion of homes with free and pay television, 2006' (2009) www.ofcom.org.uk/research/cm/cmrnr08/tv/.

Ofcom, PSB Review Interactive Executive Summary: Glossary (2009) http://comment.ofcom.org.uk/summary/glossary.html.

Office for National Statistics, Consumer durables – trends over time, table 4.19, consumer durables, central heating and cars: 1972 to 2002 (2009) www.statistics.gov.uk/lib2002/downloads/housing.pdf.

Olly, Mark, biography (2009) www.media53.co.uk/clizone/treasures/series1/mo.html.

Pettie, Andre, 'Tony Robinson's Crime and Punishment', Telegraph.co.uk (2008) www.telegraph.co.uk/culture/tvandradio/3673824/Tony-Robinsons-Crime-and-Punishment.html.

The Way We Were (2009) http://forums.itv.com/thread/742786.aspx

UKTV History 'About Us' TV (2007) www.uktv.co.uk/?uktv=standarditem.index&aID=527826.

Wollaston, Sam, 'Last Night's TV', guardian.co.uk (2008) www.guardian.co.uk/media/2008/jun/02/television.tvandradioarts.

Transmitted programme sources

Bradsell, Michael, *Making Reel History* (trans. BBC Scotland/BBC1, 15 April 1996).

Barnett, Correlli, *That Was the Great War That Was* (trans. BBC2, 22 February 2003).

Brooker, Charlie, *Charlie Brooker's Screenwipe* (trans. BBC4, 25 November 2008).

Cave, Julia, *That Was the Great War That Was* (trans. BBC2, 22 February 2003).

Forman (Sir) Denis, *A Tribute to Denis Mitchell*, Granada Television (trans. C4, 6 December 1990).

Fraser, Nick, *That Was the Great War That Was* (trans. BBC2, 22 February 2003).

Jay, (Sir) Anthony, *That Was the Great War That Was* (trans. BBC2, 22 February 2003).

Keegan, John, *That Was the Great War That Was* (trans. BBC2, 22 February 2003).

Loach, Ken, *Making Reel History* (trans. BBC Scotland/BBC1, 15 April 1996).

McGrath, John, *Making Reel History* (trans. BBC Scotland/BBC1, 15 April 1996).

Paxman, Jeremy, *The Victorians* (trans. BBC1, 15 February 2009).

Toovey, Barry, *That Was the Great War That Was* (trans. BBC2, 22 February 2003).

Wark, Kirsty, *The Making of Culloden* (trans. BBC4, 3 July 2006).

Watkins, Peter, *Making Reel History* (trans. BBC Scotland/BBC1, 15 April 1996).

Wheeler (General) Earle, *Dear America: Letters Home from Vietnam* (trans. HBO, 1987/BBC2, 1990).

Index of programme and series titles

General index

See also Index of programme and series titles, p. 218.

Lightning Source UK Ltd.
Milton Keynes UK
UKOW06f0028300915

259535UK00003B/66/P